# TEACHING HOPE

# TEACHING HOPE

## STORIES FROM THE
## FREEDOM WRITER TEACHERS
### and ERIN GRUWELL

BROADWAY BOOKS · NEW YORK

www.broadwaybooks.com

BROADWAY BOOKS and its logo, a letter B bisected on the diagonal, are trademarks
of Random House, Inc.

Library of Congress Cataloging-in-Publication Data

Teaching hope : stories from the Freedom Writer Teachers / Freedom Writer Teachers ; with Erin Gruwell. — 1st ed.
    p.  cm.
   1. Teacher-student relationships—United States—Anecdotes. 2. Motivation in
education—United States—Anecdotes. 3. Teachers—United States—Anecdotes.
4. Teachers—United States—Attitudes. I. Gruwell, Erin. II. Freedom Writer Teachers. III. Title.

   LB1033.L458 2009
   371.102'3—dc22                                             2009000447

ISBN 978-0-7679-3172-4

Printed in the United States of America

Design by Gretchen Achilles

10 9 8 7 6 5 4 3 2 1

FIRST EDITION

TO THE STUDENT IN ALL OF US . . .

# CONTENTS

## DISILLUSIONMENT     171

## EMPOWERMENT 309

# FOREWORD

ANNA QUINDLEN

Any columnist who makes sweeping generalizations is looking for trouble, but I once did just that in an essay I wrote for *Newsweek*. "Teaching's the toughest job there is," I said flatly, and the mail poured in. Nursing is tough. Assembly line work is tough. Child rearing is tough. There were even a few letters with some of those old canards about the carefree teacher's life: work hours that end at 3 p.m., summers at the beach.

I imagine that the people who believe that's how teachers work don't actually know anyone who does the job—if they did, they would know that classes may end at 3 p.m., but lesson planning and test correcting go on far into the night, while summers are often reserved for second jobs, which pay the bills. But I'm lucky enough to know lots of teachers, and that's why I stuck by my statement. More important, I've taught a class or two from time to time, and the degree of concentration and engagement required—or the degree of hell that broke loose if my concentration and engagement flagged—made me realize that I just wasn't up to the task. It was too hard.

But if hard was all it was, no one would ever go into the profession, much less the uncommonly intelligent people who, over the years, taught me everything from long division to iambic pentameter. I don't remember much at this point in my life, but I remember the names of most of the teachers I've had during my educational career, and some of them I honor in my heart almost every day because they made me who I am, as a reader, a thinker, and a writer.

So when I first read about Erin Gruwell and the Freedom Writers, it came as no surprise to me to discover that the truth about teaching was that it was sometimes a grueling job with near-miraculous rewards, for students and for teachers alike. In Erin's first, internationally known book, *The Freedom Writers Diary*, you saw this mainly through the eyes of her high school students, young men and women living with combative families, absent parents, gang warfare, teenage pregnancies, and drug abuse. Above all, they lived with the understanding that no one expected them to do anything—not just anything great, but anything at all. They'd been given up on by just about everyone before they even showed up in class.

Except for Ms. G, as they called her, who was too inexperienced and naïve to get with the surrender or the cynicism program. Her account of assigning her students to write candidly about their own lives and thereby engaging them in the educational process, of how many of them went on to college and to leadership roles in their communities, is a stand-up-and-cheer story. That's why it was turned into a movie, and why Erin's model has now been replicated in many other schools.

That first book contained the stripped-bare writings of those students, but in this one, it's the teachers' turn to give the rest of us a window into how difficult their job can be. In a way I never could, they answer the naysayers who question the rigor of their jobs. Here are the real rhythms of a good teacher's life, not bounded by June and September, or eight and three, but boundless because of the boundless needs of young people today and the dedication of those who work with them. These are teachers who attend parole hearings and face adolescents waving weapons, who teach students they know are high or drunk or screaming inside for someone to notice their pain. "Sitting at the funeral of a high school student for the third time in less than a year" is how one teacher begins an entry. There are knives and fists, and then there is the all-too-familiar gaggle of girls who are guilty of "a drive-by with words," trafficking in the gossip, innuendo, and nastiness that have been part of high school forever. One teacher recalls a reserved and friendless young woman with great academic potential and a wealthy family, and the evening the maid found her "hanging, as silent as the clothing beside her, in the closet." Another gets a letter from a former student with a return address in a state prison, with this plea: "I know you're busy but I would be very grateful if you would write to me."

Yet despite so many difficulties, these are also teachers who weep when budget cuts mean they lose their jobs, teachers who quit and are horrified at what they've done and then "unquit," as one describes it. Some of them have faced the same problems of racial and ethnic prejudice or family conflict as their students, and see their own triumphs mirrored in those of the young people they teach and, often, mentor. One, hilariously, writes of how she is "undateable" because of the demands of her work: "I'm going to have a doozy of a time finding someone willing to welcome me and my 120 children into his life."

Teachers had an easier time when I was in school, I suspect. Or maybe back then the kinds of problems and crises that confront today's students existed but were muffled by silence and ignorance. Certainly I was never in a classroom where a student handed over his knife to the teacher. I never had a classmate who was homeless, or in foster care, or obviously pregnant.

And yet many of the teachers here speak my language: of pen pals, class trips, missed assignments—and, above all, of that adult at the front of the room who gives you a sense of your own possibilities. "Isn't that the job of every teacher," one of them writes, "to make every student feel welcome, to make every student feel she or he belongs, and to give every student a voice to be heard!"

And so I stick with my blanket statement: It's the toughest job there is, and maybe the most satisfying, too. There are lives lost in this book, and there are lives saved, too, if salvation means a young man or woman begins to feel deserving of a place on the planet. "Everyone knows I'm gonna fail," says one boy, and then he doesn't. What could be more soul-satisfying? These are the most influential professionals most of us will ever meet.

The effects of their work will last forever. Each one here has a story to tell, each different, but if there is one sentiment, one sentence, that appears over and over again, it is this simple declaration: I am a teacher. They say it with dedication and pride, and well they should. On behalf of all students—current, former, and those to come—let me echo that with a sentiment of my own: Thank you for what you do.

# PREFACE

ERIN GRUWELL

When I made the decision to become a teacher, I enthusiastically studied the principles of pedagogy at my university, but the moment I stepped foot in Room 203 at Wilson High School, I discovered how really unprepared I was for the difficulty of working with vulnerable teenagers. Like so many idealistic college students who watched movies about education, I suppose that I expected my students to stand on their desks and say "Oh Captain, My Captain," as the students did in *Dead Poets Society*, or to overcome all obstacles like Jaime Escalante's students in *Stand and Deliver*. So there I stood in front of a room full of unruly, apathetic freshmen, with chalk on my butt, a pained smile, and a fragile facade. My students took one look at me, with my white polka dots, my white pearls, and my "white privilege," and immediately began to make wagers on how long I would last. Luckily, my naïveté shielded me from their foregone conclusion that I would give up by the end of the week. One of them folded my syllabus into an airplane and threw it at me; some called me naughty names in Spanish; and too many defiantly carved their gang affiliations into their desks. It became painfully obvious that every theory I had memorized in my graduate courses paled in comparison to the raw lessons I would learn every day in my urban classroom.

I planned to teach my students about Shakespeare and his sonnets and about Homer and his tale of an odyssey, but I quickly realized that my students couldn't care less about figurative language and metaphors. At fourteen, everything in their lives was literal, focused on reality. When you feel the pang of hunger in the pit of your stomach, that's reality. When you are shot at on your way to school, that's reality. When you have been a pallbearer at your friend's funeral, that's reality. In order to reach my students, I would have to understand their predicaments and make my lessons reflect their reality. Shakespeare's sonnets would have to mirror the eulogies they gave at their friends' funerals, and Odysseus's struggle to return to Greece would have to personify their everyday struggles to make it home alive.

Once I recognized the importance of seeing my students as individuals, I realized that in order for them to embrace any academic lesson, I would have to build a bridge between what they already knew and what I wanted to teach them. One of the activities I used to engage them was the Line Game. I separated the class in two, divided by a piece of tape on the floor, and then asked students to walk to the line if my questions pertained to them: "Stand on the line if you know where to get drugs." "Stand on the line if you've visited a relative in jail." "Stand on the line if you've lost someone to senseless gang violence." Prior to this provocative exercise, my students' journal writing had been perfunctory and uninspiring. One student, Maria, had written in her composition book, "I hate Erin Gruwell! I hate Erin Gruwell, and if I wasn't on probation, I would probably shank her!" Yet when Maria and the other students courageously walked to the line, exposing their vulnerabilities, they realized that everyone has a story; they just needed the opportunity to be heard and an entrée to the healing power of writing. Suddenly, their journals began to bear witness to the death of a cousin, to a father being incarcerated, or to the shame that came with being homeless. We saw one another with new eyes, and as a result, we treated one another differently. Room 203 became a safe haven for students to be honest, to write about their most painful moments, and to dismantle the barriers between us.

As my students became more like a family, I was surprised by how difficult a balancing act being a teacher really is. At the end of each day it became more impossible to leave my students' problems in the classroom. Then there was the fact that my social life was beginning to implode, and I was spending way too much of my own money on school supplies.

All too often, after a brilliant lesson failed to make any noticeable impact and I feared I wasn't getting through to my students, I began to question myself: "If they don't care, why should I?"

When I sought solace from my colleagues, the naysayers in the teacher's lounge often made me feel worse. To them, I was idealistic and burdening my students with unrealistic academic expectations.

As I packed up my students' work to take home with me at night, I often felt as though I was shouldering every student's burden. But when I got home, I had problems of my own: student loans to pay; a husband who would rather have me make dinner than grade papers; and the all-too-noticeable effects of sleep deprivation. And after another late night of reading students' journals, before I knew it, it would be 6 a.m. *again* and I would have to muster up the courage to face my frustrations *again*.

As I made that forty-five-minute commute back to work, contemplating how to make my lesson plan relevant this time, I tried to ignore the nagging voice that often asked, "Do I *really* want to be a teacher?"

But every time one of my struggling students had an aha! moment, I knew that I had made the right decision. Those priceless moments when students' faces lit up, their hands flew in the air, and I knew they "got it," validated all the sleepless nights and began to ease my self-doubt. The small victories rejuvenated my spirit and set the stage for my students' legacy. To pay homage to the 1960s civil rights activists the Freedom Riders, my students decided to band together and call themselves Freedom Writers. However unlikely it had seemed when we started, the Freedom Writers now follow in the footsteps of authors who came before them, those same authors on my syllabus that was once folded and thrown at me.

When *The Freedom Writers Diary* was first conceived, it was 150 stories photocopied and bound at Kinko's. Even though the book was sprinkled with expletives, the brutal reality of racism, and the heart-breaking ramifications of sexual abuse, an underlying message of hope resonated. When a New York publisher agreed to publish the book, we were ecstatic. Far surpassing our wildest imagination, *The Freedom Writers Diary* became a best seller. We knew that many students suffered through experiences similar to my students', but we didn't anticipate that so many readers would identify with their tragedies. Our readers were no strangers to depression, addiction, abuse, alienation, and disappointment. *The Freedom Writers Diary* united their voices in a way that spoke to each person who read the book.

With the success of *The Freedom Writers Diary,* the Freedom Writers and I began to understand the importance of sharing our story. When Miep Gies, the woman who had hidden Anne Frank, told us that we must "bear witness," we realized that indeed we must use the book to make a difference in the lives of others. That lesson became even more urgent after we visited Auschwitz concentration camp in Poland and witnessed firsthand what happens when voices are silent. Holocaust survivors challenged the Freedom Writers and me to "never stand idly by," heightening our determination to make a difference.

After the Freedom Writers graduated from high school in 1998, I began to teach at the same university where I had learned how to become a teacher. My graduate classes came alive each and every time the Freedom Writers "guest lectured" about how dyslexia impacted their ability to read and about how their home environment affected their ability to do their homework. They spoke about the transformative power of picking up a pen rather than a gun. As I watched my graduate students frantically take notes, ask questions, and shed stereotypes, I realized that my Freedom Writers had become teachers. Together they and I replicated some of the unorthodox techniques I had used to engage them in Room 203, such as filling plastic champagne glasses with sparkling apple cider and making a Toast for Change to inspire future teachers who wanted to reach their students in a similar way.

At the same time, I was immersed in the halls of academia with professors who studied theory, and I began to learn that some of the practical lessons that I often devised on a whim actually had academic merit.

After visiting different schools around the country, the Freedom Writers and I were humbled and exhilarated by teachers who were using our book in their classrooms. This was the impetus for the Freedom Writers who worked beside me at the Freedom Writers Foundation to re-create the magic of Room 203 and build a teacher's institute that used our own curriculum to replicate our success.

With the Freedom Writers' help, I began to assemble teachers from across America and Canada until I had recruited 150 Freedom Writer Teachers. Recruits had to believe that every kid could make it; they had to believe that one size does not fit all; and, most important, they had to teach to a kid and not to a test. The seeds of revolution were planted.

These teachers came to Long Beach, learned techniques directly from the Freedom Writers and me, and then went back into their classrooms and had even more success with their students than I'd had with mine. The results were amazing. Not only did their students excel, but the teachers did as well. Their students began to graduate, and the teachers got promotions and many won prestigious teaching awards. But the most important element of our program was the collegiality and sharing that took place at our training sessions in Long Beach and in the virtual classroom we created online. Suddenly, there was someone to listen to these teachers, validate their experiences, and make them feel that they were not alone.

As the Freedom Writer Teachers continued to collaborate, I

saw how important it was for each teacher to share his or her story in the same poignant way my students had shared their challenges. Through sharing their journals and blogs with one another, they invited us into their classrooms. In doing so, they also sparked controversy. One teacher was targeted by the Ku Klux Klan for using our book; another was criticized on the air by radio hosts; and one lost her job. But what we learned from being thrown into the center of the censorship storm by those who tried to ban our book was that controversy makes more teenagers eager to read it and more innovative teachers want to integrate our book into their curriculum.

As we were forced to come to terms with the difficult choices in our lives and in the lives of our students, I saw similarities between these 150 Freedom Writer Teachers and the original Freedom Writers. Many of the teachers were just as bound up in insecurity, doubts, and fears about using their voices to tell their stories as the Freedom Writers. Oftentimes, teachers' real voices are muted or gagged, so when it comes time to speak out, they get caught up in an inner struggle. On the surface, our teachers may have different backgrounds—different religions, ethnicities, or sexual orientations—but here was an opportunity to work together and speak in an honest way to anyone who chose to listen.

The technology available to the Freedom Writer Teachers allowed us to work side by side even when separated by geography and time zones. Unlike *The Freedom Writers Diary,* which was created on computers donated to Room 203, this book was created on laptops donated by Hewlett Packard in a virtual classroom managed by Microsoft.

At the request of the original Freedom Writers, the Freedom Writer Teachers laid open their lives, confessed their fears, and exposed the painful truth behind teaching. It was not an easy process. This would not simply be an anthology; it would be the collaboration of a newfound family. The Freedom Writer Teachers wrote and rewrote stories that cut deeply into their pasts. In mentoring and editing one another's stories, their bonds were solidified. Some of these teachers struggled more than their students realized. When a husband leaves one teacher, she goes back to work the next day. When another's student is shot, the teacher still goes back to work. When a school is bombed, yet another teacher has to make the students feel safe. Teachers return because their students need them.

Occasionally, I embraced my old cheerleading ways and rallied their spirits. When deadlines loomed, it was the Freedom Writers who took great pleasure in helping me ensure that the teachers turned in their stories on time. In the end, through much cajoling, herding the cats, and too many Keystone Cop moments, we had our 150 stories.

This book mirrors the yearly cycle in teaching—the anticipation of a new school year, the challenges students face, attempts to engage students, the feelings of disillusionment that often creep in, and by the end the rejuvenation the teacher feels to empower his or her students. Each section is filled with the personal stories offered up honestly by the Freedom Writer Teachers from their own experiences, both successful and sometimes utterly painful. Some rose to the challenge, some suffered in silence, some were fired, and some succeeded. These are their very human stories.

I wish I'd had this book before I began my journey as a teacher. I would have had more realistic expectations about the power a teacher has, and also about the barriers that spring up all around to challenge that power. Freedom Writer Teachers have come together to share poignant stories from their classrooms: the ups, the downs, the triumphs, and the tragedies all candidly presented to frame a new understanding of what it means to be a teacher.

I am hopeful that this book will speak to your favorite teacher, and that that individual will find a piece of her or his life within these pages. I am hopeful that you will feel empathy and compassion for educators. And I am hopeful that teachers can see themselves in the faces of their courageous colleagues who have shared their insecurities in the classroom and the little victories that sustain them. Through this book, the Freedom Writer Teachers have become teachers to all of us.

# INTRODUCTION

Think of that teacher, that one teacher—the one who made the difference, who saw you and pushed you to find out who you wanted to become. This book is written by 150 people who attempt to be that teacher in the lives of their students, every day. We come from elementary schools, middle schools, high schools, and universities. We teach in public, private, parochial, and charter schools. Our students are urban, suburban, and rural. While they may not travel uphill both ways to get to our classrooms, many must work to learn in spite of their lives.

We are the first-year teacher facing his class for the first time. We are the veteran who has changed young lives for more than thirty years. Our lives revolve around our students, more than is probably healthy. Though our official titles may not be "teacher"—some of us are called social worker, professor, guidance counselor, administrator, school board member, even mayor—we all work to educate the students in our charge.

Beyond our shared commitment to educating each of our students no matter what challenges are thrown our way, we are also bound by a shared experience. We've all traveled to Long Beach, California, multiple times and been trained by Erin Gruwell and the Freedom Writers in an attempt to re-create the magic of Room 203 in our own classrooms. In the process, the bond that formed between the Freedom Writers has been manifested among this family of 150 teachers.

This book is meant as a rare window into the workings of education. We know we can never truly capture every moment, but we have done our best to share our highs and lows. Each section represents a psychological phase in a teacher's year. Beginning with the anticipation of the first day of school, working through the challenges of engaging students, the disillusionment and rejuvenation intrinsic in the school year, and the empowerment of students by year's end, these stories tell what was happening when that teacher—that one teacher—was working to help you find out who you wanted to become.

# TEACHING HOPE

# ANTICIPATION

So many emotions go through the mind of a teacher at the beginning of the year. Thoughts like "Am I ready for this?" and "Do I really want to be a teacher?"

Before my students walked through the door on that first day of school, I was positively giddy. Armed with a meticulously typed syllabus and inspired by the literary canon, I was prepared to bring literature to life. Yet as my disengaged students sauntered in, my enthusiasm quickly turned to panic. Within moments, I realized my students didn't like reading, didn't like writing, and didn't like each other. But like so many teachers, I had hope: hope that my students would find themselves within the pages of a book, hope that they would find their voices in their writing, and hope that they might find a friend or two.

What I quickly found out was that there was too much work to be done before the first bell and even more work for me once my students finally went home. My days often started before dawn and continued into the wee hours of the morning. I would have to manage my own expectations. I learned that I had to be quick on my feet when a student challenged me, flexible when my best lesson plans failed, and willing to embrace every teachable moment.

The stories in this section expose the day-to-day emotions and expectations that every teacher, regardless of experience—or lack thereof—faces at the beginning of the school year. Some are terrified but mask their well-founded fears; others are seasoned and their passion is palpable. Still others are desperately trying to justify their career choices after leaving the private sector. The Freedom Writer Teachers share the daily grind of lesson plans gone awry, trying to reach reluctant learners, all the while remaining steadfast in their mission to teach even the most *unteachable*.

# 1.

I stood in front of the class and faced complete silence. Shuffling feet and blank stares were all that echoed back to my question: "What makes you unique?"

For middle school students striving their hardest to fit in and to conceal their differences, it was a challenge. On their first day of the school year, I saw it as a grand opportunity for them to answer my inaugural question and begin breaking down barriers. Multicolored index cards lay unmoved on desks as my eyes ventured around the room. No pencils moved. It was as if the ballad of street crickets who accompanied me in my attempted sleep last night packed up their fiddles and banjos to serenade my classroom.

As my first teaching minute squirmed around the clock, a seed of doubt crept into my mind. Scanning the room for a glimmer of hope, I started to worry. Can they read my anxiety about starting the year? Will the sweat from my hands leave marks on the desks of my students? Will my students respect and welcome one another? Could we form a classroom built around tolerance?

The students craved the normalcy of the first day. They weren't expecting to think or reflect; they just wanted to check out who was seated around them. They damn sure weren't answering any questions other than their name and schedule.

The night before, I had envisioned students frantically filling in the back of the index cards with their beliefs, personality, and defining moments. The scene before me was something else entirely. Some struggled to write a single thought. Watching the seconds tick away, I repeated my question in other words: "Look around the room. If I took you out of the equation, what would we be missing? How are you different from anyone else in here?"

Something clicked. Stories of summer glory, faded vacations, family secrets, hidden treasures, and teenage life flashed behind my students' eyes. The wait time was paying off, and finally almost all of them had scrawled at least one aspect of themselves.

I glanced over shoulders: *I won the championship for amateur goat tying. I flew to the Bahamas for a summer of sun. I'm one of eight children in our apartment. My grandmother taught me everything I know. I'm not unique*—I stopped at this one.

Miguel was tapping his pencil. How could he be trapped in school for another year? Education had lost its appeal, simply because he had no voice. The look in his eyes told of expected failure, whittling chances, and exceeding apathy. The first lesson I learned from my students is that I'm up against their past, present, and future. I pressed to know more.

"Where were you born?"

He casually responded, "San Antonio."

I quickly recognized he was the only student of Latino descent in the class. I ventured further: "Were your parents born in Texas?"

Lowering his voice, he said, "No, they're from Mexico."

What does it say about our community, our education system, and our nation if a thirteen-year-old boy feels uncomfortable asserting his cultural identity? This was my first chance to connect with one of my students.

"Feel free to write whatever you think makes you unique, but I hope you at least feel comfortable writing real stories."

"What you mean real stories?"

I spoke up so the entire class could hear: the ones who scribbled something in one second, the ones who elaborated infinitely, and the ones who just started thinking about the question while drawing their name in bubble letters.

"Everyone in here will be posed with a dilemma in writing and also in life—to be either lightning, which changes every moment it flashes, or a stone watching and yearning in deafening silence. Which one will you be?"

I asked again, "What makes you unique?"

Miguel sat and thought about whether I had answered his

question. He erased his former reply, wondering where he should go now. I walked around the room collecting the finished products, all the while with an eye drawn to the side following his pencil. I knew I had asked difficult questions of my students. Had it been too much? I berated myself, picking away at the scab of first-day desperation. I picked up Miguel's card last and walked back to the front.

*I was born.*

## 2.

My feet hurt; my head hurts; my whole body hurts. Today was the first day of school, and all the hard work of getting my classroom ready was hardly noticed by my students. Why *would* they notice, though? They have no idea how heavy the boxes of books were. All they see is the colorful spines lined up on shelves, waiting to be pulled out and read. How could they possibly know that sweat had dripped from my forehead as I knelt on all fours and scrubbed the rug to remove spots from last year's soda dribbles? Would the welcoming signs and flowers on my desk even register with them?

As I surveyed the room, I felt deep satisfaction. I liked the way it looked. I liked the neat rows of books and the shiny floors. I liked the welcome mat at my door and the bulletin boards waiting for student work. It was worth it—those late nights of work after a day full of district staff development. The chorus of complaints from teachers who never have enough time has died down now because everything was, in fact, ready. This morning, 2,253 students arrived, went to classes and lunch, and rushed out at the end of the day. The cycle has begun again.

Never does a school year begin without a skip of my heartbeat and a late night of last-minute preparations. I know that every student who walks through the school door does so with new hope—hope that *this* year things will be just right.

"*This* year the teachers will like me, and I'll like them," they think. "*This* year I'll do my work—go to class—stay out of trouble. *This* year I will not repeat my mistakes."

I feel the same way. *This* year I will grade papers quicker and return them sooner. *This* year I'll learn my students' names faster. *This* year I'll be more organized.

A clean slate every August. A new opportunity to try again to get it right—or at least do it better. Is there any other place that renews itself with hope every year as school does?

"Are we going to keep this pace and do this same kind of activity every day this year?" asked one of my students as he left my class on the first day of his last year in high school.

"Well," I said hesitantly, not knowing if his question was going to be followed by a complaint or a compliment, "probably— why?" I feared he would tell me it was too slow, too fast, too boring, and too irrelevant.

"Because if every class is going to be like this one, I think it's going to be an awesome year."

### 3.

I'm so scared my hands are shaking. My mind is moving fast. Am I ready for this? Do I know what I am doing? I could easily walk out the door right now. The sound of the bell. Here they come. I hope this was the right thing to do.

A few students enter, but most hang out by the hallway, leaning up against the drab gray wall. I can smell the disinfectant from where the janitors scrubbed pencil marks off the walls outside my classroom. A couple more students enter my room, looking around at the brightly decorated walls.

The tardy bell rings. The students slowly come into the room. Most are wearing shorts, flip-flops, and remnants of summer tans.

"Hello. My name is Mrs. Lancing, and this is my first day of teaching. I'm excited to be here and to get to know each of you. I really love literature and reading. I used to read book after book when I was your age."

Okay, that sounded stupid. They could care less what I did at their age. Looking around the room, I see a couple of the girls smirking at one another. Is it about me? My mind is full of white noise at this point. I know I'm supposed to say something, but what?

Gulping a mouthful of air, I ask, "Do you have any questions for me?" My voice sounds weird.

These guys are going to eat me alive.

I notice the boy before he speaks because his massive frame looks to be about six feet tall sitting down and he must weigh over 250 pounds. God, I hope he never starts a fight in class. He asks, "How come you ain't be a teacher before? Did you get fired?"

"No. Although I am an adult, it took me a bit longer to decide what I wanted to do, so here I am."

My college professors said new teachers shouldn't reveal personal information, but I feel these students need to understand why I am here.

"I thought I didn't need to go to college. My husband was making good money, and I was doing okay in my different jobs. I thought having a job only meant making money to pay the bills. I didn't realize a job could also be a calling."

From the corner of my eye I see a boy with a bright red football jersey uncross his legs and turn toward me, so I keep going.

"I graduated college the same year my daughter graduated from high school. It was very hard to study and take care of a home and be there for my kids. They needed help with homework and theirs came before mine. Sometimes I was up past midnight working on assignments while washing clothes and making grocery lists."

I was also incredibly shy, but I'm not sure I want to say this to the students. Do they really have to know that I hated speaking to anyone? Or that I would hide behind my mama's leg and stare at people? When I did talk, I sometimes stuttered, which was another excuse to not talk. Less nervous now, I move on: "Anyway, I was really shy and hated talking. I even stuttered so that gave me an excuse to not have to."

I stop and swallow the lump in my throat just as I hear a voice ask: "So when did you start talking?"

Looking across the room, I can't tell which student it is.

"Not till I was about twelve. I started reading, and one of my first books I fell in love with was a book about a little girl trying to survive the Holocaust, and it was called *The Hiding Place*."

The students are actually listening to me. The room is very quiet. The only sound is the ticking of the clock over the chalkboard.

"I had a calling to do this and I had to do it. As soon as I made the decision to do it, I felt like I was a whole person." Shivering from chill bumps, I wrap my arms around myself.

## 4.

Today is the first day of the school year, and I wish I could bottle up all of the feelings I have and save them for the entire year. After last year, I thought that I would be anxious and nervous, but I am only excited. My students are 150 new personalities ready to burst through my classroom door and into my life.

The best part of my day is seeing my students from last year, who greet me with big smiles and hugs. I imagine that some of them are a little surprised to see me return. I'll bet some thought that I wouldn't have the nerve. The last time I saw any of my students was a little over a month ago when I came face-to-face with one of my ninth graders in a juvenile courtroom.

As we were preparing for finals last spring, Shanece returned to class after a long absence, the result of several attempts to run away from home. Before entering my class on the day of her return, I asked Shanece to tuck in her uniform shirt. Shanece refused, and as she began to protest, an administrator passed by and immediately pulled Shanece into her office.

Thirty minutes later, Shanece burst into my classroom. Her eyes were wild and brimming with tears, her arms full of books, shoes, and pictures torn out of her newly vacated locker. She threw her books on the floor and yelled, "You got me put out of school! This bitch got me put out of school!"

Shanece crossed my classroom, yelling, until she stood just inches away from me in the far corner of my room. The next thing I remember, someone was holding Shanece in a bear hug as I dashed to the front office. As I ran out of my classroom, I had a strange and surreal realization: Shanece just hit me in the face.

The next time I saw Shanece, she was being led out of the school in handcuffs. I was taken into the school's conference room to complete a victim's report, followed by a meeting with my administration, who encouraged me to press charges against Shanece.

My gut reaction: Hell, no.

However, after a long conversation with my administration, I became convinced. If Shanece could enter a counseling program through the juvenile system, they said, she could receive the help that she needed.

When I arrived at the juvenile center for Shanece's trial a month later, I was escorted to a waiting room and met by my "victim liaison." She told me that in most cases students plead guilty and the sentencing occurs without any testimony at all. She led me into the courtroom, where I saw Shanece and her parents for the first time. For an entire school year, I had tried every day to win her trust. Now, I was just another person working against her.

The judge called the court to order, and when Shanece was asked to speak, she began to cry. She turned to me for the first time since entering the courtroom and apologized. I bit my lower lip and tried my best to hold it together. I hope she knew that I was sorry, too.

A moment later, Shanece pleaded guilty and was assigned a juvenile parole officer.

As I listened to the terms of her probation, I became confused and concerned. Shanece wasn't assigned to a counselor or to an anger management program. Six months of supervision by a parole officer? What was happening?

I started to protest, but I had no idea what to say, and before I could act, the trial was over. The entire process lasted less than fifteen minutes.

After the hearing, I demanded answers from my victim liaison. She informed me that the charges against Shanece had been changed. She was charged with verbal assault so that she would be more likely to plead guilty and the case could be moved more quickly through the court. Because the charges had been changed, she didn't qualify for any of the counseling programs.

I left the courtroom appalled. Throughout the entire process, I had been labeled a victim. But the only victim in this scenario was Shanece. She was the victim of a community that taught her that in moments of desperation the only answer is violence. The victim of an educational system that lacks the resources to educate its children. The victim of an exhausted judicial system that views our youth as cases on a docket instead of children in need.

Shanece is the reason I am sitting in my classroom today, the reason I am ready to begin a new school year. There are 150 students entering my room, and I am determined that they will not be victims anymore.

## 5.

"You've been so successful. Why are you giving up now?" "I hear you've changed careers. Why?" "You're going to do what?" Family, friends, and strangers could not believe that I would leave my career as an attorney to become a high school teacher. I had practiced law "only" four years, some of them said. "Why would you leave now?" But I'd had an epiphany and I knew I had to follow my heart. Many of today's teenagers are apathetic—about their education, their futures, their lives—and I was going to do something about it.

As an attorney, I saw kids as young as twelve who had given up on those daring, delicate dreams first imagined when they were five and six years old. Dreams of becoming a doctor, a lawyer, or a firefighter were set aside on a dust heap of hopelessness. I met teenagers who were more willing to risk going to jail than graduating high school. I had discussions with young men and young women who trusted and admired the drug dealers and gangbangers who were destroying their communities more than they trusted the teachers and mentors who were providing those same students with tools necessary for a bright future.

The apathy stunned me. But rather than putting my head in my hands, I tried to understand why so many young people simply didn't care about their future. Why would they willingly forgo college, settling for increasingly inadequate minimum-wage work? Why would many students view their teachers and principals as enemies and gangs as friends? After a lot of thought, I decided that many youth lack a support network. Our young have been devalued by society. They have been repeatedly characterized as lazy, disrespectful, and selfish. They have been shown that their thoughts and feelings do not matter. And they have been told one too many times that "children are to be seen and not heard."

But our youth reflect society's beliefs about and expectations for them. If young men or young women don't think their teachers care about them, how can we expect them to trust? When we treat them as expendable or worthless, how else are they supposed to view themselves? Our children are more than adults-in-waiting, and their worth and their rights begin long before they can drive, vote, serve their nation in the military, or drink alcohol. They deserve our attention and our respect, and we owe it to them and to ourselves to treat them with dignity. If our children are starving for love and support, then it is up to all of us to meet their needs.

As a high school teacher it is my goal to love and support my students unconditionally, to be their cheerleader. Educators are charged with the responsibility of providing their students with more than a strategy to pass a standardized test. We must pass on to our students those lessons that will enrich their lives, lessons that will sharpen their ability to think critically, lessons that will help them grow into the men and women they are capable of becoming so that they can become productive members of our society.

I love and support my students the way I love and support my own children, and I urge other educators to do the same. I champion their successes and help to empower them when they fail. Above all, my students know that even if no one else believes in them, I expect great things from them; when no one else is willing to listen, I will be their sounding board; when they have no one else to ask for advice, I will talk to them openly and honestly. As an educator, I am more than just a classroom teacher; I am one of the cornerstones in the foundation for their future success.

When I am faced with those questions of why I left law to become "just a teacher," I remember a letter I received from the mother of one of my students:

*I want to thank you for whatever it was you said to David the other day. Whatever you said really touched him. . . . He told me that it was not until after the two of you spoke that it hit him that "this is it for high school and it is all fixing to be over in a few days. Therefore, I had better start making some decisions about my future." He said he did not want to sit around wasting time in and out of part-time jobs here and there, trying to decide what he wanted to do with his life. . . . Thank you, for your kind words, your understanding, your patience,*

*but most of all, for all that you have done for David his final
year in high school.*

That is why I am a high school teacher.

## 6.

I was once a lawyer in Mexico, a good lawyer. Now I'm a teacher
in America, a good teacher. My road from the courtroom to my
classroom was a tough one, but it has been *mi camino a la verdad*
(my journey to the truth).

I never saw myself doing this job. When I discovered I
couldn't practice law in the United States, I needed a job and I
wasn't going to operate a leaf blower. My chance came from an
elementary school principal and a program for foreign professionals to become educators. My assignment was first grade. Piece
of cake, right?

A few days later, I was in a classroom in front of six-year-old
kiddos. What do I teach? I was trained to deal with judges and
criminals, not with children. I made many mistakes my first year.
One of my students was sleepy almost every day.

"Pedro, why are you always sleepy?" I asked him.

"I stayed up late last night. My mom let us watch television
until twelve a.m.," he said.

"How come she let you do that?"

"She doesn't care."

I wanted to hug him, but instead I said, "I'll talk to your parents to see if you're telling me the truth." However, I never got
in touch with them because I didn't know how to handle a parent conference.

I was always afraid that the principal might come into my
room and see Pedro asleep and realize that she'd made a big mistake by hiring me. I woke Pedro up as often as I could. But he
wasn't able to keep his eyes open for long. I used to deal with the

most stubborn, most difficult judges with ease, yet this sleepy little six-year-old was getting the best of me. My job depended on how well my students learned, on how well I could adjust, and on how effectively I could engage kids like Pedro.

I attended many training sessions, but I struggled to make progress. Students didn't have the slightest clue what I needed from them. I improvised my lessons and felt desperate when they didn't work out. Most days I just wanted to leave school for good, and when the school year came to a close, I was extremely relieved.

Somehow God made me stick it out because He always had this bigger plan in mind for me. The following year I made a pledge to myself to be the best at what I was meant to do. I went back to college and enrolled in a teacher training program. I learned how factors and needs affect children's behaviors. I put this knowledge into practice immediately. I could see a huge transformation in my kiddos. With every success I felt invigorated. The classroom was alive with learning. I was transforming from attorney to teacher.

My students also began to see the potential in themselves to transform. Lolita, a nonreader, suddenly discovered that a veil had been lifted from her eyes.

"Maestro, ya puedo leer, mire." [Mister, I can read now, listen.] She read fluently a small paragraph.

"Awesome job!" I said. "How did you make it, Lolita?"

"Usted me dijo que yo podia hacerlo si lo intentaba aunque no pudiera. [You told me I could do anything if I try hard.] Mi abuelita se va a poner happy, maestro. [My grandmother is going to be happy.] Gracias, maestro." [Thanks, Mister.]

I remembered how much she had struggled. I gave her the courage and the necessary tools because I knew she would be able to do anything with guidance. Her excitement was contagious. The class had witnessed a true transformation right before their very eyes.

Lolita could read.

An unexpected letter from Lolita's grandmother arrived on my desk. It said, "I want to thank you for your time and dedication in teaching my granddaughter. She will never forget what you have done for her and neither will I. You will be in her heart when she receives her diploma."

This kind of recognition was definitely better than winning a case.

Gracias, Pedro and Lolita. Thank you for helping me find *mi verdad.*

### 7.

Not everyone stays. Even fewer return. First lady Michelle Obama did. And so did I. I grew up in the shadow of Dr. Martin Luther King Jr.'s legacy, and I studied in the same high school as the Nobel laureate and civil rights martyr. When I realized my calling to become a teacher, I knew that I would return. This profession is a privilege—to usher the next generation of leaders to realize their potential; to serve the Atlanta neighborhood that gave, and continues to give me so much; to bind myself to the legacy of service Dr. King challenged us all to live. Every day I ask myself, "How can I fulfill my own dreams and those of my students?"

Marian Wright Edelman reminds me that "it is the responsibility of every adult . . . to make sure that children hear what we have learned from the lessons of life and to hear over and over again that we love them and that they are not alone."

Teaching is an art that must take place both in and outside of our schools in order that our students may see the connection between learning and serving.

My relationship with my students is a special one. Because I walked the same halls and sat in the same classrooms when I was a student, they relate to me in a way few other educators are fortunate enough to experience. And even though many of my students are high achievers and scholarship earners, there is often darkness behind the light.

Skill is often not enough. One of my students is a great debater and was given the opportunity to compete in a national tournament held in Washington, D.C. Sadly, he could not attend because the registration required that he have health insurance—insurance he no longer had because both of his parents lost their jobs at the GM and Ford plants. I realized that even those students who delve deep into their studies face barriers.

Another student maintains a 94 grade-point average, a winning attitude, and a thirst for putting pen to paper. But, caught up in her academic success, she was dehydrated. Drained, every day she fought the fear of no longer having her two HIV-positive parents in her life.

I keep seeing this child in my mind's eye. I see her in class working away as if no care in the world presses upon her. I see her writing away to earn A's across her report cards. How do I separate my role as teacher from that of social worker? When she tells me that she needs "just a couple more days" to gather the money for a trip, because the money she had set aside had to be used to buy her parents' medicine, how can I remain fair to the other students? Do I give her more time? Do I pay for her trip myself?

Another one of my students admits that he wants to murder his father, because his father refuses to pay child support. He still bears the scars of being forced to watch his mother being dragged across floors only to see the man who abused her abandon his family and forget who and what he left behind.

When the students have done all that they can, where do we and the education system meet them? It is heartbreaking to teach students who have talent but no stage on which to perform because of where they live; who have artistic ability but no canvas on which to express themselves because the school district keeps cutting back. It is heartbreaking to teach students who come from torn homes that have fostered broken definitions of what romantic love really is and should be, and students who are so young but already convinced that they'll never be able to live debt-free because half of their family's bills are in their names.

For many of my students, I am all that they have. And I am giving all that I am to move them beyond their present circumstances. Teaching is my life. Helping my students become their best selves gives my life purpose, meaning, and hope. Today is a better day. I am what my students need. I am a teacher.

## 8.

I am looking out at the largest audience of educators to whom I have ever presented an autism workshop. I am lit onstage, and they are sitting in darkness. It's a beautiful state-of-the-art theater, which I would rather be exploring, touching, playing in, but I am here on a mission. There is too much ignorance, and I can help solve that. I look down at my service dog, Shakespeare, whose soulful eyes encourage me. I launch.

"My name is Joy Marie and I am autistic. I am middle-aged, overweight, talented, and articulate. But it hasn't always been this way. I have always been odd. I didn't talk until almost four, didn't read until fourth grade, and I was always picked last for sports games. How many of you were picked last for sports?"

Out of 250 teachers, close to half raise their hands.

I continue: "This is interesting to me that those who are teaching the leaders of tomorrow, so many were not the winners. Yet here you are—encouraging, enlightening, and empowering the next generation!"

There is soft laughter. After some anecdotes about my childhood that establish my humble autism beginnings, I ask questions.

"What do you think of when you hear the word 'disability'?"

Hands are raised, and voices call out: "Broken." "Hurt." "Alone." "Incapable."

"Are these positive attributes? Of course not." I pause. "What about the word 'autism'?"

They respond: "Lost." "In their own little world." "Closed off." "Socially inept."

My work is cut out for me.

"In third grade," I say, "I was tested for IQ at 85. I didn't read or talk in discussions. Now I have twelve hundred books in my home, and I certainly talk a lot!" There are more titters. "I began reading a lot in sixth grade, and then in seventh I began writing. In tenth grade I was retested, and my IQ was suddenly 150. How many of you think you can predict the future of a two-year-old? What will that child do? Who or what will she become? Do you know?"

I close my eyes and walk about the stage and remember that I am up *high*. Shakespeare has walked in front of me near the edge of the stage. "Good dog!"

"I want you to imagine something. What are you wearing now? Can you feel the seams? The tags? Your feet? Do you have on socks? Sandals? Clogs? Feel your feet. Feel your clothing. Feel the seat, your butt. Look around you at the colors everyone is wearing! Browns, red, blues, black, yellow—there's an orange shirt. Look about this theater! Look at the ceiling! Cool patterns, parquet, look at the walls with the swirling fabric! There are circles and *stripes* on the carpet. So much input!

"While you are gazing about, keep your mind on your feet, your clothing, and the chair you are in. This side, I want you to sing 'Row, Row, Row Your Boat.' " They begin, tentative then strong. I move to the other side. "You are to sing 'Jingle Bells.' " This group starts out loud, no encouragement needed. I yell over the din, "How do your toes feel? Your back and arms? Keep looking about you at the colors and people!"

I pause center stage. The chaos is wonderful. I have to shout: "Now turn to someone in a different row and have a conversation!"

Total bedlam. I motion for calm. They are well-trained teachers.

"This is life for many on the autism spectrum! Your students begin the day—if they slept—with alarm clocks, family noises, maybe other kids, maybe a dog barking. They have to choose clothing, take a shower—can you imagine feeling each pellet of water, the scratch of a towel, the overwhelming scent of shampoo and soap? Then the bus ride to high school? The crowded hallways and pathways of this campus? Then you expect an autism student to learn anything at 7:30?"

Shakespeare barks. I pick him up, calm my own sensory overload, and look into the dimness.

"Every person is a gift. Your autism students experience the world differently. They are artists—have you ever asked to see their drawings? They are poets—check out their Facebooks. They are sensitive and, yes, often lost."

Scratching my dog's ears, looking up at the lights shining from the theater pipes, the patterns and chaos all about me, I have one last salvo.

"Each of you has a gift, a talent. If you are a visual person, be the eyes for your autism student. Describe this world. If you are a historian, frame this experience, create a scaffold for interpreting life. If you are a word person, define words, read the dictionary. Make sarcasm illegal. Each autistic person is a gift. Your mission, should you choose to accept it, is to find the gift. Change your words—the words 'broken,' 'lost,' 'wounded.' Opt for words that lift up, such as 'creative,' 'unusual.' Change yourself, and maybe by making the world safer, friendlier, we just might choose to come out of the universe in our minds and to join the universe that is yours."

Let there be Light.

## 9

Like so many lessons, my story is not perfect or refined. It doesn't make any attempt to meet any benchmark or standard, and it doesn't prepare anyone for a standardized assessment. It is simply a life lesson that I share with my students. It is a lesson from my soapbox, but the soapbox is sturdy, tried, and true.

Since I am not an architect, composer, or celebrity, I don't expect buildings, songs, or stars to be named after me. However, if my students understand the Three Birthdays on their own terms, not mine, I will help their human spirit rise to levels that they would have not experienced otherwise. My legacy will live within my students.

Many of my students are at-risk and have been removed from the traditional classroom. Most have a parole officer, are documented truants and runaways, and have been to juvenile detention or family court.

During the school year, my students and I learn a lot from each other. They arrive with the enthusiasm, the curiosity, and the apprehension of children. Finally, they are no longer children but responsible adults in training. They wear the freshman badge, much like a trainee on the first day of a new job.

They can't fathom or understand their new roles in society, so it is up to me to guide them through the first days of the rest of their lives. I set them up by asking, "How many birthdays do you have?" Their responses vary from the number of celebrations they have had to the number of milestones their parents and grandparents have experienced. But I tell them, "You have only three birthdays." The rest are just recognitions of another year of life—in my opinion, they are milestones, not birthdays. In disbelief, they ask, "Mister, what do you mean?" And so their first lesson begins.

"Your first birthday takes place at whatever age you enter

high school," I tell them. "Your actual age is unimportant because many of you have entered high school at different ages.

"The world no longer looks at you as a child," I continue. "Now, you're a young adult, one of life's trainees. Your parents and your community believe that the time has come for you to take on some responsibility. You have begun your ascent into adulthood.

"In middle school, you had a taste of having more than a single teacher all day and the freedom of moving between classes without adult supervision. In high school, the practice is over, and it's game time. The road toward adulthood has been set."

They nod a bit, so I continue.

"Then, there is your eighteenth birthday. Whether you're still in school, graduated, or dropped out, you'll be considered an adult. Responsibility is wrested from your parents and placed squarely on your shoulders. You must now become accountable.

"No longer are your parents required to feed, clothe, or provide a roof over your heads. Great freedom comes with this 'second birthday,' but you must also be ready to bear the responsibility."

I give them an example: If they are caught shoplifting from a convenience store at seventeen years, eleven months, the manager will call the police, but the police will most likely call and release them to their parents. However, if they are caught shoplifting from the same convenience store at eighteen years, six hours, the manager will call the police, and they will most likely go to jail, with one phone call and bail set. From age eighteen on, I tell them, "the person responsible for the choices you make, good or bad, will be you. With the 'second birthday,' you can vote and die for your country."

Then, I ask them if they can guess the "third birthday." I get a few takers, probably because this is the birthday that most teenagers long for. "That's right," I say, "your 'third birthday' is when you turn twenty-one years old. It is a rite of passage. After three years of practicing responsibility and accountability, society feels you're ready for any and all that the world has to offer.

"On your third and final birthday, you can finally party like a rock star, and you have unlimited access to alcohol. No longer do you have to ask your older relatives to buy you alcohol, sneak alcohol out of your parents' cabinet, or bribe a stranger to buy it for you. Now you can have as much or as little alcohol as you like. So, how is this your final birthday?"

I like to tell my students a story about a commercial that was on TV some time ago. The commercial starts with a bartender and a blender. The bartender pours some mixers and then some alcohol into the blender. Before the bartender puts on the lid, he drops in a set of car keys and then he starts the blender. The sound of grinding metal reminds you of nails across a chalkboard.

Because my students live in a community that is plagued by alcohol abuse, I feel compelled to tell them that chaos ensues when you add alcohol to any situation. In the hopes that maybe they can break the cycle, I tell them that alcohol affects you on every level. It heightens your emotions, slows your reflexes, and clouds your judgment. I tell them that I hope that during the time between their second and final birthdays they mature into responsible and accountable adults able to deal with these choices.

Some of the students ask, "So, Mister, what about your twenty-fifth, thirtieth, or even fortieth birthdays?"

I tell them, "Those are simply milestones. In high school, you learn to be responsible. On your eighteenth birthday, you became accountable. On your twenty-first birthday, you must be both while having complete and unlimited access to alcohol. Besides those three birthdays, you have celebrations and anniversaries, and you achieve milestones.

"Happy birthday, and welcome to the rest of your lives."

## 10

I knew that Dad was sick, but I had the hope that he would get better. No such luck.

The first day of school had me excited and ready for what was going to be a great year. During preplanning I had laid out everything so that I knew everything I wanted to do and when I would be able to do it. Then on the way home my mom called me to let me know that the doctors had told her Dad had days or, more likely, hours. I headed to the hospital. After my sister arrived, we all took turns saying our good-byes. Of the three of us, I went back to his ICU room the most frequently. I had to apologize for the things I had done that had hurt my parents. I wasn't always a good son, but at Dad's bedside I knew that I would try harder to be the best son I could be. As my mom, sister, and I left to go grab a quick bite to eat, I straightened Dad's hair.

I left the hotel where we ate on foot and walked back to the hospital because I needed some alone time. As I neared the hospital, a little voice told me to go back and see Dad. I went in. They had moved him to a room on another floor. Once I found his room, I went in and sat down and watched him. The man who always towered over me now looked much older and frailer. I watched for an hour. As I watched, I realized that his breathing was slowing and he was having a harder and harder time catching his breath. Thank God he was sleeping, due to the drugs.

Finally, the little voice announced its presence again and told me it was time to go home. I had cried a bit every time I had seen him, but this time I knew I would never see my dad again. I wept as I had never done before. I again straightened his hair because he never went outside with messy hair. I then walked to my car and began the drive home. As I drove, I kept thinking I needed to go back, but the little voice stepped up and reminded me that Dad would not want me to see him die because he had watched his own father pass and it had always haunted him. I got home and went to bed. At 5:30 a.m. he passed. I took off the rest of the week for the funeral and to help out Mom.

My dad is dead. These are the worst words to have to say.

The only real comfort that week was remembering my dad saying he was proud of me. One of the most memorable occasions he said that to me was when I decided to become a teacher, and the other was for being selected to be a Freedom Writer Teacher.

I teach because I love a job that is never boring and always has surprises. When I entered my class again before the school day started, there was a giant homemade card on my desk. It was signed by all of my students, the faculty, and the administration of my school. I set the card down and cried for joy at the blessing of being in a place where I am so loved.

### 11.

Sitting at the funeral of a high school student for the third time in less than a year, I was struck by a disquieting feeling of how unnatural it was. Nature is not operating in its proper form. I am reminded of a similar feeling I experienced about seventeen years ago.

When Hurricane Bob struck our island, he howled with winds as high as 115 miles per hour, but he came without rain. The salt picked up from the ocean's twenty-foot waves dried out the leaves on trees and bushes. Tall, aged trees were ripped from our sidewalks and toppled onto the cobblestones. Approximately fifty-five feet was eroded from our southern shoreline. This happened on August 19, 1991, and for the rest of the summer and into the fall, I couldn't shake this eerie, unnatural feeling. One of the most beautiful things about our island is the light, and it now was all wrong. For me the light is most beautiful from the summer's end through the last lingering weeks of fall. Without the season's buffer of the leaves, the light felt too harsh—unnatural and unnerving. The moors that had been parched grocery-bag brown in August never created their amazing display of vibrant vermillion shading off to magenta. Nature, taken off guard by this early death, tried to have spring in the fall, as frail buds and blossoms appeared. Try as I might, I couldn't shake the weird unsettling feeling lurking just beneath my consciousness. Our island still shows the scars from what Bob unleashed upon us and will forever.

A different scourge on our small community will leave deep, unending scars as well. The psychologists and newspapers tell us we are in a "suicide cluster," where the threshold for students to harm themselves has been lowered. I understand the experts, but living here, I can't see this larger picture. I see and feel the loss of three distinct and wonderful young people. Perhaps nature will right itself and a healing will occur.

Two weeks ago, beyond numb, I attended another young man's funeral. Another adolescent, with every dream to live for, had taken his life. Four deaths in eighteen months: it is beyond words and sense.

As a teacher, I think of this unendingly. These were my students, my friends. In this small, intimate town, our families are entwined.

Last school year, I lost a member of one of my classes in January. By that time in the school year, I have cemented the number of students in each class in my head to allow me to take class attendance efficiently. I count the students in the room, allow for absences, et cetera, match the number, and off we go. As late as June, I was struggling to make the number come out. On a few occasions, I went so far as asking the students in that class to help me figure out who was missing. When the realization would happen, it was as if I was a boy again. I have just been punched hard in the stomach. I can't breathe, and I want to cry. I cover my lapse with a joke about senility setting in, or the good fortune for them that I am not their math teacher. But, unerringly, my eyes focus on the empty seat where hope and life used to sit.

There are twenty-one students in the room, and they are my priority. I look at them, at their eyes. They buoy me up and give me hope and purpose. I breathe and we move on.

As we start a new year, I am excited. Five times a day, fifteen to twenty students enter my room, deserving the best I've got, and they get it. All children, our greatest assets, are at-risk. The students we have lost were on their way to becoming stars, and it saddens me that we will never see their light.

Still, I am optimistic. I have not yet shaken that unnatural undercurrent haunting me below the surface. I use it to motivate me, to heighten my awareness, because failure in what I do is unacceptable.

## 12.

I swallowed hard and rose from my desk to welcome my class for the first time. Two thousand miles and what seemed like a lifetime in school couldn't possibly have prepared me for what lay in store.

One month into the school year, I was hired over the phone for what should have been my dream job: eighth-grade social studies in a suburban area of the city. However, I arrived as scheduled the week before last and was introduced to a low-income school as an eighth-grade language arts teacher.

The students filed in, taking their seats where they pleased. I had been told that many of these kids were rough, and I was not sure how to prepare for it. I mean, come on, how is a suburban white girl supposed to know how to deal with kids who didn't even want to be in school and were there only because their parole officer told them it was either school or juvenile hall?

I stood firmly at the front of the classroom with my armor on and ready for battle. No smiles graced my lips. I stated the classroom rules and began the first language arts class of my career. If the students only knew that I really had no idea what

I was doing . . . I passed out the syllabus. The students were quiet as they sat back assessing me, looking for a soft spot in my armor.

"How was the first day?" a colleague asked.

"Great, it is going to take some time, but I know they will come around eventually," I said. "I pulled off my tough-guy impersonation."

Other teachers offered unsolicited advice: "Don't smile until Christmas," "Just get 'em through the system."

"Good luck with *those* kids," a seventh-grade teacher said. "You know, a teacher quit halfway through the year last school year because he could not handle them."

There was bitterness in their voices, but I got through the first couple of days with success.

Then the middle school social studies teacher began returning my homeroom students because they were a "behavior" problem. I took it in stride at first. I got it: Rookie teacher gets the behavior problems. "Okay," I thought, "I can handle this." This was just a test of my battle skills. Don't think I'm talking about only one or two kids. Oh no, I was seeing four, five, and at times six of my homeroom kids walk through my classroom door while the rest of my homeroom students were in social studies. They angrily stalked in as hot tears rolled down their cheeks because they had been belittled as being stupid in front of the whole class.

"Why are you in here?" I asked a student who had just walked into my classroom.

"He kicked me out of social studies," she replied.

"Why?"

"I don't know. He just kicked me out."

"Why did he kick you out?"

"Because he's racist!"

I had been taught to build relationships with my students, no matter what their background was, fostering those relationships and encouraging the students to succeed against all odds.

At home, I reflected on my first week of teaching, staring at the numerous books that came with the language arts curriculum. I realized that these kids couldn't care less about verbs or parts of speech. They needed someone who would listen, have patience, and show them that she truly cared about them as individuals. They needed someone to teach. I don't know if I can do this job, but I know one thing: I am going to try my hardest.

## 13.

Education is music, and music is education. The relationship between the two didn't occur to me until I met Tommy. His long, messy blond hair and interest in skateboarding set him apart from the other students. It didn't help that Tommy joined my class late and knew very little about what we were studying. From other teachers I found out that Tommy was running into the same type of trouble in all of his classes. I noticed that during lessons he was more interested in looking at the world map on the wall next to his desk than in paying attention to the points I made. Each time homework was due, Tommy's was missing from the pile.

Not too long after Tommy became my student, I was at home preparing for a weekly performance with my band. Because you always want to get the best sound from your instrument, my first preparation is to tune my guitar. By loosening or tightening the strings, the musician can manipulate the frequencies to sync up and create a smooth, harmonious sound. At first, it was my dad who tuned my guitar. I depended on him to make the guitar sound good before I practiced. After I learned to do this on my own, I was no longer dependent on someone else to help me.

It occurred to me that the same could be true of Tommy's experience in school. There was the possibility that he wasn't in tune with what we were working on at school. Much like the strings on my guitar, Tommy had to be on the same frequency as our class. An idea occurred to me, and I wrote a few notes. Then I grabbed my guitar case and headed for the gig.

The following week, I took Tommy aside to find out what he knew about World War II—which we were studying at the time. Tommy didn't know much about World War II. He knew so little that I soon realized all of the information was new to him.

I thought that even if the information was new, Tommy could get in sync with the rest of the class if he had good study habits. I asked him, "Do you study or take the time to try to finish your homework?" He looked away for a minute before answering with what seemed an eternal "Ummm . . ."

I decided to go to his house and find out for myself why he avoided my question. When Tommy opened the door and saw me on his doorstep, I thought he was going to shit his pants. Tommy lived with his grandmother. When I sat down with her, we talked about several ways to help her grandson be successful in school. I suggested to her that his homework be finished before he was allowed to go outside to skate or hang out with his friends. We created a homework area in his room, and all three of us sat down and established some daily after-school expectations. I tutored Tommy twice a week after school, helping him to catch up.

My goal in doing these things was to help Tommy tune his habits and his mind-set to the same frequency as my other students. When he began to be engaged in class discussion and started to turn in homework, I could tell that once again my classroom was in perfect pitch. Like my father, I needed to teach Tommy to finely adjust his learning so that eventually he could do it himself.

One thing that a guitar player must always remember, though, is that a guitar never stays in tune. It requires constant attention to make sure that the waves of notes are all on the same pitch. One must pay attention to how the strings sound when they are played. There is never a time when the strings don't need to be loosened or tightened. For a teacher, students are the same. Once a teacher knows how to tune the strings in the classroom, the sound created is beautiful.

## 14.

The class was a mess.

Shortly before winter break, the teacher for the first four months of school was asked not to return because of poor performance. I had walked by many times and seen the previous teacher standing in front of the class leading a lesson while students were arguing, wrestling, and playing card games in front of him. Considering the extremely dysfunctional atmosphere of the previous year, a year in which I saw exactly seventy-one hired people come and go, many of the students were under the impression that they could run any teacher or faculty member out of the school.

The funny thing was that I identified with these students. My own experiences as a black Latino male who attended public schools in California had created in me sensitivity to being judged by teachers—the kind of teachers who allow little room for feedback. They treat their students like empty vessels that need to be filled up with information and not as people who have real and valuable experiences with something to say and lessons to teach. These teachers are often unaware of the prior experiences, the differences in culture and values that their students carry with them, and the realities that so many of their students attempt to navigate between every day. And many times, even when they do recognize these differences, they fail to find ways to validate and involve these aspects of their students' lives.

On this big day, the month's work was going to be put on display. I had invited the principal and some parents, who created a buzz in the room, an uneasiness that encouraged students to choose their words carefully and be mindful of their behavior. But this day was not about the adults. The students were beside themselves with pride and eagerness to share the secrets of who they were and what they had learned about themselves. They sat still, but I could tell they felt as if they were on fire.

Although the theme for the year was ancient Eastern cultures and I had taken over four months into the school year, my students had not yet studied any ancient cultures. It was unfortunate that my students had not engaged in any meaningful work that would have allowed them to explore ancient peoples and past cultures, but at least I could start from scratch. I decided to give them an opportunity to teach each other, and me, about themselves.

I assigned a personal history project. The purpose was for students to learn more about their own backgrounds and their own cultures, to communicate with family members, to research, to gather data and information, and then to teach their peers and teachers about where and who they came from. We tackled the broad subject of culture by breaking culture down into its many aspects, such as geography, background, themes, attitudes toward the unknown, food and drink, political structure, economics, family life, communication, arts and aesthetics, and recreation. Some of the students who usually flew under the radar—the shyest and least confident, or even the sneakiest ones—sat stiffly in their seats awaiting their turns, biting their nails. My alphas— the students whose names you remember the first day of class and repeat more often than any other names because the individuals' energy and will to be reckoned with demands it—smiled nervously and sat silently. The room smelled delicious. Many students brought food from home that they had prepared the night before with their parents and grandparents. I was starving. I had encouraged students to bring in "your people's food." Hip-hop, samba, salsa, bachata, reggeton, reggae, and other styles of music that students brought in were playing on a small boom box while we waited for everyone to settle in.

One brave and very shy student volunteered to present first. With a huge smile that he tried to hide, he strolled to the front of the class.

"Hi, my name is PJ and my parents were born in Brazil," he began.

Just then, one of my machismo alpha males, Miguel, yelled out, "Why you lyin'? You black!"

I gave Miguel a hard stare and pursed my mouth in disapproval. He leaned back and announced, "Well, he look black. How I'm supposed to know?"

PJ shuffled the note cards in his hands. I nodded to him and he continued. He proceeded to tell everyone that although most people thought he was African American, he was Brazilian and he was proud of it.

He told the story of his parents' move to the United States and described some of his visits to Brazil. Miguel declared, "Yo, they got some bad girls in Brazil. You seen that Snoop video?" All of the boys nodded in agreement and giggled like the eleven-year-olds they were. PJ continued, "They do have beautiful women in Brazil." Then he smiled. "But we have good music too."

PJ asked me if he could play a CD. I put his CD into the player. The room was silent. Grins surrounded me, and I looked over at some of the parents, who were whispering and smiling at PJ, who swayed from side to side, still smiling. When I pressed the Play button, the distinct sound of the bacteria, the drum section of a samba band, captivated everyone. For a few seconds, the only thing that could be heard was drumming and the piercing whistle that accompanied it. Suddenly PJ broke into dance. Still smiling, he shouted over the music, "This is samba! And this is how you dance to it!"

A few students looked at me, smiling, a bit embarrassed because no one saw this coming. But I had the feeling that some actually wanted to join in. I asked if there was anyone who wanted to try, and a few girls nodded. They got up and stood beside PJ, who stopped dancing to show them the steps.

Gradually more girls went up, and eventually a few boys joined in. Pretty soon some parents went up and participated. I stood in the back and tried to soak up what I was witnessing. My principal came to my side and squeezed my arm. She told me that it was beautiful. I had to agree.

## 15.

Walking to this new bus stop was agonizing. I used to enter this white, affluent neighborhood only to go to the store. This time I was going to stand in an area of this bus stop where no African American had ever stood. I made the left turn away from the route to my old bus stop. My heart began to beat faster. My palms were sweaty, and my deodorant was working overtime. Conversations grew quieter as I approached.

The smells of cologne, deodorant, cigarette smoke, and peppermint candy filled the air. The hot August sun beamed down. These boys wore dress pants, belts, oxford shirts, and penny loafers. I was wearing new pants, a new shirt, and new shoes with laces from the local discount store.

"Where are you going?" one boy sneered.

"To school."

"Why are you going to our school?" asked another boy.

"I needed a change."

"What grade are you in?" came from another boy.

"Eleventh."

The bus approached and stopped.

The bus driver asked, "Are you at the right bus stop?"

At the next stop, a white girl got on the bus and said, "There is a damn nigger on the bus."

When we arrived at the school, all the students went to the auditorium first, where we were welcomed by the principal. He was a big white man with broad shoulders, a pointed nose, and thinning hair. He told us that this was going to be a good year despite all the changes. I think he meant that even with this thing called "integration" this was going to be a good year.

If I had stayed at my previous high school for my last two years, life may have been easier. I wouldn't have known this type of rejection. However, it made me a better person and a better teacher. Many of my students have been rejected, too. Some have been rejected because of race, where they live, the kind of jobs that their parents have, or their lifestyle.

Three years ago, a white girl walked into my classroom. She had transferred from another school because she was having problems. She was very smart but didn't fit in well with other students or adults. One day, I asked about her home life. She said, "Don't go there." Later, she confided in me that her parents were fairly well-to-do but had divorced.

I connected with her because like her I'd felt out of place when I was in high school. It seemed as though very few people had understood me in high school, and I could see that even though this girl was very intelligent she was not connecting with others.

When she got in trouble in other teachers' classes, she came to my classroom to plead her case. I always listened and then gave her advice on what she should do. She often got in trouble because of her tardiness in first period. On one occasion, she came to my room after the people in the front office told her that if she was tardy one more time she would be withdrawn from our program. I told her that she must not be late for school, and that she didn't have time to go to a restaurant in the mornings for breakfast. She and I came up with a plan to get her to graduate early. She worked hard by staying later in the day, and she completed her requirements for graduation early.

Recently, I ran into her when I was in a store shopping. She approached me and gave me a big hug. She said, "You just don't know how much I appreciate what you did for me."

I asked, "What are you doing these days?"

She said, "I am attending college and working."

Trust wasn't part of the equation when I went to high school, but trust is part of my equation. I don't agonize going to the bus stop anymore.

## 16.

"I've never seen a black person in real life before."

I stared with disbelief for a moment at the new student in my class who had whispered this to me. I had just asked him if everything was all right because I noticed that he kept glancing around the classroom nervously with his light green eyes.

"For real?" I blurted out.

I didn't get it. Here we were, living in one of the most multicultural countries in the world, and just because this kid moves two hundred miles from his small town up north, he's now a stranger in a strange land.

"What do you mean?" I asked.

"I mean, like I've seen black people in movies and TV before, but never one up close."

Shane had moved to our school district from a small northern town with a population of only about three hundred. For Shane, being parachuted into this cultural stew was foreign and unsettling. His whole town was white and Christian, and everyone was well acquainted with one another. Where he came from, news about his exploits reached his house before he did.

Now, Shane's pale skin and blond spiky hair made him stand out like a sore thumb in our class. His brow furrowed whenever he heard students speaking a different language, as though he was worried they were talking about him. Shane felt a bit awkward around his new classmates, but he wasn't the silent type and hated not knowing things. He bombarded me with questions when we were alone.

"What's with these Muslim kids starving themselves during Ramadan? Man, I could never skip lunch."

"Does that kid take his turban off when he showers or just put a plastic bag over his head?"

"Hey, sir, you're Chinese, right? How come you need two New Years? Does that mean you get to get drunk twice?"

He continued to observe his classmates and tried to piece it all together. All these different students were getting along even though they did such different things and believed in such different gods. No one seemed to argue or fight, and everyone just went about his or her business. Some students experienced light-bulb moments in my class. Shane had strobe lights.

The more he learned, the more he realized how sheltered his former life had been. His initial fear gradually evolved into an understanding that there would always be something new that he wouldn't totally understand about his classmates.

"Man, if my friends back home could see me now . . ."

His homework had just begun.

## 17.

"If you do it standing up, can the girl still get pregnant?"

My "inappropriate" alarm went off when he asked me the question. I thought that he might be putting me on.

"Really?" I couldn't help myself, I had to ask.

I can remember when I was his age and sex ed was taught. Everyone involved—teachers and students—wanted to be anywhere else, doing anything else. I remember all the handouts and filmstrips to which nobody was expected to pay attention. A couple of fill-in-the-blank tests later and we could move on to something that was less painful for all involved. What I don't remember was ever having an honest and frank discussion about sex with anyone who could have given me a straight answer. I don't remember if my parents ever had "the talk" with me, and I certainly don't remember my health teacher ever telling me anything other than just the rudimentary biology behind pregnancy. I do remember wanting to know more than anyone was willing to tell.

"Yeah. Well, can she?"

"Yes, she can get pregnant any time you have sex," I replied, careful not to give away the fact that this was the most uncomfortable moment of my entire teaching career.

"Oh, okay . . . Thanks."

I was really hoping not to encourage anyone else in the class, but I couldn't stop myself from asking, "Why did you want to know that?"

"Because we just finished learning about sex ed, and they wouldn't let us ask questions. All we did was worksheets and overheads and that's it. I had heard that a girl couldn't get pregnant if she was standing up but I didn't believe it, so I asked to check."

It was out of my mouth before I even knew that I had said it: "Who told you that?"

"Just some guy."

It was pretty apparent to me that nothing had changed with the way teachers teach sex ed or the way kids talk about it. Maybe, I thought, I could mention to the health teacher that for next year she could allow the kids to ask questions or maybe have a question box for students . . .

I was stopped midthought by the waving hands that were now up in the classroom. I knew at that moment that I could be like all the other teachers and parents who failed to have a frank and open discussion about sex and sexuality or I could answer some questions that would make me incredibly uncomfortable. I opted for the latter, and with one deep breath, we were off.

"If you use two condoms, can you still get pregnant or catch a sexual disease?"

"Can you get pregnant from anal sex?"

"If you pop a girl's cherry, will she gush blood?"

This went on for the next sixty minutes. Hand after hand went up. Almost everyone in the class had a question to ask, and those who didn't were paying close attention to the answers. I covered everything from basic hygiene to dealing with HIV/AIDS. The kids had a thirst for knowledge, and the longer the discussion went on, the more comfortable I became saying things like "penis," "vagina," "clitoris," and "anus." The kids didn't laugh or giggle; they just listened and asked more questions. I figured if they were brave enough to ask the questions, I could muster the courage to give them the information they really wanted to know.

As the day ended, the kids packed up their books, and the student who started all of this with the first question said, "Thanks. I knew you would answer my question. You know a lot of stuff, and you're not the kind of teacher that's afraid of things. Sorry it kind of got out of hand at the end."

"Hey, no problem," I lied.

But then I figured the only thing scarier than the questions would have been if they didn't have anyone to answer them at all.

## 18.

Although my students grew up in a small farming community three and a half hours from the closest metropolitan area, they sat quietly as Erin Gruwell and a dozen Freedom Writers shared their personal stories. They enjoyed Erin's comments, but it was her students—the Freedom Writers—and their individual tales that broke down the facades my students had constructed and touched the raw sores of their inner lives. Confusion flooded their faces when an African American Freedom Writer shared the story that he had been advised not to come on this trip because people in our area drove pickup trucks. He told them that he feared pickup trucks because of the stereotype of racism and violence. A black man in the South had recently been dragged to death behind a pickup. Finally, tears gave way to laughter when the young man said he had ridden in nothing but pickup trucks for the past three days and his experience in our area had enabled him to overcome some of his own fears and prejudice.

It was a great day of hands-on activities and intense sharing. My students couldn't stop talking about all the great things that had taken place that day.

I had barely entered my classroom when one of my aides came up and told me we had a problem.

"What do you mean?" I asked.

"One of our students stole a book," she said.

"Stole a book? Who steals a free book?"

"It gets worse. He actually stole two books. And one of them was the mayor's."

"Are you kidding? The books are personally signed by Erin and the Freedom Writers and have someone else's name in them."

"Uh, he took care of that problem by tearing the front page with all the signatures out of both books."

Extremely embarrassed and frustrated, I called Erin and told her I needed to order a couple copies of *The Freedom Writers Diary* because one of my students had stolen two books, including the mayor's. When Erin finally stopped laughing, she told me not to worry. She said she would cover the cost of the books if I would turn the incident into a teachable moment, and she insisted the cost of the books was a small price to pay for a great lesson.

Afterward, I took the student aside and asked him why he stole the books.

"I just wanted to see if I could pull it off without getting caught," he said.

"Did you stop to think about the impact the theft would have on the person whose book you stole?"

"What's the big deal? It's just a book," he replied with a shrug of his shoulders.

I sat the rest of my class down, filled them in on what had

happened, and asked for their comments. While a few students looked at the ground, the majority turned and stared at the guilty student.

"What were you thinkin', man?" one student asked. "Everyone already thinks we're a bunch of losers, and then you gotta go and steal a freakin' free book. How stupid is that?"

"Yeah, you take those books, and we all get a bum rap," a girl across the circle said, her eyes were like red hot lasers.

"You don't get it, do you? All day, that lady and those guys from L.A. talked about how we need to make good choices and do the right thing," another guy said. "Weren't you listenin' at all?"

Jazzed up about the day's experiences, my students unloaded on their classmate, letting him know how they felt about his theft. For the rest of the period, I sat back and listened as my students taught the day's final lesson.

## 19.

My coworker Mr. Johnson and I were on hall patrol. The break between bells lasts only four minutes, but it seems like an eternity with staff yelling: "Go to class!" "Pull your pants up!" "Get on the right side of the hall!" "Not so loud!" "Stop cursing!" "Stop pushing!" "Hurry up out of the bathroom!" The tardy bell rang, and it seemed that all students were in class. Mr. Johnson and I walked back to my office, talking about how crazy the week had been, when we were startled by what sounded like a small explosion. *Boom!*

The sound came from the boy's bathroom, which was right up the hall from where we were. Mr. Johnson and I ran to the bathroom, concerned that a student might be hurt. When we entered the restroom, we saw one of my favorite students, Donte, standing in a puddle of toilet water and broken porcelain. His pants were splattered with water, and the look of embarrassment on his face was priceless. We made sure he wasn't hurt, given all the broken porcelain that was scattered across the floor. After the initial awkward glances and silence, Mr. Johnson said, "I am glad whoever was in there flushed the toilet or you would have been in some serious shit!" We busted out laughing, and despite his embarrassment, even Donte had to laugh, too.

"What happened?" we asked. Donte admitted that he had been standing on top of the toilet to smoke. "That way," he said, "when people look under the stall, they don't see my feet, and I am high enough to see over the stall to see who's coming." At that moment, I thought to myself, "Smokers sure are a determined group of people. They will do the most ridiculous things to get their fix." Donte was no exception.

Situations like this don't stay quiet for very long, and it didn't take much time for the incident to become the source of jokes for days with Donte on the receiving end. It was hard for Donte to be the butt of the joke because most times he was on the giving end. Hearing him being teased constantly, I couldn't help but think how this was a perfect example that what goes around comes around. A couple of days later Donte said, "Mr. Carter, I think I'm going to try to start doing the right thing." Who knew that public humiliation could get someone to do the right thing?

The fact is teenagers are going to mess up, and they need someone to help pick up the pieces. Donte's incident reminded me of the time I made a bad haircut decision and my dad flipped. I can still remember that day vividly.

"Boy, what the hell have you done to ya head? Damn, you done lost your mother-fucking mind?"

Terrified at my father's anger and not knowing what to say, I blurted out, "Mr. T on *The A-Team* has one." After I had taken some old hair clippers and cut my hair in a Mohawk in middle school, all I knew was it looked cool to me and Mr. T had one. That's all I cared about.

What I have learned over my ten years in education is that life's often unexpected moments such as this can help even the most confused individuals make sense of it all. Donte learned his lesson, it seems, but only time will tell. Before this moment, I could never get Donte to 'fess up to his wrongdoings. To hear him say he wanted to change was indeed a first step. Some of us can be told to change, many of us have to fall on our asses multiple times before we change, and the rest of us have to stand in the shit we've created.

## 20.

It was a mistake to bring my $300 in rent into the weekly book club and creative writing session I teach to sixteen- and seventeen-year-old boys charged as adults at the jail. At the end of class my empty wallet, driver's license, and credit cards were strewn in the corner.

My colleague Leslie and I had been the victims of a simple yet effective plan. Antonio, a shy, pint-size boy who hid his big, sad eyes behind long braids, had approached me. He'd been telling us for weeks that he didn't "do the writing thing." Then suddenly this week there he was, standing in front of me with his journal open and asking, "Um, can you give me some writing topics . . . lots of them?"

It was a teacher's dream, a real breakthrough. I set to work excitedly listing prompts: "If You Really Knew Me," "The Scariest Day of My Life," "I Wish." Four or five students then joined in, circling me and asking for their own topics and shouting out questions.

While I was reveling in our success, a second group of students, led by Delonte, the resident class clown and instigator, grabbed the cash and began dispersing it. When I realized we'd been duped, I tried to console myself with the thought that at least they were working together on something. We were constantly trying to foster a supportive brotherhood among all the boys, who often had been enemies on the street.

I couldn't justify their actions, but $300 in cash out in the open in my bag was a very tempting get. The hard reality in the jail is that they need money for even basic necessities like toothpaste and deodorant. If you don't have someone from the outside who can put money into your canteen, you have to find the money on your own. But I still felt sick to my stomach, a queasy combination of shock, disappointment, and embarrassment for my own naïveté. I guess I had subconsciously thought a bond had been created in the classroom that gave Leslie and me immunity from any harm.

I notified the correctional officer taking the boys back to their cells about what had happened and endured a verbal dressing-down from him for bringing cash into the jail in the first place. As I left, I wondered how I would ever be able to turn this into a teachable moment.

I wasn't expecting to get my money back, so when the security officer slapped on latex gloves and reached for a clear plastic bag full of bills, I felt as though I'd pulled a lever and gotten three cherries. I thought it was odd the bills were in a bag, but I chalked it up to protecting the evidence.

"Ma'am, I suggest you decontaminate," he said.

Decontaminate? What was he talking about? "Sir, can you explain a bit more for me? How would you recommend I decontaminate?"

"Ma'am, I've got a jail of two thousand people to secure. I don't have time to give you a lesson in decon. There is two hundred eighty dollars here, fourteen twenty-dollar bills. We couldn't get at the last twenty, sorry."

Couldn't get *at* the last twenty?

When I got home, I called Leslie and asked her what she thought "decon" meant. Her laughter grew louder, and finally she blurted out, "Oh my gosh, you've got poopy money!"

What? It all started to become horribly clear. The officer explained it further at our next class. After I had alerted him, he'd pulled all the boys into the gym and strip-searched them. The money had been evenly distributed. I wondered if they had taken a recent book we read on socialism to heart.

At our next session I was so nervous my voice was shaking. I began, "I felt really hurt last week, and I'm trying to understand why you all did what you did." They squirmed in their seats, and most eyes fell to the ground. I went on to tell them how their actions affected me, how much I cared about them and wanted to forgive them. I also told them that a trust was broken between us that we'd have to work hard at repairing.

After a long silence Antonio mumbled, "I'm sorry for what you went through." Then others began to share and offer their apologies. Several said they were not involved, but for the most part it was a time of real exchange of feelings.

Leslie asked, "Have you ever thought about what your other victims have gone through?" Stories flowed out about how most of them had been victims of assaults and robberies themselves. Their own victims were faceless and anonymous to them. They hadn't really considered what the emotional effects could be. Many had never heard the word "empathy" before. We asked them to imagine how they would feel if their own mother or grandmother had been harmed, instead of a nameless person they didn't have to think about.

I lost my naïveté that day, but I gained new understanding and passion for restorative justice, where victims and offenders meet so healing can begin.

I really don't know how much of our discussion got through, but I do know that Antonio is one of our best writers now and Delonte stays in touch through letters from federal prison and wants to be a counselor when he is released.

I also know that twenty-dollar bills scrubbed down with bleach, microwaved, and placed in the dryer don't hold up too well.

# CHALLENGES

A guidance counselor told you that you have all the important character traits: organizational skills, multitasking, problem solving, seeing the best in everyone. So the decision to become a teacher was easy, right?

What no one told you was that you'd be overwhelmed with stress, have an unmanageable workload, and have no option but to break up even the worst of fights wearing pantyhose and your good pair of heels. When the Freedom Writers came into my class, they carried with them all kinds of baggage. Some of my students had been homeless or faced teenage pregnancy, and others claimed to have "attended more funerals than birthday parties."

Initially, my students did not want to reveal these wounds to me and tried to hide the scars. They were afraid that I would call child protective services or turn them in to the police.

When their stories began to pour forth onto the pages of their journals, I was taken aback. All I had to offer them in return were my own life experiences. But even when my students were in pain, it was difficult to decide how much of my past I should reveal. "Keeping it real" was always a brutal balancing act.

The stories in this section expose some of the most heart-wrenching testimonies about what life is really like as a teacher. Many of the Freedom Writer Teachers have students who come from disturbing realities. Too many of the stories in this section reveal tragic parallels between a student's current situation and a teacher's painful past—surviving child abuse, persevering through foster care, and overcoming suicidal thoughts. But the teachers' struggles to honestly reveal these parallels created the safe environment where students could come and ultimately begin their own healing process.

## 21

In come my students, eighteen alpha males incarcerated for violence and/or drug abuse. There's Jose, five-foot-eight, with a round tub of belly. His face is straight and expressionless. There is Samson, always smiling. His smile is warm and inviting even when he's doing something horrible. There is Jack, a foot shorter than everyone else. He is constantly gabbing away.

"Samson and Jon got in a fight during rec therapy," Jack begins. "Samson lost his level, Jon is at the nurse's, we played dodgeball, I have a court date coming up in a week . . ." I scan the room to see Samson smiling and poking Jose with a pencil, ". . . we all finished our work in history, this room smells weird, Jose is on pencil restriction . . ."

I approach Samson and take the pencil from him and put it firmly on the table in front of Jose. "Stop antagonizing him," I say.

"He likes it," Samson smiles.

I look at Jose. His face is straight. He doesn't acknowledge Samson or me. I turn to Samson, "Don't mess with him."

I have never seen Jose show expression. "Hi, Jose," I say. "How are you today?"

Jose's eyes are locked on the air in front of him. He breathes loudly, his belly moving in and out.

Samson moves to the front of the class, where a couple of kids are play-fighting.

Jack is still talking, ". . . lunch was ham and cheese sandwiches again, and our morning snacks tasted like cat food . . ."

The airtight, windowless room catches and traps every unwanted scent. The eighteen bodies coming from a workout raised the heat about ten degrees. Body odor, cleaning supplies, damp air. My head hurts. There is only one option. "Okay, everyone, it's nice outside. Let's go to the courtyard and read. Grab your books."

I usher Samson out of the room with the rest of the stragglers. The others are already with the two adult supervisors, lining up in the hall.

"Count off," one of the adult supervisors says. They begin counting. I scan the classroom to make sure nothing is missing. I shut and lock the door and run to the head of the group.

"Let's go." I begin walking, and they follow. I lead them through many locked doors to the enclosed courtyard.

"Find a spot, sit down, and read."

My students sit down on the grass and begin talking to one another.

Jose sits away from the others. He has his back against the side of the building. I roam around and quiet everyone up. I too sit down and begin to read.

I am impressed at my students' calmness today. They are all reading, it seems, and I can breathe.

Times of peace are short.

Jack runs over to me and says, "Call a code blue!"

A code blue? My mind is reeling through all of the various codes that can be called in the case of emergencies. Code green: A resident has escaped. Code yellow: There is a riot. Code brown: A resident has defecated in an unorthodox spot. I have never called a code blue.

"Why?" I ask, trying to remember.

"It's Jose," Jack says. "He did it again."

Jose has his hand on his right cheek. He removes his hand but leaves behind a smattering of blood that is dripping onto his shoulder. *A code blue is a medical emergency, of course.* I run over to Jose. His left arm is bleeding profusely. A bloody pencil is on his lap. He punctured his left arm numerous times with the pencil. One puncture bore deep into his subclavian artery. Blood spurts from the hole rhythmically.

*Holy shit.* I grab the courtyard phone and punch "Page All" and yell through the receiver, "Code blue courtyard, code blue courtyard!"

I run over to the nurse's station and knock on the door. Carla, a nurse, opens it.

"We need you in the courtyard now."

"What happened?" She asks as she is grabbing some supplies.

"It's Jose," I say. "He stabbed himself."

She sighs. "Not again. I guess I'll need more of this." She reaches down and grabs a stack of gauze pads.

In the courtyard, all of the kids are gawking at Jose. He is an angry bull. He charges those who come too close. The supervisor tells the kids to back off. Jose's head shrugs forward, his body too weak to support it. Blood still spurting from his wound, he falls to the ground.

Carla crouches down before him, puts her hand on his shoulder, and asks, "Are you okay?"

Jose shakes his head. His eyes roll back. His wounded arm rests on his plump belly. Carla straightens his arm out to inspect it. She inspects the blood on his face and doesn't find a wound. She looks at his blood-soaked arm. She tries to lift up his shirt, but Jose shrieks and holds it down with both arms. The nurse looks behind her to see the other seventeen kids watching intently.

"Everyone turns around," she says. They do. She looks back to Jose and says, "It's okay." Jose lets her lift up his shirt to inspect his abdomen. She finds no wounds. She applies gauze to his bleeding arm, wraps it, and takes him to the nurses' station.

Two days pass.

Jose has been on bed rest and suicide precaution. He is still on pencil restriction.

I see him in the hallway as he waits to see his therapist. His left arm has many scabs, all undressed.

"How are you, Jose?" I ask. "I've been worried about you."

"Not good."

"Why did you do that the other day?"

"I don't know."

"Are you going to do it again?"

"Yes."

## 22

"I can't do this no more—I want out of this crazy, fucked-up life!"

Sierra stands across from me, lips pursed in anger. She is five-foot-two and just over 100 pounds, but she terrifies me. At fifteen, she has a facial piercing and a lifetime of stories that she wears like a bulletproof vest. Pacing, throwing her rage and sadness around the room, she screams, "Nobody knows what I go through! Nobody!"

Her tattered words reveal more emotion than her tearless, bloodshot eyes. I don't know what to do. I am a first-year teacher. No education class prepared me for a suicidal student. I freeze. I trip over my words: "Sierra . . . have you talked to someone like a counselor . . . about this . . . about feeling this way?" She can see through me, sense my fear. I feel myself unwinding. I try to utter something wise, but it feels forced: "I think you have every reason to feel angry and depressed."

Sierra sits down, puts her hands over her ears, and taps her foot anxiously as she mutters into the desk, "Some people just don't belong, and it's better that way."

I timidly touch her shoulder. She slowly raises her head. Our eyes lock for a moment. There is something I want to share, but I hold back and mutter instead, "Sierra, I think we need to get you help."

Sierra sits up, holding herself, then bolts out the door, betrayed.

I chase after her, fearing the worst—that she will run outside into the busy street and throw herself in front of traffic. We pass the glass front doors, dodging the street, and turn into another hallway. Where is she going? What am I doing? Why the hell am I the one Sierra came to? Should *I* be running out the door?

Are Sierra and I really that far from each other?

Our footsteps echo down the empty hallway until I corner her. My instincts take over, and I throw my arms around her. She resists until her thin frame hangs limp, unresponsive. Then she sobs, all her toughness slipping away: "Why can't I be normal?" It's like looking in a mirror.

I am the survivor of four suicide attempts. The first time I was fifteen, and the last time I was twenty. I was so disconnected from myself, from the people around me, and this was the only way I knew: I tried to kill myself to kill the pain.

But how can I tell any of this to Sierra?

Weeks later, when she returns from a stay in the psych unit, I am nervous. I know what she saw there, and I know the journey she has ahead of her. I smile when I see her, but I receive an empty stare hidden behind her black bangs. I recognize that look. The look of tired—tired of being at war with oneself, of living, of failing at living, of trying to die, of failing at death.

At first, Sierra sleeps in the back of the class, her hoodie pulled over her head, shut like a shell. Then, weeks later, she sits at the front of the room, rolling her eyes, tapping her foot, sighing, and muttering, "This is bullshit." In a matter of months, she explodes: "I hate this fucking class! You don't do nothing to help us out!" The tension between us grows unbearable, to the point that a social worker is present with Sierra during my class, to the point that I want to give up or give in.

But Sierra journals. Even on days she doesn't have my class, she has her journal. I can tell it's broken in by the worn corners and the contrast between the wrinkled pages and the crisp, smooth ones. I am curious about what she writes. Then, as I am passing out papers one day, she discreetly asks me to read her journal.

"Which entry?" I ask, shocked.

"Any." She slips me her journal and turns away.

That evening, I read it cover to cover. She writes about her mom, about their tumultuous relationship. She writes about the night she witnessed her friend's murder, about wanting to bring him back, about wondering why she's left here. She writes about her other suicide attempts, about her hospitalizations, about wanting to get better but not knowing how. Between her harsh, angular words, there's an element of softness, of vulnerability, of poetry, much like Sierra herself.

I cry as I read, knowing I should do more. I hug her journal when I finish. Now I understand the stories behind those eyes. I understand the pain and the anger and why she wears them both like armor. I understand how lives overlap in the classroom. Finally, I begin to write: "We're both survivors . . ."

## 23.

Kate strides into the room with purpose. She walks quickly and takes her seat adjacent to my desk. She rests her bubblegum-pink backpack, the one that engulfs her four-foot frame, on the floor. The backpack outweighs her. She carries all of her books, refusing to use a locker in order to avoid "wasting time in the halls." She takes out a mechanical pencil and places it horizontally on the desk in front of her. She takes out a piece of lined paper, preprinted with the heading required, and places it next to the pencil. Another zip of the backpack reveals *A Separate Peace*, by John Knowles; she begins reading. Period 3 starts in fifteen minutes. It is snack time, but instead of talking with friends out on the grass, she sits at her desk, camouflaged by my classroom. In Kate's world there is no downtime, and when I greet her, she simply looks up, smiles without showing her teeth, and nods.

Driven and analytical, she devours every assignment regardless of the point value attached to it. A product of Ivy League parents, Kate navigates her way with ease around the academic game of high school. Her battleground remains the social side of campus. Kate rarely engages in conversation with her peers. She isn't really one of them. She skipped a grade in elementary school.

During class she pleads with me to let her work alone rather than with a partner or in a group, professing to "work better that way." The work she submits convinces me; I allow her to work independently. She seems so self-confident academically that it doesn't appear to matter to her that she doesn't have a date for Homecoming. I can't really picture her at Homecoming; I can picture her discovering a cure for cancer, quietly, alone in a dimly lit laboratory. When her peers rally around beating the rival school in football, she ignores them. When they talk of their experiences with dating, art classes, or student government, she nonchalantly looks the other way. Her energies focus on reading and her mission: completing assignments. And her work isn't just complete, it is brilliant. I figure this social adjustment will eventually work itself out, even though she is so stealthy and quiet. A member of the Animal Rights Club, she explains to me one day while taking refuge in my classroom during the snack break that "animals don't really have a voice, so someone needs to stick up for them." When the bell rings and while students discuss their capricious first loves, she asks if I will recommend her for the honors class next year as she rubs her sweaty palms together and pushes her glasses back to the top of her nose. I assure her I will.

She never comes to visit me during her junior or senior year. I see her walking through campus, negotiating the student land mines standing around every corner. Her quiet demeanor makes her an easy target for verbal assault. Students whisper insulting bullets about her clothing, her childlike choice of folder, her pink sparkly ponytail holder. She flies by seemingly impervious to their comments. The devastation of their words subsides when she is not in firing range as they speak. Sighing, I hope she has an outlet for her creativity and at least one friend who shares her accomplishments, even though I rarely see her walking with other students, only around them.

One day in May of her senior year Kate came home from school and went straight upstairs to her room. Concerned when she wasn't present at the agreed-upon time for dinner, the maid went to check on her. Walking into a still room, she found Kate hanging, as silent as the clothing beside her, in the closet. She slipped out of this world intentionally and without a sound. When I heard the news, my heart dropped like an elevator with its cable cut.

Poised adjacent to the desk wherein Kate used to sit rests my Teacher of the Year award and, while it slightly obstructs my view to her old desk, in its reflection I will always see Kate.

## 24.

As Patty walks by to take her seat, Jen says just loud enough so the girls who act like a pack of wolves circle in for the kill, "Oh my God, what a slut."

"I would never wear something that makes me look so cheap and whorish," replies Sandy.

"Did you hear what she did at the party?"

"I know, it's all around the school, stupid girl. She is ruined here, and I'm going to make her life hell."

These words flow so freely from Jen and Sandy, two of my students. They think I can't hear them, and I wish I couldn't. The smiles of the beautiful are razor sharp, enough to cut through the toughest Hollister or Abercrombie exterior to slay someone's spirit. I know how bad the girls in my class hurt each other because I read their journals:

> My father has told me to be more like my sister. Why can't I be like her? My sister is a skinny, perfect, beautiful prom queen, amazing at everything she ever did. Then the rumors. I cried so hard that it was a dream, this couldn't be happening to me. My friends have left me. Friends! What friends! I want to curl up every time I think about them. There is too much pressure. Enemies! Making up rumors, telling false stories behind my back.

The girls slowly kill one another. They do a drive-by with words, verbally killing any sense of self-confidence or hope. Today's victim ended up here by accident, her four-inch heels clicking across the floor, the Louis Vuitton bag clutched to her chest, the makeup perfectly done.

I had had enough.

I kept thinking about a new assignment. It had the potential to be great or to fail miserably. The students got armed with a pack of Post-it Notes. They had to write a short note to everyone in the class. Two rules: All positive, and everyone must get one. Go.

An excited moment, energy filled the room; they bought into the idea. Simple kindness, this was what was missing in their lives. I watched the interactions closely. Separate tribes, the haves and havenots, the cool and the left behind, all running around the room dropping notes to each other.

"You're not as mean as I thought you were."

"I hope we can be friends outside of class."

"Remember when we were friends? I want it back."

"I have a secret crush on you."

Patty, the most recent victim, sat at her seat, her petite hands sifting through her notes, much as one sifts through ashes of the past. She started crying softly. No one heard her at first; they were too wrapped up in their own worlds. Patty was sobbing uncontrollably now, hands in her face. The class froze. I knocked over my chair as I furiously jumped out of it.

"What happened? What's wrong?"

The dragon was ready to come out of my six-foot, 200-pound body and rip someone apart.

Patty held up a single Post-it Note. It said, "I am happy you're here, please forgive me."

She wiped her eyes and looked right at the mean girl who had written the note. She said, "My dad found out I was bulimic. My friends left me. I tried to commit suicide."

I was stunned; I knew Patty was battling problems, but I didn't know this.

"This note meant so much to me. I thought about trying it again," she said. "But this class helps give me strength because I can be myself. No one feels my pain except in here."

Patty didn't even look up while she was talking.

I recovered from my shock and did the only thing I could do, gave her a hug and said, "Let's go talk to the counselor and get you some help."

As Patty looked back across the class, only two pairs of eyes followed her the entire way out of the room: Jen's and Sandy's.

## 25.

By being promiscuous, I discovered, I could quickly fit into my new "dark cloud city." The early sex, the name-brand clothes and the attention they brought, and doing things I thought my Momma would never find out about hurt the people I loved most and threw my life off course.

I grew up in the rural South. From the outside looking in, my family life seemed blissful. Mom and Dad fought a lot, but that didn't stop us from doing things. We went out to eat, skated, visited talent shows, toured parks, shopped, bowled, and worshipped in our local church. We took twice-a-month trips to my grandmomma's house, come hell or high water, even if Mom and Dad had fought the night before. My mother worked two jobs, and Dad was self-employed. We didn't want for anything, not even attention. My father even had us a house built in a gated community. I didn't know it at the time, but our house was built with dirty money. And dirty money leaves a trail. I remember the chief of police coming to our home and telling my parents (Dad in particular) to stop dealing the drugs 'cause Dad's name had come up next on their list to be busted. Dad didn't listen, but Mom did, so within two weeks we were all packed, ready to board the train to a big city—which is now known to me as a "dark cloud city." There is where my story really began.

This new city was way bigger than the rural area we had come from. "Wow," I thought, "a city bus." In the South, we walked almost everywhere. Thank God my oldest sister and other family members had moved to the city before us and could now show us around.

Within a month I landed in a school that was bigger than the town we lived in down South. They didn't paddle students for disrupting the class like in the South, but they did hand out 72s—slips of paper to be taken to the office. I quickly learned that getting a 72 was my ticket to skipping school without Momma ever knowing.

Middle school city kids were cursing, drinking forty ounces, having sex, skipping school, and abusing drugs. My sisters and I were shocked 'cause we were still saying "Yes, ma'am" and "No, sir." I couldn't help wondering what the city students did when they skipped school, and soon enough I became subject to the wrong environment. Smoking weed, cursing, drinking, and skipping school were all I thought about. The "jump-down girls" clique was my clique now, too. I went from "Yes, ma'am" and "No, sir" to "Fuck that" and "Kiss my ass." I was a hot mess, to say the least.

At fourteen, I was pregnant. At fifteen, I had a baby with no daddy in sight and little clue to who the father might be. I'd even had sex with my sister's boyfriend, so anybody's guess was as good as mine. I learned my way around the "dark cloud city" with my legs wide open and my eyes shut.

Now here I sit, eleven and a half years later, and it looks to me as if history is repeating itself. My daughter is starting to skip school, and it seems as if she is too friendly with the boys in our neighborhood. Fear creeps in, but I can't allow the "dark cloud" to close my eyes this time. Older, wiser, and remembering what curiosity did to this cat, I won't permit it to steer my child in the wrong direction.

I chose to go back to school and get the education that was long overdue. I had to take responsibility that being promiscuous at an early age caused me to become a teenage mom.

Where I was once frustrated, I am now determined. Where I was detoured, I have righted my ship. Where I was delayed, I am making up time in a hurry. The many directions of my life have not left me broken but strong. The pain that once hovered over me like a dark cloud can be turned inside out—into an outpouring of inspiration to rain over my daughter, my future students, and my new life.

## 26.

There is a knock on the classroom door. It's Mandy.

"Miss, I need to talk to you."

There's just twelve minutes until my next class and I promised that all their tests would be graded, but I hear myself say, "Come on in." I smile, but the look on her face is grave, not her usual.

"You know that Steven and I have been seeing each other for more than a year now and I know I said I was a virgin but last month we decided to be together. I know, I know, I went to the clinic and I got birth control. No way was I gonna be stupid."

"You do realize that the pill only protects you from pregnancy, not diseases, and it only protects you if you take it every day?"

"Yeah, I know but it's not that though. It is Anthony."

"Anthony? From our class?"

"Yeah, he's my friend and my brother's best friend and he found out about me and Steven and told my mom. Last night, in the middle of the night, she came bustin' into my room. She woke me up. Miss, she was ranting about me having sex and screaming that I was probably already pregnant. She said she was

gonna beat me and my sister with a belt because Lisa said nothin'
and must have known, and that it was a disgrace to find out from
a stranger."

I feel a little unsteady. I reach for the corner of my desk. Focus, I tell myself, focus.

"I was begging, 'No, Ma! No, Ma! Lisa had nothin' to do with
it. I never told her nothin'. Don't even touch her, Mom. It's all
me, Ma!' And then she did it. Miss, she hit me with the belt. She
was yelling all kinds of shit, saying that she should throw me out
into the streets like the whore that I am. My sister was screaming
for her to stop but it just seemed to make it worse. She said she'd
send me to Mexico and make me live with my father. Mexico?
I'm an American. I can't ever live there. Besides, I never even met
the guy. He left before I was born. Miss, she said that she'd make
sure I'd never see Steven again. Look, I know that she'd never
throw me out in the streets, but she might send me away. I think
she might actually send me away."

"Mandy, come over here."

She hesitates, takes a few baby steps, stops, and starts again.
This child is making her way toward me with eyes lined like Amy
Winehouse's, that piercing on her delicate nose, and those long,
crazy, clear acrylic nails rimmed in black. I hug her. Was that a
wince? I think that might have been a wince. Is she bruised and
hurting under that denim jacket?

"Are you all right?"

"Yeah, I'm fine."

"Do you want to go see your guidance counselor?" Did I
really just say that?

"Huh, no! I wouldn't talk to him about nothin' like that."
Mandy bristles.

Shit, she is insulted. I lower my head. I cover my forehead
with my hand. The tips of my fingers begin to rub the space between my eyebrows in firm circular motions. They move a little
bit above that spot and press more firmly.

"Has your mom ever done that before? Hit you with a belt, I mean." I'm looking so deeply into her eyes I feel like Alice about to crack the mirror.

"No! Never. She just totally freaked when she found out I wasn't a virgin anymore."

"Mandy, you do realize that as a teacher I am a mandated reporter."

"A what?"

"By law I have to report any incident, any suspicion even, that any of my students might have been hurt or abused."

"It's not like that, Miss. I'm okay. I'm all right. I wasn't even worried about that. I was just so scared she'd send me away. You can't tell. Don't tell nobody. This is the longest I've ever lived anywhere, and I graduate in June. Miss, don't say anything. It's not like what you say. It's not like that. I'm okay. Don't you know? I trusted you. You gotta trust me."

Don't I know? Don't I know what? Don't I know that she is okay or that she trusted me? I don't know what I know.

"Mandy, it's the law. It's my job. I don't have a choice here."

"We always have choices. You said so. You said we got to think for ourselves."

Mandy's big green eyes plead, but they don't have to because I won't say anything. I knew I wouldn't even before I said the words "mandated reporter."

## 27.

"Damn! I'm sick and tired of these boys in this school," Imani yelled as she walked into class fifteen minutes late. She quickly policed the room, seeking a seat in the back, where she never sits. She must have gotten into a fight with Jamal, her boyfriend, again. They argue constantly.

After ten minutes of teaching, I went by Imani's desk. "Are you all right?" I asked her. She lifted her face and tears fell from her eyes. I knew it was something serious. Imani never cries. I asked my support teacher to watch the class as I led my student into the hall.

Imani leaned against the lockers. "Ms. Bryant, you cannot tell anyone about this!"

"As I always tell you, Imani, I care and am responsible for what happens to you. Therefore if what you tell me endangers your life, I will share this conversation with your guidance counselor."

With tears streaming down her face she blurted, "Ms. Bryant, I am three months pregnant, and Jamal and I are not ready to become parents. You know I have always kept it real with you, Ms. Bryant. I am only sixteen trying to get my life together."

I asked her who else knew that she was pregnant.

"I only shared this with Aunt Liz and Jamal, for I'm too afraid of telling my mom. My mom would be so hurt and disappointed. Besides she already has enough to deal with. She is currently caring for my seventy-two-year-old sick grandmother, my fifteen-year-old brother is in and out of the detention center, and she is just simply trying to make ends meet financially. Although my aunt Liz is disappointed with me too, for not taking my birth control pills regularly, she is willing to support me in my decision."

We had spent many hours discussing life issues in the Gear Up program last year, and I thought Imani would have been more responsible.

"Can you forgive me, Ms. Bryant?"

Of course I could forgive her, just as I had forgiven myself.

I began: I too was afraid to tell my mom that I was pregnant, especially being pregnant at seventeen for the third time. After pacing the floor back and forth for several days, I decided to have another abortion without telling Mom again.

As I was riding the P12 bus to the hospital that Tuesday morning, I was still wrestling with whether or not I was making the right decision. Although I knew of the fasting after 12 a.m.

from my last two abortion experiences, I chose to eat my butter roll. Part of me was hoping that this doctor would proceed anyway.

The woman in bed next to me began sharing about the blessings of having children. She shared that children are God's beautiful creations. Then she asked, "Why are you here?" I was uncomfortable and scared, but I told her because there was something special about this woman. She prompted me to share my feelings toward why I was choosing to abort my baby. I answered truthfully: I was scared as hell. I was only seventeen. I wanted to be the first in my family to graduate from college, and I knew it would be a struggle, especially since I didn't know if I could count on the father for support.

The woman shared that although she got married before her children came, she still had her struggles in her marriage. She said, "God has a way of bringing unique challenges to help each person mature. No matter what decision you make, God will always send his angels to get you through the struggles. You must forgive yourself and not feel shame about the decisions that you have made."

Tears fell from my eyes. I thanked her as the nurse came in. "Did you have anything to eat since last night?" she asked. I said, "Ms., I was so hungry while waiting, I had to eat my butter roll."

She left to tell the doctor what I had eaten. Within ten minutes, she returned and informed me that the doctor would have to reschedule for tomorrow. I said okay, thanked the woman for sharing, and quickly left the hospital room.

Could I raise a child without being married? How could I graduate from college and be a single parent? Would God really send an angel to come along and support me? Could I really provide a great life for my child?

Throughout the night, I tossed and turned, thinking about whether or not I should have the baby. After praying and contemplating, I decided to keep the baby. Because I was still afraid to tell my mom, I did not tell her until two months later. She said, "Marie, I already knew that you were, and I decided to wait until you said something first."

Mom was disappointed. She read me the riot act, but she said she would support me as much as she could.

As I finished sharing my struggles with Imani, she stood there for a moment, silent, considering what I had said. Then she replied, "Thanks, Ms. Bryant. I just don't know. Guess I better tell my mom?"

I hugged her. "Whatever you decide, Imani, I am here for you. Remember that."

## 28.

"Some say I was lucky." I gently close the tattered and frayed pages of the book I am reading to my class and glance at the soundless students sitting in front of me. As I begin to explain the premise of the book to my seniors, my voice shakes: "Alice Sebold, the author of *Lucky*, was raped at the age of eighteen. Her memoir was written to save her life and, in return, it saved mine." My heart begins beating louder and harder. I close my eyes so that the tears filling my eyes can stay hidden. I take a deep breath and do something I never thought I would do. I begin recounting my own rape.

I remember that night as if it were yesterday. I am in a room. With a man. Paralyzed by booze and fear. Music blaring—the sound of Queen drowning out my screams. It is just the two of us. I am trembling; he is in control. I am scared for my life; he is growing more powerful and determined with every "no" I scream. I am a virgin. He is stealing my innocence; I am letting him walk away. I tell no one. And he rapes six other young women.

I take a deep breath, open my tear-filled eyes, and place myself back into the classroom, where I am no longer *just* a teacher; I am now a person, a victim, a human. The students are silent and dazed, and as I glance around the room, my eyes are drawn toward Angela. I can see the once-twinkling eyes become blurry. Just moments ago she was giggly and energetic. Just moments ago she was the girl who seemed perfect. The beautiful blond-haired girl that every boy wants to date and every girl wishes to look like is suddenly clothed in terror. Angela, the typical American girl who has been accepted into her dream college, who is a member of the Homecoming Court, who has many friends and receives good grades, is falling apart before my eyes.

As the class departs, Angela stays glued in her seat. I walk over to her and wrap my arms tightly around her. She begins to sob. She was raped only two weeks ago, and I am the first person she tells.

She is at her first college party, posing as a sophomore from a nearby university. The cup of beer in her hand is never empty. She has caught the attention of several young men, but one will not leave her alone. He refills her drink, telling her how beautiful she is, calls her his "dream girl." He is saying all the right things. As the room begins to sway, she realizes she should leave. But he has other plans.

"He kept telling me how beautiful I was . . . He started . . . and then . . . I can't . . . oh my God . . ."

Her sobs are deep, and her breath is becoming more labored. I cradle her in my arms, wishing that I could make her hurt disappear. All I can do is listen and understand. As I hold her, I can feel her body shake as her tears mix with my own.

"Angela, I am here, I am right here. I am not going anywhere."

"It was not . . . supposed . . . Oh my God, what am I going to do?"

"It's going to be okay. I promise, you are going to be okay."

"I feel so dirty . . . I feel so . . . Why did I go? Why did I believe him? Why did this happen to me? It was all my fault . . . I should have never . . ."

"Angela, I *never* want to hear you say that it was your fault. It was *not* your fault. You did nothing wrong. You are a beautiful and amazing young woman, and he had no right to harm you. He had no right to rape you!"

I grasp Angela by her arms and stare into her broken eyes, realizing that what I am about to tell her is something I wish had been said to me years ago when I needed it most: "I love you." I whisper those three simple words over and over as we rock gently together, alone in an abandoned classroom, crying for something we know we can never have again, knowing we will overcome.

We are lucky.

## 29.

Among my English-as-a-second-language students, Laura brought to light memories I thought forgotten and showed me that strength is always embedded in weakness. She was a shy, fourteen-year-old recent arrival from Mexico, always clad in blue jeans and loose shirts, who rarely uttered a word.

By midsemester, her shoulder-length hazel hair was not trimmed anymore. She began getting to school late and sauntered half asleep to her seat. One day I noticed rings under her eyes and asked her if she was okay. "I feel drowsy because I stayed up late last night," she replied.

Some of the warning signs of sexual abuse in teenagers are sudden changes in behavior, withdrawal, falling grades, untidy appearance, and the empty look that seems to say, "Though you see me here, I am not here."

Alarm bells went off, and when I was alone in my room, images of an almost forgotten incident flashed through my mind.

When I was twelve years old, I left home for the seminary because I wanted to become a priest. Six years later, I questioned my vocation and quit the ecclesiastical studies. I made a last trip to the seminary to pick up the clothes and books I had left behind.

Since it was my last time there, I wanted to go to the city of Guanajuato, and I asked Father Camacho if he could give me a ride. We'd visit some places and dine, and I'd take the bus back home that same night.

In Guanajuato, we set out to visit several places in the colonial downtown. It was past midnight when we finished our tour, so we decided to stay overnight in a hotel and leave the next morning. Father Camacho would drive to the pilgrimage shrine he was in charge of, and I'd take a bus back home.

In the room, I let the priest have the bed and I took the folding cot. As I was falling asleep, I felt Father Camacho's heavy body on top of me. "Hug me, just hug me," he pleaded, clinching me.

"Just put your arms around me," he kept asking me while I tried to wiggle myself out.

Desperately, I began jerking.

"What's happening?" he asked.

"I need to go to the restroom," I mumbled, frightened and shaking. "I want to throw up."

As soon as he stood up and I felt free, I sprang off the cot, snatched my pants, and darted barefoot out the door and down the stairs. I told my story to the front-desk clerk.

"Do you want me to call the police?" he asked me.

"No," I replied after a while. "He's in charge of a very famous pilgrimage site, and many people would lose their faith."

Later, Father Camacho came out hastily from the hotel. He was visibly agitated and told me he was going back to the sanctuary. Back in the room, I was afraid he'd return and I wouldn't escape a second time. So I secured the door the best I could and tried to sleep on the cot.

Years later, my students were discussing a story published in a newspaper about a young girl who had conceived her father's child as a result of repeated sexual abuse.

"This only happens among poor and illiterate families," Alex said. "Don't you think, sir?"

"It may happen everywhere, blockhead," snapped Sarah. "Doesn't it, sir?"

"When I was in the seminary, a friend of mine had a traumatic experience with a priest," I told them and then shared my own experience under an assumed name.

After I finished my story, a heavy silence set in. When the bell rang, all the students dashed for the door.

"Sir," I heard a shy voice calling. "Was that a true story?"

As I traced the voice, I saw Laura standing in the doorway, looking down and clutching her books against her chest.

"Yes, Laura," I nodded. "Unfortunately that's a true story."

"I cannot believe that happened, sir." She replied, walking back into the classroom. "My mom is very religious and we go to mass every Sunday."

"It's my own story," I confided to her.

"You're not the only one, sir," she assured me, sitting across my desk. "My mother's boyfriend began making passes at me, and one night, while she was working, he got in my room and touched me all over. I was shocked and didn't know what to do. After that, he abused me every night my mother wasn't at home. Two weeks ago, she came home earlier and found him in my bed and kicked him out . . . I'm still afraid."

Laura's voice broke. She hid her face with her arms and started to cry.

"I'm so sorry, Laura," I mumbled. "Somehow we all are survivors. If I got over it, you will, too. Sometimes writing about what happened helps heal the wounds."

She was sobbing and shaking while I stood still at my desk staring at the wooden cross on the wall. After a while, she wiped the tears off her face with her hands and started walking toward the door.

"Oh, I don't know if I can, but maybe one day I'll give it a try, sir," she promised before leaving.

When I was in the seminary, I wondered if one day I'd regret not becoming a priest, but I am glad I didn't. As a teacher, I've come to realize teaching isn't just imparting knowledge from the books, but learning life's daily lessons as well. As a teacher, I strive to turn around the lives of my students and encourage them to find their own voices.

## 30.

From the depths of despair can come great hope. I am living proof.

With little effort, I can close my eyes and re-create the feeling that literally paralyzed me that early March morning. The mere thought of it can still take my breath away. I am an alcoholic and a criminal, and a teacher.

As I lie in that jail cell, still legally drunk but painfully aware of all that is around me and all that awaits me, my helplessness sinks to utter despair. I want to will myself the ability to turn back time, to undo what I have done. But I realize that no amount of will can help me explain this to my friends, my family, all those to whom I have promised, "This will never happen again." It *has* happened again, and the only way I can relieve the pain is to avoid, avoid, avoid . . . and to end my own life.

Whatever it is that allows a human being the ability to muster up the very last ounce of strength when there is nothing left emerged from within me at that moment. The courage I found was barely detectable, in fact, but it was enough to make my heart stop as my head acknowledged I could not actually kill myself. I would, instead, have to face the future that I had just created for myself by becoming a repeat-offender drunk driver. Paralyzed by fear, I couldn't move, I couldn't rationalize, I couldn't cry. I could barely breathe. Alcoholics spend countless hours trying to be something we are not. We try to cover up our hangovers and lack of sleep, make excuses for our mistakes, and laugh off our memory losses and embarrassment. We can be very good at it for a very long time. Often, few know the true stories, our true existence. I hid my secret very, very well. Getting caught with no escape route means hitting bottom—this time, I cannot lie to myself or anyone else that something has gone horribly wrong. Now that my double lives have collided, I must admit to the world that I am in an outrageous amount of trouble because I drink and my drinking is out of control. I finally understand that if I continue to drink I will eventually end up in jail, if I am lucky; dead, if my luck runs out.

It is at this moment that a switch is flipped. I realize that the rules that I have made and changed for myself over and over again have not kept me safe and have in fact almost killed me. I also realize there is something inside me that knows better, that recognizes that this is not the person I was brought up to be and that I am robbing myself of the life God created for me. I finally admit that my drinking is a cover-up for great pain. But beneath the pain is a bright, insightful, well-educated person; an award-winning, well-respected teacher; an athlete—so many things worth saving.

Partly out of fear, and partly out of ardent determination, the desire to drink has not entered my life again since that night I was in jail. I have broken the glass prison of alcoholism. The switch flipped, and I got it: It is not the *last* drink that pushes me over the edge; it is the *first*, and that is the one I must avoid. I got it.

I rarely share my story. Most people around me have no idea and would never guess it could be true. I do not want to be defined by my alcoholism. But sometimes I wish I could say more because mine is actually a great success story. The person struggling in that jail cell is long gone, barely recognizable to me today. The beauty of my job today is that I am a teacher working with kids who also struggle, some with chemical dependency, many with parental dysfunction of all kinds. Most of them lack hope in their lives and have yet to learn that change begins from within. It is something I understand at a deep level, but I have chosen hope and I teach hope. I have come from the depths of despair and am living proof that what defines you one day need not define you the next. I have the opportunity to reach students through literature—better known in my class as "the study of human behavior"—to help them learn about themselves through their relationships with one another, and to challenge their fears through personal empowerment. They must be taught that life is full of promise. When they learn to trust me, to trust one another, and to work together, we walk, one step at a time, in a new direction. My students need not know my motivation for teaching change, but they certainly recognize my determination to help them also discover the amazing resiliency of the human spirit. I am living proof.

### 31.

My father sat on top of my mother and banged her head against the floor. Her wig started coming off. She was crying, saying that she didn't know where his keys were. I was sitting in our overstuffed Archie Bunker chair, eating from a boxed pint of vanilla ice cream with a big spoon. Vanilla ice cream was my favorite. I never had to wonder or wait when I tasted it because it was always the same: plain. But my ice cream was getting all melty because I wasn't eating it fast enough. If my father kept banging my mother's head like that, I didn't think he was ever going to get her to help him find his car keys.

PO 5-1313. I kept saying that number in my head over and over again as I ran to the phone and called the police. "My daddy was beating up my mother and I don't know what to do. I'm sp'osed to call the police because my mother ran out of the house in her slip." As I was telling the police this on the phone, I wondered if my mother would make it back in time so I could ask her if I could go to the candy truck. I'd found a dime in the couch, and I wanted to buy some Now and Laters.

I remember my mother zipping up my Picture Day dress and

hopping around frantically. "Hurry up. We gotta get out of here," she said. "Yo' daddy said that he is going to kill us all."

I'm over forty now, and I can't travel back in time. But time has followed me—not to haunt me but to help me in my teaching. Time is in the faces of my students. Time is what I have to give to my students to help them make sense of lives that have taken time away.

As I pulled in front of Robert's elderly aunt's driveway, Robert said, "I'm gonna live with my momma. This time when she gets out of jail I am going to make sure that she doesn't get into any more trouble." But earnest phrases are not wishes, and they come with no guarantees—no guarantee that Robert's mom will rehabilitate and Robert will have a home with her.

When I was little, we kept going back home to my daddy no matter how many times my mother ran away with us. Sometimes we went to stay with my grandmother on the South Side of Chicago. Once my mother even pawned our little black-and-white TV set and we took a Greyhound bus to Gary, Indiana, to stay with one of my mother's friends. I don't know how my daddy found us that Christmas, but he did.

I made a point to go and visit Mason in the hospital one week after he'd been shot. Mason was one of my favorite students. Even though he was a total goofball, I loved him because we understood each other in a quiet, unspoken way. He never combed his hair and always wore his sleeves two inches too short. I never combed my hair and wore clothes that puzzled everyone. We greeted each other by our initials: "What's up, J. H.?" to which I'd inevitably respond, "Nothing much, M. L." Some of my students had been to see him, and they said he was conscious and talking. But I was not prepared to see big, lumpy Mason in his hospital bed, hooked up to tubes. Mason didn't say so, but I could tell that he was kind of rattled for me to see his catheter filling up on the side of his bed while I talked to him. Three months later I was the one rattled at our high school graduation ceremony as Mason wheeled down the aisle in the procession of graduates.

Once my mother and I didn't get away from home in time, and my mother stabbed my father in the chest with a butcher knife. She didn't mean to do it. It was an accident. My father had the knife at my mother, and somehow my mother got my father with the knife instead. There wasn't that much blood on the floor. Mostly the blood was all over my mother and splattered all over the kitchen walls. My mother wasn't stabbed, but she didn't look that good either. Me and my mother sat up all night waiting to hear from the hospital. My mother kept asking me if I thought he was going to die. I don't think she really wanted the answer from sleepy, eight-year-old me. I think she just wanted my company that night because she was scared.

The teaching staff got the news the day after he was shot that Mark was dead. Mark was a bright kid and a talented artist. That didn't matter to the kids who pulled up alongside his car and shot him. I think it mattered more that Mark and his crew were planning to shoot them first.

Sometimes people ask me if I am afraid of working with "at-risk" kids in "high-risk" neighborhoods. They don't understand that the question they are really asking is if I am afraid of me. I am not afraid of me. Although my students have had hard-core life situations thrust upon them, my students are not hard-core.

I love my students like the children they are. When my students discovered I had no intention of hitting them or embarrassing them, they treated me mostly kindly. They would crack up when they asked me what I'd do if confronted with physical violence. "Run," I said.

My students respect my squareness. When I came to my first hour upset because my disgruntled neighbor's son dumped trash in front of our house, my students wanted to go and beat him up for me. My students are just kids in shitty circumstances put on them by adults. Yes, my students sell drugs, rob, have sexually offended, and have done everything else in between. But really they are my students first, and often that is enough. They are my students: It's a bond and it's everything I need to have my students in my life to help them through theirs.

## 32.

How could a petite, four-foot-eleven-inch chocolate-complected businesswoman hurt a 300-pound man so badly? As an adult now, I can call it love, but as a child I knew it only as the home-cooked meals, bedtime stories, and family outings that all ended once my mom began smoking. It wasn't the pack of Virginia Slims that she smoked on a daily basis that broke my heart. It was some type of white substance that she smoked privately.

The first time I witnessed my mother smoking dope, I was peeking through a crack in our bathroom door as she sat on the edge of the toilet seat. Her back was hunched over as she focused on something she was holding in her hand. She had a glass Gerber jar, and she lit the lid with her favorite purple lighter and, through a candy-cane-like straw, sucked the smoke in. I ran off after I saw that, and she never knew I'd seen her. She began using cocaine routinely. Eventually my father found out, and it destroyed my family like an 8.0 on the Richter scale. That's when the homelessness, sleepless nights, and abuse began. She was like Jekyll and Hyde. First, she would lecture me for hours, and then she'd hit me like I was a stranger off the street, but she knew not to hit me in any visible places. My only escape was school, and sometimes I would miss class because she beat me so badly.

Initially my family tried to contain my mom's habit and abuse but they couldn't. Child protective services got involved, and I was eventually placed into foster care. It all happened so fast, and all I knew was that I wanted my mom back. I no longer cared about her hurting me, and I couldn't function without my mom in my life. Twenty years have passed, yet I am still hurting.

I'm hurting, but I can't even imagine the pain and distress many youth endure that I encounter on a daily basis. I work with youth who have been in more severe situations than myself, also by no fault of their own. And to make matters worse, these youth are institutionalized, sometimes for eighteen years of their lives. It seems like these young, innocent victims are being punished but haven't committed any crimes. Many individuals and social service agencies can't understand why they see so much anger. You would think that professionals would be more empathetic or compassionate to the behavioral issues or dysfunctions of these youth.

I try to help youth look beyond their current situations and plan for the future. I work with a team that opens a window of hope with these youth. I can't help but think about one youth named Cole, who would always go AWOL. On his way out he would yell, "I'm out! Y'all don't understand me because you don't know what I've been through." And I would respond, "You're right, but help me understand what you have been through!" This battle went on for months until Cole came to me one day and told me that the only reason he stayed around and kept coming back was because I took an interest and never gave up on him. This story and many others are tattooed on my heart. The youth's voices echo in my soul and stitch the open wounds of my past.

## 33

"My mother is not dead. She is addicted to crack and living on the streets." Ashley's words resonated throughout the classroom as she read aloud. Her voice began to fluctuate as tears flowed down her face.

"When I was seven, I remember being home with my sisters by ourselves one night when we heard a knock on the door. It was a lady and a man that I had never seen before. My mother was MIA again so these people came to pick us up in a truck to take us away. I can remember a strange white lady leaving me at some lady's house that I didn't even know. My momma was no-where to be found."

To avoid facing the reality and embarrassment of having a crack-addicted mother, Ashley hid the truth behind a fabricated story of a deceased mother. She was mortified that the same woman who brought her into this world was the same woman who landed her in foster care. Time stood still. Her fellow class-mates consoled her, comforted her, and validated her feelings. I had never witnessed so much compassion from my students.

Lisa interjected, "I lived in foster care for five and a half years. When I was two, me and my sisters and brothers were taken by the department of social services because my mother was on drugs and she often beat us." Lisa continued with her head bowed as if she were praying. "My mother would not bathe us or feed us for days. She would leave us on the doorstep at the day care and would not pick us up. I can remember being taken away and separated from all of my sisters and brothers. We all bounced from one foster home to another. I still don't know where they are. I miss them. I still miss my mom even though she doesn't love me."

By the time Lisa reached middle school, she already had a reputation of being "easy" with the boys. Now it was clear that Lisa's behavior was simply a desperate plea for love and acceptance. I never would have guessed that these girls had once been in foster care. Would they have guessed that I had a secret of my own?

Should I tell them that I too grew up with a parent who had an addiction? If my students were courageous enough to share, why couldn't I? My mother has been deceased for almost twenty years so why was I still so guarded?

My students had opened their hearts and allowed me and their fellow classmates to see beyond their masks. Now it was time for me to remove mine. Though still hesitant, I blurted out, "My mother was an alcoholic."

There was dead silence. There, I said it. It was the only way I knew how. Eyes widened as one child in total disbelief said, "For real, Mrs. Sullivan?" My confession totally caught them off guard.

"Yeah," I muttered softly. "I often remember the horrors of seeing my mother drinking, all the while turning into a different person. My sober mother had a kind and gentle spirit. However, with every sip of alcohol, she became increasingly agitated. Transforming into an unknown being, she would often lash out at me, inflicting both emotional and physical scars. There were even times when social services questioned me, but out of fear, I would never admit to it."

Hanging on to my every word, my students were totally astounded. Quite honestly, I surprised myself. This was something I never admitted to *anyone*.

As we cried and continued to embrace one another, I truly connected to the hearts of my students. I was no longer the professional teacher dressed in high heels and a suit. I was no longer perfect. I was a wounded soul just like them.

It has always been difficult to talk to anyone about these painful memories. I have never been one to share my fears, my pain, or my desires. However, the irony of this encounter was that I was empowered by my students. It was their freedom of expression that challenged me to uncover a truth about myself. I allowed them into my heart. I allowed them to see beyond my mask. I allowed them to see me.

## 34.

The pungent smoke of sweet grass drifted over the computer console and across the middle of the English classroom. A blanketed powwow drum rested quietly in the center of a circle of desks. Someone from a morning class had left sentence-structuring directions on the dry boards. American Indian artifacts were hanging from the ceiling, and powerful faces of legendary warriors stared silently from posters. This classroom is mixed-blood just like many of the Indian kids drifting through the doorway. They follow the welcoming smell of a room blessing and the dying beat of a powwow CD called *Young Grey Horse*. Some of the American Indian kids in this Montana high school call this room the Rez Room.

Jamie walked into the classroom, dropped into the wing-back chair, and wouldn't look at me. I scooted over from the computer and teased her as usual. When she looked up, my heart jumped in my chest. Her bruised eye and stitches grabbed me by the throat.

"God, what's with the stitches?"

She just shook her head quietly and looked away.

"Jamie . . . ?"

"I got hit with a frying pan."

"A what . . . ?"

Knowing I'm hard of hearing, she smiled and repeated for me as she always does.

"I got hit with a pan."

That quick smile says it all about many American Indian kids. Blood and bruises are an everyday thing. Fighting and hurting are no big deal. Bureau of Indian Affairs statistics tell of this about the Rez, but I've learned being Indian follows you everywhere.

"Looks sore," I said and turned to see some of the other kids staring at one another. Jamie tried smiling again but only sighed and slipped away. Later, I made my way to Jamie's counselor. Her sad eyes told me she knew why I was leaning on her door. "Yeah, I saw her earlier today. She and some people had been drinking and some older woman smacked her in a fight." That evening, I cornered a police officer I hang out with. I knew he would look into the situation, but deep down, the whole thing settled over me like something dead.

Like many of us, Jamie is a long way from her reservation. After her dad left them and her mom had finished treatment, she told her mom that they needed a place where they could start over. They came to the city, where off-the-reservation Indians become urban Indians. Public housing was a start for Jamie's family. Jamie makes it to classes because public housing is across the street from the school. For the first three years, she didn't make it often. The reason was simple: No friends. No extended family. She was an outsider. A Rez kid without the Rez.

Jamie is a tall, athletic Northern Cheyenne who loves basketball. She tried out for the team two straight years but was cut from the program each winter. So what kept her coming back to this school each year? Maybe trips back to the reservation helped. Maybe she just got used to this place. She's not really sure. All she'll say now is she wants to graduate and go to a tribal college across the mountains. I asked her what her mom said about college. "My mom? She just asked me how I was going to eat." Both of us laughed. It was a good Indian joke.

I glanced at that new sliver of a scar around Jamie's eye. All I could think was, How in the world are you going to avoid another one of those? Instead, I asked her, "How do you say in Cheyenne, 'It's okay. It'll be good'?"

She didn't hesitate: "Ish'p'va."

I nodded and said, "Ish'p'va," as she walked out the door.

## 35

I took out my white crayon—dulled from use and broken in several places, though the wrapper is completely intact and holding it together. I held it up to the class, took a deep breath, and started.

"This crayon represents me for several reasons. First, it is white. That may seem like a pretty obvious comparison to me, but it's deeper than that. Unfortunately, that's sometimes all some people see when they look at me. A white woman. They don't see my love of languages, of cultures, or my respect for differences. They don't see that I love to travel around the world and immerse myself in cultures that are different from mine. They don't always see those things about me because they are blinded by the white."

I glanced around the room and saw some of my students nodding. Good, they were still with me.

"My crayon's wrapper is completely intact; it's not ripped or torn off or even scratched. That's because I usually prefer to keep certain things about my life under wraps. I put on a good front, most days. What most people can't see is that, under this perfect wrapper, my crayon is broken. It has several breaks, and so do I. My father called me 'stupid' all my life and would hit my brother often. Then, after thirty-five years of a rocky, emotionally abusive marriage, he left my disabled mother so that he could marry his new Internet girlfriend in Singapore. I've also dealt with depression since I was in middle school; there are days, even now, when it is hard for me to get out of bed and to face the world. You see, by keeping my wrapper intact, by hiding all these cracks and breaks, I thought I could keep my crayon together. But I've also learned that means that the cracks and breaks can't get fixed—because they're never seen—and so that is why I'm willing to share this with you today."

My students were quiet; some were nodding, some staring at

the boxes of colorful crayons on their desks. I continued: "Today, I want you to choose a crayon from your box, and do whatever you need to do to it—break it, sharpen it, unwrap it, whatever— so that it can become a metaphor of your life. Then I want you to write down exactly how that crayon represents you and your life. And remember, you only have to share what you want with me."

My heart leaped as the room burst into action. The room was filled with the noises of their movements as they manipulated the forms of their crayons and settled down to write their metaphors. Jackie, the extremely intelligent, introverted "Goth" girl who usually tried to read teen romance novels during class rather than participate, thoughtfully stared at a black crayon for a moment before swiftly putting it down and selecting a chartreuse one instead. My eyes scanned the back of the room and fell on Maricela. Her eyes appeared to be focused on the corner of her desk, her thoughts turned inward and her paper unusually blank; she normally was a "fast and furious" student, working hard and finishing long before her classmates. Angel, my talkative "cholo" (gangster) was actually writing—using paper and pencil, rather than a permanent marker and the desk. My usually chatty sophomore class was absolutely silent, working on their assignment until after the bell rang at the end of the period.

During my planning period, I settled at my desk, cup of tea in my hand, and was totally absorbed in my students' stories. Many felt ignored, some felt discriminated against, used, or sad over the loss of friends or loved ones. There were heartwarming stories, too, of helping disabled friends and overcoming obstacles in their own lives. As I reached the last paper, however, I choked on my sip of tea. Filled with dread, I reread the first line: "I chose a dark blue crayon to represent me because my dad gives me a lot of bruises." Maricela. She was one of my best students. Both she and her older brother had been placed in my classes after testing out of ESL classes. They struggled with their English, but they worked hard, were quiet, and never got into trouble at school. After describing the abuse she suffered at home in heartbreaking detail, she wrote, "Please, never tell this to nobody . . . because if something happens to him, my mother will never forgive me." My shoulders sagged and I put my head in my hands; I felt as though I had aged a hundred years in ten seconds. I had told the kids at the beginning of this unit that I had to report any information about abuse or neglect, so why did she turn this in? Why is she telling me this now, three days before summer vacation? Does she really want me to do nothing, or is this a cry for help? What do I do now?

I knew what I had to do. Not just because the state requires me to report abuse, but because if I ignored this information I could never forgive myself if something more serious happened to Maricela or her brother.

Feeling as though I was moving underwater, I photocopied her paper and walked it down to the guidance office. Her assigned counselor sighed after she quickly scanned Maricela's paper and informed me that she would "take it from here."

I insisted on being in the office when they called Maricela down from last period that day. I wanted her to know . . . something. I didn't know what. That I was sorry? That I wanted to help her? I didn't know what to say. After her initial shock, she laughed during the interview, insisting that it was just a story and she felt she had to write something sad—but it felt wrong to me. Maricela's face and body were turned totally toward the counselor and administrator in the room, her attention completely on them. I suddenly didn't exist anymore. She was deliberately not looking at me.

The next day, Maricela arrived to class late. After class, as her peers dashed out of the room, I stood in front of Maricela. Her eyes focused on her book bag as she stuffed her notebook into it. She apologized for scaring me. "Really, Miss, it's nice to know you care so much, but it was nothing," she mumbled. I nodded stupidly. As she left the room, I tried to get her attention,

"Maricela—" but she was already gone, out of earshot. I missed my chance.

The following day was the last day of school, and she was absent. After the chaos of the day, I sat at my desk, sorting through papers and watching the students scatter away from the school outside my window. And I wondered if there was something more I could have—should have—done. . . .

## 36.

"Okay, ma'ams and sirs. Settle down, let's get started. You have a test on *Fallen Angels* tomorrow, so we need to review. How would you characterize Pee Wee and Ritchie?"

"Pee Wee crazy," replies one student.

A few giggles and confirmations follow this remark.

"He try to act like he ain't scared, when we know he is," remarked another.

"Please raise your hands, so that I can hear all of your comments."

Hands go into the air. I recognize a student. "Okay, JaQuan. How would you characterize Pee Wee?"

"Crazy. Scared of the war, but not people, 'cause he'll talk junk to anybody."

"Good," I reply. "Anyone else . . . Toya."

"I think he is a coward, and that all the stuff he does is a big front."

"So you don't think he ever shows any signs when his feelings have been hurt or when he is afraid, Toya?" I ask.

"I mean he did when that girl broke up with him, and when he and Perry are in that hole, but most of the time he puts up a big front."

The discussion goes on, and I tune most of it out. Aaron raises his hand as I call for the last comments.

"Okay. Aaron."

"I mean I think they both heroes 'cause they both from single homes, and they just trying to make some money so they can help take care of their family and . . ."

At this point, several hands go in the air. Everybody has some kind of story or remark about the single-parent household, and how hard their mothers work, and how shiftless their fathers are. The rest of them want to discuss the fact that they have never seen their fathers, and how they have to take care of their little brothers and sisters.

They always do that when I ask questions, and I never really gave it any thought until I received a letter from one of my quiet students during dismissal. This student, Nicholas, is one of my quiet A students, so I really didn't know what to expect. He expressed his frustration with the one-sided discussions in class. It seems that he feels alienated because there are hardly ever any discussions about good fathers, middle-class families, middle-class values, and other issues with which he and a couple of other students in the class are familiar.

I sat down and wrote a letter to him:

*Dear Nick:*

*I am not sure that the students who talk about their mothers and their family struggles don't view having bunches of kids out of wedlock and living in the projects as a "badge of honor" as you say in your letter. I just think they are talking about what they know. I am like you in that I grew up in the suburbs with both of my parents, my father and I spent lots of time together, and I (like you) really can't relate to a lot of the things that some of the students who live in public housing talk about. But there is another side to the story. People criticize public schools, but one good thing about them is that children of all races and all socioeconomic levels are in one place. This has the potential to benefit all parties involved. You and I and other people who grew up in the suburbs should have a greater appreciation for our parents for working hard to pro-*

*vide a stable, more comfortable home, and the students who live in public housing can hear your stories and know that there is hope. Hope that there is a different kind of life. A life in which fathers and mothers are there to raise their children; a life in which shootouts in public places are not the norm; a life in which the heat, the water, the cable, and the electricity are always on; a life in which you never have to look your children in the eyes and tell them that the food is all gone.*

*This is the kind of hope that inspired America to elect its first African American president. So instead of hating them for sharing their stories, listen to theirs and tell yours, and remember that there is no perfect life, there is only life, and it is what you make it.*

*Yours truly,*

*The teacher who understands what it is like to be you*

## 37.

A knock on the door interrupts my class and my thoughts. The school counselor and a little girl with mouse-brown hair and a look of fear on her face step into the room. "You have a new student," the counselor announces.

Adding students to class was usually an annoyance, but something deep inside me said, "Relax, she needs you."

The counselor says, "This is Cindy Johnson, but she would like to be called Angel Williams, as she will be adopted soon."

I struggle to focus on the counselor's words. The same fear I see in Angel filled my eyes when I had to start over.

Ten years ago, my middle school English teacher asked me, "Do you want to move and live with my parents? I know that you are miserable with your mother, and I would take you if I could, but I just got married, and it is not the right timing for me. You understand, don't you?"

No, I didn't understand. Why couldn't I just stay with her and her husband? Her parents were old and didn't even know me. Why would they want me to live with them? Didn't they know how screwed-up I was? Twelve-year-old children are not supposed to make life-changing decisions, but I stepped up and made a decision.

"I guess I can give it a try for a few weeks." My voice shook and tears rolled down my cheeks. She held me tight. "I love you. You know that, right? You'll really like it. I did when I was a kid." I was not convinced. I knew that I would be happier with her.

We called my biological mother for permission before taking any legal action.

"Tina, this is Mr. and Mrs. Walker. Samantha has been staying with us while she's been here visiting and has decided that she would like to stay with us permanently. We need you to sign over your parental rights. We can send you the documents to sign. Are you okay with it?"

"Sure, just send me the papers, and I will sign them for you," she responded with no sense of emotion or loss in her voice. It was as if she had been asked her favorite color but couldn't answer because it didn't matter.

Life was not the same for me. I was still Samantha Michaels, but I wanted to be called Samantha Walker because I was going to be adopted.

My thoughts quickly shift back to Angel. Her head is down in defeat, her hands are shaking, and her eyes are welling up with tears. But my fear keeps me from hugging her and saying, "Angel that is awesome! I understand how you are feeling and what you are going through. I am adopted too."

## 38.

They say that a person's past is always a part of who that person becomes, that what happens to us shapes the way we think and the way we live. Sometimes, we put the "bad times" behind us, thinking that if we just forget about those things they will miraculously disappear. But sometimes when you least expect it, those memories can quietly creep back.

I had a student in my class who always wore dirty clothes and looked as if he never slept and never combed his hair. But what he lacked in grooming he more than made up for with kindness shown to me and his classmates. The other students ignored his smiles, though, and they always talked about him; and he was never chosen to play on any team. When I handed him his copy of *The Freedom Writers Diary*, he gave me a little grin, and I couldn't wait to read what he had to say. A few weeks later, he asked me to "please" read his diary.

"My mom told me last night that we'd have to move soon," he had written. "She said that we were being evicted and would have to sleep in a tent for a few days. My classmates have no idea what I'm going through."

As I began to cry, I found myself reflecting on my own dark past. Memories of neglect, abuse, and homelessness swept over me.

When I was growing up, I never had a father around so my mom struggled a lot. At school, I was the kid who never had nice clothes; I was the one who always got picked last; and my mom and I always had to move from place to place. Unfortunately, I never had a teacher who even noticed that there was something wrong, never noticed that something was on my mind and bothering me.

When my mom got married to my stepdad a few years later, the bad became worse. My stepfather beat the crap out of me, and one day, his torture put me in the hospital. As I lay in the hospital, I thought of my mom and how she did nothing to stop the constant abuse. I used to dream of hurting my stepfather while he slept. I dreamed of the day that I would escape the prison I was living in.

I guess my mom finally got smart and got tired of him hitting her, too. So she packed our bags and we left for good. I never got over the fact that she let him touch me. And I resented my mother almost as much as my stepfather. As soon as I turned seventeen, I was out; I left home and just stayed wherever I could. I remember so clearly not having a place to stay and sleeping on the cold, lonely streets of despair. One night it was so cold I took some cardboard boxes and made myself a little tent for the night. I was so scared—that I was on the streets, that my life had spiraled into darkness beyond what I had already endured. Going back to my mother's house was not an option, so I had to live with the choices I was making. I was alone in the world, but at least no one was putting their hands on me.

I slowly started to get my life back on track, and although I suffered a lot, I wouldn't change anything, not even when I was homeless and alone. I told myself that my experiences would one day make me a better person and that if I ever ran into someone who was going through what I went through, I'd be better able to help them. As I read more of my students' diaries, I began to notice similarities between my life and the lives of many of my troubled kids. I knew that I had to do something. Many of these kids lacked a father figure; many came from poor families; many of them just wanted to please everyone around them to feel accepted.

The next morning, I saw my student who was being evicted from his home. I hugged him and told him how important he was to our class. I called his mom later that day. She told me that they were being evicted because she couldn't pay the rent and that they would have to move out of town in three days. I asked her if it was okay if I bought her son some clothes. She paused, and I thought I heard her begin to cry. Then she said, "Okay. No one has ever given us anything, so thank you very much."

After school that day, we went shopping at the mall, and I let him get whatever he wanted. A few days later, he was gone, and our class changed. In his last entry he wrote, "I feel as though I have to hide who I really am, for no one accepts the 'true me.' "

As teachers, we have to know each one of our students, so that we can reach them in order to teach them. I encourage us to be that teacher who cares for those who are labeled "lost" and for the students called "unteachable," because the only thing that kids really want is love.

## 39.

Like so many homes in the New Orleans area, from Kenner to the Ninth Ward to Buras, Gabbie's home was completely destroyed by floodwaters caused by Hurricane Katrina.

After her return trip home to survey the damage, I just finally blurted it out: "Gabbie, how was it going back home?" The other ten students who had found refuge in our tiny town in Iberia Parish listened intently with a communal, understood silence of respect for Gabbie.

She said, "We got to Buras and it was like a war zone. The town is a mess, Ms. T."

Her eyes glazed over a bit.

"Are you all right?" I asked. "You don't have to go on. I know this is difficult."

"No, it's okay." She continued: "My house looked like a box of dropped toothpicks. I went through the pile of garbage and found just one glass animal ornament from my glass collection that was in my room. It was full of sludge but not broken. It was my favorite, and I was going to keep it. But just before we left I threw it back into the pile of wood."

It was her way of dealing with the loss and finding closure. I also think this was symbolic of a brand-new start and leaving the past buried.

It was rather strange when the others did not chime in with comments of support, or share their experiences of going back to a home that no longer existed. The class remained silent, almost as if in solidarity and support. One young lady, Liza, put her head down on her desk and sighed softly.

Gabbie's eyes reddened a little. She ended with, "Dad's buying a house here in New Iberia. This is where we will call home now."

I knew Gabbie would be welcome here because of our community spirit of helping others in need. The devastation could have easily affected us but it didn't. We were fortunate and now needed to extend a hand of kindness and help our new residents adjust. Everyone did their part. We realized they were going to stay, and it was okay. We just needed to understand that it would take time for them to realize this was now home.

Gabbie's a senior now. Yesterday was Senior Portrait Day. How radiant she looked as she posed in her cap and gown. Her smile did not belie the loss she felt in her sophomore year of a childhood home in Buras, Louisiana. I have watched her rise and fall and have seen her take giant steps toward finally putting the ghosts of Katrina to rest.

### 40.

"Chase, you're a good kid, with a lot going for you, but right now everyone thinks you're a pain to have in class." This is what I told this young man, the instigator of most of the problems in my classroom so many years ago. He had moved around frequently, and his family struggled with finances. It was easier to be a discipline problem than to make friends.

Growing up, athletics provided stability for me. We moved often, fifty-eight times to be exact, and not always with much warning. One time my family moved while my oldest brother was gone at church camp. When he returned, his ride dropped him off at an empty house. He had no idea where we had moved, so he just sat outside and waited. In my family it never came as a surprise to hear the words "we're moving." I've known what it's like to be the new kid on the block and try to remain as inconspicuous as possible. It was hard to invest in relationships you were certain would be short-term.

Financial management never was a strong suit for my parents. I remember my dad always made a decent wage, but by the end of the month there was never any money left. I remember answering calls from bill collectors demanding money and greeting people at the door threatening us for nonpayment. One winter morning the sheriff came as I was getting ready for school. He came to take my mother away for writing bad checks. I can still hear her crying as the handcuffs were placed around her wrists.

Dad had a strong work ethic, working incredibly long hours driving a truck for a local company and never missing a day. I never doubted that my father and my mother loved and were proud of me.

By my senior year of high school, we moved west and left the Rust Belt of America. This was my third high school, and money was still tight. I had become accustomed to having my things sold at garage sales before our moves to pay bills. I lived on bologna, hot dogs, and fried-egg sandwiches and coped with the turmoil by immersing myself in sports. My senior year I had to meet with the counselor for a graduation check. He condescendingly asked about my plans for my future. I told him I really wasn't sure but I would probably learn a trade. He told me I was not college material, and he hoped I wasn't planning to attend college. It was an affirmation of everything I had learned: Kids like me can never succeed at anything.

During my senior year, my parents divorced. It was then I also found the girl of my dreams. In her family the expectation was that everyone went to college. I began to imagine that maybe there was a possibility to take the one thing that gave me stability and a connection—basketball—and become a coach and teacher and be part of a school, the stable piece of real estate that didn't change addresses. I worked after graduation and by second semester I was enrolled in college, on a path to a dream unheard-of in my world. I wasn't looking back.

The phone rang at 12:30 one night. My wife answered, "Hello?" Scared it was some emergency at that hour, I quickly sat up, fumbling for my glasses. She told me it was a former student of mine—Chase. Well aware of his history, she said, "I wonder what's happened to him now."

As I took the phone and listened, I heard an excited young man on the other end. Years earlier he had been the young discipline problem in my class. Now he was different. He told me, "Mr. Kosper, I wanted you to know I finally graduated! I've been going to a community college this last year. I was calling to thank you for believing in me."

When everyone wanted to fail him, I kept telling him he had so much potential. I believed in him and knew if he wanted to, he could do anything. He called because he had been offered a full-ride scholarship to play Division I baseball. We visited for several more minutes. As I hung up the phone and listened to the steady breathing of my wife in the stillness of our bedroom, I realized Chase had made it, and so had I.

### 41.

"I'm from Butler Projects. You gonna mean mug me? Are you crazy?" an angry tiny girl bounces around the cafeteria, aiming for a fight.

Someone yells, "Take your ass back to the projects." The room is a sea of faces thirsty for a moment's excitement, but she's got everyone solidly at bay. I search for the source of her agitation, and the tension in the room swells. We're nanoseconds from a throwdown, but no obvious target emerges. A group of popular girls slip quietly away from the throng.

Stealthily, I move toward Moesha. I put a gentle arm around her shoulder. Not sure what to do, she quickly pastes on a half grin, still poised for a fight. I guide her away from the cafeteria crowd and toward my classroom. She doesn't resist, but tears are now forming in her eyes and slowly smothering the fire that blazed so fiercely only moments before. There's an awkward silence between us, and I let it ride.

"Butler Housing Projects, huh? Is that where you're from?" I ask.

She nods. I continue, "So that makes you a gangster? Girl, you're just a Wangster. I'm from the Cabrini Green Projects in Chicago—I'm a real GANGSTER!"

At the thought of a teacher living in the projects, she laughs, softly at first, and then her laughter grows with intensity until she's laughing and crying at the same time. Tears mingle with saliva, and hair with food at the corner of her lip.

Away from the crowd, she goes limp against my arm. I carry her weight. This girl doesn't want to fight, but she doesn't know how to *not* fight.

I was a fighter, too. Before he went to prison, my father practiced with me often, sometimes moving my hands and feet into position. Frequently he offered his head as my "bag." His words still echo: "Plant your feet apart, leading with your left to keep balance. Then wait for that surprise moment and take the first punch hard with a right fist and follow up with a left jab to the nose."

"Miss . . . are you really from the projects?"

I motion for her to take a seat, and I pull up next to her. "I'll tell you, but I need to know to whom I'm giving my 411. What happened back there?"

My question hangs in the air. Moesha lowers her gaze, her head drops, and her intricately woven braids tumble onto the desk. Fine-featured and ebony-hued, she is the promise of a beautiful woman someday.

Head still down, she mutters, "Miss, it don't matter. They always fucking, I mean messing with me. They think they some-thing 'cause they live in Woodlawn." Her voice trembles with the anguish of defeat; geography is a hard enemy to beat.

"Moe, you're something too. And, yes, I grew up in the projects." She interrupts me. "But it was different back in the olden times." Her words are part statement, half question. We swap stories, and she talks freely and openly, maybe for the first time.

Before she leaves, we agree to have lunch together the next day in my classroom. A smile travels from the corners of her lips to the dancing mischief behind her golden brown eyes. I gather she doesn't get invited to lunch much.

"Okay then, Moesha. I'll see you tomorrow. Please don't knock anyone out before we can have lunch. Comprenda?"

A nod, the smile, and then a slight hesitation. "Miss, where you live now?"

"Moe, I'm just around the corner from the school, a few min-utes away."

She laughs aloud this time. "Miss, you crack me up! You got out the projects to move to Stop Six?"

Casually, I give her a "Yup, sure did."

"Why, Miss?" she asks.

I wink at her and say, "Well, Moesha, don't you think some-body has to hang around here to make sure you don't beat down the whole neighborhood?"

She heads for the door, glances back, and yells, "Miss, I like your blond hair."

"I like you too, Moesha."

The bell rings. Planting my feet apart and leading with my left, I smile inwardly and say only to myself, "This is where you're supposed to be—this is the fight of your life."

**42.**

I made the decision to stop reading my students' files a long time ago. It's easier if you get to know students before hearing about their crimes. That way, by the time you've read the reports, it's too late and they're people and not just litanies of trespasses, both suffered and committed:

> Minor stood guard while friend molested minor's 7-year-old sister. Minor's older brother in prison for raping and molesting siblings. Minor witnessed father's murder at the age of six. Minor arrested again for stealing food, due to mother chaining refrigerator shut as punishment.

When I came across the article "A Heart That Can't Be Mended," I immediately wanted to find a way to use it in my English class. It's a heart-wrenching piece written by ER trauma surgeon Mauricio Helibron Jr., who treated a child with a gunshot wound to the chest, another victim of the war that rages on in our streets. I wanted my students to see that they endangered their chances at success if they never learned to accept the consequences of their actions.

As my students filed in, I read the vibe of the class. It was tensely quiet.

"Okay, it doesn't seem like you guys are very talkative today," I said. "But that's okay, because today we're going to do something a little different. Can someone tell me who really gets affected by gang violence?"

Devon piped up loudly, "Just the family."

"Is that all?" I asked.

"What does it matter, ma'am? Nobody else cares. It's just all part of the game. That's life," Devon said.

"Really? So what you're saying is that the only people who get affected by violence are just the victims and their families?

Well, today I want to read you a little something about a person who was affected by violence. Just listen."

> *Cracking open an 11-year-old boy (he was two months shy of his twelfth birthday) is going to tear my own heart in half, I think to myself, but this is part of what I do, so I slip the gloves on and take the knife. . . . His chest cavity is filled with blood, which spills out of his chest like a macabre waterfall to the floor. There's a shredded tear in his lung, and a big, ragged hole in his heart. All the IV fluids that my associates are pouring into the patient are flowing out this hole and on to my shoes.*

I don't want to keep reading; my voice is quivering and I am angry. Will my kids even get the point of this article, or am I going to just look like an idiot up here? After all, many of them are sentenced here for gang-related violence, I think. Then I continue:

> *I put my finger in this hole—such a big hole in such a small heart—but blood and fluids still flow unfettered. My other hand finds another, larger hole on the other side of his heart. My fingers touch. His heart is empty. Mine breaks.*

Tears start to well up in my eyes, and I tell them that I don't want to read any more. Jose, a quiet student who never volunteers and rarely answers a question with something other than "I don't know, whatever," spoke up. "I'll read, ma'am," Jose said.

I passed the article to him. As Jose began, the room was completely silent. My students sat in their desks with their heads bowed. As Jose read the last word, I heard one person crying, and then another. *I don't want to screw this up.*

For one moment nothing else mattered, our differences weren't barriers, and we all "got it." I simply said, "Just write, write whatever you are thinking or feeling." They wrote and wrote. The only sounds that broke the silence were the sounds of flipping pages, furious writing, and the sharpening of pencils.

At last, one after another, my students put their pencils down and sighed—heavy, burdensome sighs that seemed to lessen the heaviness in their chests. Terry, one of the boys who was moved to tears, asked if he could share what he wrote. Terry stood, smoothed out the wrinkles in his tan government-issued shirt, cleared his throat, and began reading.

"Why do people hurt each other? As I was listening, all I could think about was my little brother. Man, I love him so much." Terry began to cry, and his whimper became a shoulder-shaking sob. Devon reached over and put his hand on Terry's shoulder.

"It's okay, man, go on," Devon said.

Terry wiped his eyes and nose with the back of his hand, took a deep breath, and continued.

"I don't even know what I'd do if I lost him. All I could think about is how I haven't been there for him, to show him right. I know he loves me, and I don't want to be the one who leads him the wrong way. This kid in the article didn't deserve to die. He was just an innocent little kid."

Soon, the entire class was crying. Eighteen wounded boys were grieving and in need of comfort. Devon stood up with glistening eyes and wet cheeks. Instead of their usual squaring off, he stuck out his hand and pulled Terry closer, hugging him. Devon needed it as much as Terry.

## 43.

My classroom is so cold I can practically see my breath.

"Is anyone as cold as I am?" I ask as I add a sweater to my two layers.

"Sam White's even colder, I bet," says Sequan, laughing nervously. There is a visceral groan.

"That is just ignorant," Tara says and starts to cry quietly in the desk in front of mine.

"What's going on here?" I say.

"Miss, haven't you heard? Sam White got shot last night," Julia bursts out.

"Is he a student here?" I ask.

"Yeah, he's a freshman. I mean, he was a freshman," Barry says.

Tara begins to sob, "Miss, I was just chillin' with him yesterday, and today he's gone. It's not right!" As she rocks back and forth, wearing pajamas and slippers, her hair disheveled, both her style and confidence shaken, she looks as if she's aged ten years overnight.

"It was gang related."

"It was a setup."

"The killer is still at large."

The rumor mill in full force, I listen to the stories my kids tell me of their friend.

"We are all saddened by the loss of freshman Sam White. Grief counseling will be available," crackles over the P.A. system.

"They are just looking for information, and I ain't going to give any," shouts Joe.

"These people are no better than the cops," Brie maintains. "They don't understand what we face every day."

Over the next few days, absenteeism is rampant as students attend Sam's wake and funeral. It seems Sam was the victim of a premeditated murder.

In the days that follow, another one of my students goes MIA for a week. I ask Rob, his buddy, "Hey, where is Scott?" As he replies that he doesn't know, I sense that he does know but will not rat out his boy. A few days later, Rob says, "Hey, Miss, Scott moved out of state."

I stop my lesson when the normally raucous class is quiet. "Moved out of state?" I ask. "Why? Was this planned? Where did he go?"

Rob's silence is the only answer.

Strangely, the next day, Scott saunters into my classroom after class has begun. I ask him about his move. He replies, "You heard about the shooting last week? That happened in my apartment. He died in my arms." What do you say to a fifteen-year-old who witnesses such a heinous event? Bile rises in the back of my throat, and I throw my arms around him and take him to the school counselor.

As my heart pounds, I march right up to see Scott's guidance counselor and the vice principal. "Why didn't anyone tell me that Scott was a witness to murder?" I inquire.

As they look back and forth from one to the other, the vice principal sheepishly says, "What do you mean? We didn't know anything about it."

My blood starts to boil. "You didn't know that a murder of one of our students took place at Scott's house one week ago? Didn't the police contact the school? Not to mention the fact that the suspect who committed this crime is still out there, isn't he? What if this eighteen-year-old gangbanger showed up looking for Scott because he can identify him? What if he came to my class looking for Scott? Shouldn't I have been made aware that there was a potential danger because my student, Scott, was a witness to a murder?"

The counselor and vice principal look at me blankly, then rush back to their respective offices. "We'll check into it and get back to you."

Knowing that I will get no answers, I storm out of the office. I never see Scott again.

As I enter my classroom and contemplate the events of the day, I stare at the space where my classroom door used to be. I begin to shiver but not from the cold.

## 44

I walked up to the pulpit and looked out at the crowd. No professor's lecture or college textbook prepared me for the words I was about to say, how to say them, or the feelings hell-bent on erupting at any moment:

"I will always remember Aaron for his personality and for his spirit. He knew how to be a kid one moment and transition to an adult the next. And it's one of the reasons that brought so many of you here today." *Jesus, what am I doing up here? I'm only twenty-seven years old, and I'm eulogizing one of my sixteen-year-old students. No one told me this could happen.*

"While laughter may be inappropriate for most eulogies, Aaron would be disappointed if we simply mourned for him and cried because he is not here. On the contrary, he is very much here—here in each of us because of what we were able to share with him during his sixteen years." *If I stutter or pause one more time, I'm going to lose it. Get it together, Jim. This is for your boy. This is for Aaron.*

Aaron gave two classmates a ride home after school on a cold, snowy February day. On his way home, he hit a patch of black ice and careened into a construction vehicle.

"I suppose the most fitting words about Aaron are those that tell you what he was like as a student. We all know he was the angelic student who turned in all of his homework and aced every test." *Good, laughter. Whew! I swear, I am never doing this again.*

"Truly, what sets Aaron apart from his peers is how he approached life. No, he was not the most serious of students, but he brought energy to the classroom that made many admire and revere him. I mean, how many students spend an entire class period pondering how long the water tower has been rusting?" *Man, Aaron, I wish you were standing here right now to bring up another story and make everything better.*

For nine agonizing days, Aaron held on. I know he fought

the entire time, but even a youthful body has its limits. First, his kidneys failed. Then, his brain began to swell. Medicine that helped one thing hurt another.

"One of the most memorable moments was the day Aaron decided he wanted to be a teacher. He stayed after class, sat on my desk, looked me straight in the eye, and said, 'You know, Mr. J., I think I want to be a teacher. Looking at your coffee cup made me realize that is what I want to do. After all, who better to work with kids like me than, well, me?' "

Aaron basked in the spotlight, always shining in a way no other student could. As the endless train of vehicles progressed toward the cemetery, I noticed the clouds dissipating and a single ray of sunlight focusing its warmth on us. The entire world was now his stage, and Aaron was soaking up the spotlight one more time.

"One final anecdote I want to tell you confirms what you all know about Aaron. While other students were working diligently on an assignment, I had to nag Aaron repeatedly to work on his. The last time I scolded him, he looked up at me and said, 'Mr. J., do you need a hug?' Before I could say 'no' he was out of his seat, giving me a hug." *What if I had kept him in my classroom just a few minutes longer? He might never have seen those girls and would have gone straight home.*

"Aaron was more than a student; he was one of my kids. I can only hope that my future children will embody his spirit and attitude toward life." *Look at you, lying there, and so peaceful looking. I'm going to miss you, buddy.*

"I love you, Aaron."

### 45.

They say that the first stage of grief is denial. "Are you sure it was Kenny?" I asked. I was at the post office when I got the phone call that Kenny was dead—killed in a courtyard a block from his apartment building the night before. They said that an unidentified gunman speeding through the alley on a moped had shot into a crowd, and that Kenny fell to the dirt as everyone else ran.

In my hand was a stack of letters from my P.O. box, written to me by of some of the young men I have taught reading and writing at the jail for the last five years. I got into my car and started to make calls. All I had to do was find the right person, and I was sure someone would tell me that it was all a case of mistaken identity—some other boy had died. Or, if it was Kenny, surely the bullet had only injured him. He'd come too far. A bullet couldn't have taken him down. Maybe he was hurt, but he just had to be alive.

As I drove across town to pick up my son from school, the loss of my nineteen-year-old student and friend slowly seeped into my heart. I told my son the news as he got into the car. Kenny, if he was really dead, would be the fourth of my students to die because of street violence. This time it felt like too much to bear. I thought back to the first time I met Kenny three years ago. The boys at the jail were on lockdown for a disciplinary infraction. Our normal book club session was canceled, but we were allowed to talk with the kids individually at their cells.

"There's a new one today," the commanding officer said, nodding his head toward the last cell on the block. As I approached and peered through the bars, an enormous gap-toothed grin emerged from the darkness of the cell. It was Kenny. "What's up?" he said. His smile was framed by a headful of crazy braids. I could feel the *special* right away.

Unlike most of the other sixteen- and seventeen-year-old boys in the jail on adult charges, Kenny was already a reader. He fell in love with books in fourth grade. Many students in our class got hooked through novels about street life, but Kenny bragged that he would read anything. And he did. He told me he wasn't sure how or why he started getting into trouble. It's just what happened to kids where he came from. Kenny also wrote beautiful poetry. Each of our sessions ended with a creative writing as-

signment. Somehow my eyes often fell upon Kenny when looking for a volunteer to read aloud. "Ah, man, why you always
have to pick me?" he'd ask in mock shyness as he slunk down in
his seat. As he stood and read his words, though, he spoke loudly
and proudly. Ten other boys, who moments earlier had refused
to read, then waved their papers, asking to be next. At seventeen,
Kenny was already a leader.

When I got home, I took a deep breath and called Kenny's
mom, Tanya. At the sound of her voice, I knew it was true—
Kenny was dead. I went to see her the following night. Their
neighborhood had been wracked with violence between three
different "crews" for so long that Kenny once told me he didn't
think anyone still remembered how it all started.

"All I know is which blocks I can walk down, and which ones
I can't," he said. Kenny didn't see any of this as a curse, just the
hand that he'd been dealt.

The strong scent of alcohol trailed behind Tanya as she led
me through the ugly halls of the building where she shared a
dingy room with Kenny and his older brother. There was so little in the apartment that I wondered whether she was moving
out. Then I saw the living-room bookshelf neatly lined with all
of Kenny's books, including *Learning to Read Music Made Simple,*
the book we had given him two weeks earlier. A self-taught drummer and keyboardist, Kenny was just now learning to read the
notes. He had an eternal song in his heart. Throughout his
eighteen-month incarceration, while other inmates dreamed of
girls and money, Kenny made plans to book the first gig for his
go-go band. He wrote letters to club owners and other musicians.
He studied hard and obtained his GED, and after his release, he
got a job with the city. Every paycheck was being socked away
until he had enough money to buy his new keyboard. Now I
looked at the books and felt sick. What a waste.

I gave Tanya some photographs of Kenny. She needed them
for the funeral program and didn't have any of her own. Except
one. "Look what they did to my baby!" Tanya wailed as she

pulled a black-and-white 8-by-10 from an envelope. It took a moment, while my eyes focused on the photograph, to realize what it was—a picture of Kenny taken at the morgue. His eyes were closed peacefully, braids splayed across a pillow, and lips parted just enough to reveal the gap between his two front teeth. The only evidence of violence left by the bullet was a small black circle above his left eye.

Over the next several days, I seriously considered quitting my job. I felt lost as I alternated between numbness and extreme sadness. The only constant was the picture of Kenny's face. The photo felt embedded in my brain. I remembered an exercise that I had done a year before at the Freedom Writers workshop in Long Beach, California. Erin asked us to draw a picture of his or her most challenging student. We were told to remember the picture, because this was to be our motivation as we taught. If we could reach that student, we could succeed.

All of my students were challenging in one way or another. But it was their situations that presented the biggest hurdles for them and for me—the poverty, the addictions, the fatherlessness, the low expectations, the hopelessness, and the violence. I thought about the picture of Kenny and how his death embodied all of these struggles. Yet his life spoke just as loudly of the promise and the possibility. I knew I would keep teaching.

# ENGAGEMENT

A lot of the humanity in the teaching profession is lost amid number-two pencils, standardized tests, and data collection.

In order for my students to pick up a pen, rather than use their fists, the learning had to be relevant to them. An inspiring teacher knows how important it is to engage a student first, so I had to draw parallels between the lives of the characters in the books we were reading and the lives of each student. Romeo was really the awkward teenager in the desk next to you: in love, shortsighted, and headed for disaster.

I used pop culture, food, and guest speakers—anything it took to bring their education to life. It was important to me that before my students even opened a book such as Elie Wiesel's *Night*, that they not only had some context for understanding the Holocaust but could see how it related to their own lives. Thus, teaching about the Holocaust quickly became a cautionary tale about man's inhumanity and the devastating effects of intolerance.

Anne Frank's story might have been forgotten if Anne herself hadn't written it, and now each one of them, each Freedom Writer, has added his or her own story to this chapter in history.

Luckily, Freedom Writer Teachers do not subscribe to the philosophy that one size fits all. To reach their students, they too use innovative and creative techniques that don't always involve a textbook or Scantron tests. To reach some kids, you have to think way outside the box.

The stories in this section are about the breakthroughs that Freedom Writer Teachers have had with their students while reading their journals, playing interactive games like the Line Game, or provoking classroom discussions. It is those moments that they strive toward, those moments that justify the decision to be a teacher.

## 46

"You care too damn much!" Ana yells at me, slamming her book down and storming away. In my mind's eye, I see myself standing on my desk and screaming back, "Maybe I do, you little shit!" Then I imagine what that would look like—this fifty-five-year-old white woman jumping up on a desk. Can I still jump? I wonder. Screaming? God, I wish I could! Little shit . . . not even close.

I know Ana's history. After thirty years in the same community, I am part of her history. I have had her aunts, uncles, and cousins in my classroom. I know what she has lived through, why she is living with her grandparents and not her parents, why she is so angry. It's a miracle she can walk and talk. I don't know that I could survive some of the things she and many of my other kids overcome. I marvel at the resilience of their spirits against obstacles most of us know only in our nightmares. When I hear people in positions of power talk about the effects of poverty, funding, and test scores, I want to slap the hell out of them. Poverty is nothing but a word on a page of a speech handed to them to read. They wouldn't last a day in the shoes of some of my students.

I sigh, my anger deflating, and in the end, all that comes out of my mouth is, "Maybe I do."

The bell rings, and the students rush off to make the most of the four minutes before their next class. I have a planning period, thank God. A planning period—what a joke! When was the last time I really had time to plan a lesson during a planning period? My plan right now is to breathe, pee, and stay vertical through the rest of the day, then find a new strategy to try with Ana. My backup plan? Quit this job and apply for a greeter position so that all I have to do is smile and say "welcome."

I have a good idea what set Ana off. It would have been easier for her if I had screamed and yelled. That is familiar territory.

I need to try to find a way to undo the message she received somewhere that she is bad and stupid. That is always the biggest obstacle for me, because I know that it can make a difference in a child succeeding or falling through the cracks, unnoticed. These kids are the big secret in my community. They are brilliant, talented, lovable kids, and so few recognize them. What a gift it has been for me to be part of their lives.

This year I will watch one of my students cross the stage. I have known him since he was eleven. He will be twenty when he crosses. For years he struggled between school and the streets. Last summer he spent a month in jail. When he came back to school, he came to see me and said, "I'm done with that life, Miss." He made his decision and never looked back. I don't think he will ever understand how proud I am of him, how proud I am to know him—and many of my students. Their spirits have sustained me during times of sadness. Their courage has helped me stand up during times of fear when I would have much rather slipped into the shadows. They have helped keep my life in perspective, keeping gratitude and grace my goal.

Damn, there's the bell. No time to pee now, no shining lesson plan to hand in, but I am still vertical and breathing. Not bad! Laughter is echoing down the hallway as my students make their way to my classroom. It makes me smile. I walk over to the door to greet them, thinking, I won't need that backup plan after all . . . at least not for today.

### 47.

"If I know the answer in class, I will raise my hand. If I don't raise my hand, don't call on me because I won't answer."

It was the first day of school. Monique's stringy black hair was combed back, exposing big brown eyes that made her look older than your average freshman.

"My sister is the same way, but she won't speak up for herself." She looked right into my eyes.

For the first couple of weeks Monique sat quietly in the front row. We did the "Are you ready?" dance. Every time I took a step toward her, she recoiled into her seat.

As we discussed a novel, I looked at Monique, knowing that she knew an answer. She held my gaze for a second, then quickly turned away.

I tried another move during a grammar lesson. I slowly stepped toward her desk, convinced that she was ready, but she looked up and said, "I told you I would let you know."

I became really good at reading her facial expressions. There was the "I'm not ready" look, the "I may know this one but don't ask me" look, the "leave me alone" look. I knew them all, but I couldn't let up. Monique's silence was killing me.

I gave each of my students a journal: "You have a voice. Express yourself, even if it is just for you." To my surprise, they did. For the first time, all of my students were excited about writing.

They'd ask, "Are we going to write in our journals today?" and they would beg for more writing time, "Just a few more minutes!" I saw Monique writing. Was I getting through to her?

Our class developed a motto: "What is said in this room, stays in this room." We agreed that sharing personal stories outside the classroom would break the trust we built.

Days later, one student said she wanted to read from her journal. Her voice quivered as she told the class about a time when she was followed by a man who exposed himself to her. When she finished, the floodgates opened. Almost all of my students shared that day. Students spoke about physical and emotional abuse they suffered at home. Two students shared that they had been raped. Eyes welled up with tears, and jaws dropped. Just when I thought I would have to fill an uncomfortable silence, a voice came from the back of the room. The voice was strong, and clear. It was Monique.

"Sometimes I get beat, and so does my sister. I always have to do everything around the house and then my mom yells at me and tells me I'm lazy." Her eyes softened as she looked around the class. At that moment, Monique was more than a student; she was a mother, sister, father, and friend.

My class became a family. We shared secrets with each other that we wouldn't share with our families. Monique became fast friends with one of the brightest students in the school. My glances were now received with a smile and a comment, and her eyes looked alive.

One day she walked into the classroom with fancy new hair extensions and a big smile. Most of the girls in my school buy hair extensions when they are interested in a boy, when they join the dance squad, or when they get asked to the school dance.

I couldn't contain my curiosity, so I asked Monique, "What happened? You're walking around all confident. You're doing good work. You got new hair extensions. Do you have a boyfriend or something?"

"I feel safe here now. Once I knew you cared, I had a reason to do the work. I didn't want to let you down."

I didn't need to do the dance with Monique anymore.

## 48.

At the end of most school days, I read through my students' journals. The journals allowed my students to think and write about issues important to them, and reading them helped me to know my students better. I was allowed to read them, though, only if the students gave me permission.

The orange notebook sitting on the top of the pile belonged to Alli. I flipped it open. As usual, the corner of every page was folded over, which was the signal to me that I was not to read that journal entry.

Alli had arrived in my class about a month into the school

year. She had an air of maturity and an exotic beauty, and she certainly drew the attention of the eighth-grade boys. She was quiet and reluctant to offer much personal information, but I had coaxed out of her that she lived with her older sister Ruma and Sam, her sister's husband. She was studious and courteous, so I really had nothing to complain about, but I was curious about her background.

One Friday, Alli called me over to her desk. "Sir, I would like you to read one of my journal entries," she said. She gave me her journal and left for the day.

I sat down to get my first insight into Alli. She had written, "Ruma and I just don't get along any more. She yells at me all the time, and I can do nothing right. I miss being her best friend."

The next Monday, I asked Alli to speak with me after class.

"Is everything okay at home?" I asked.

"Yeah, sure" she replied.

I pressed further. "Well, your journal entries suggest otherwise."

"She just bosses me around all the time, and I'm tired of it," she said.

It was the first real honesty I had seen in Alli. "I think your sister must be under a lot of pressure. Maybe she doesn't know how to be like a parent and a friend at the same time," I said.

"You just don't know what it's like to not have your mom around when you need her!" Alli stammered as she hurriedly left the room.

The next day, Alli came to see me again.

"Sir, can I ask you a favor?"

"Of course."

"Will you read my journal?" she asked meekly.

"All of it?"

I'm sure she sensed my utter shock and giggled as she handed me her journal. "Yes, I think I would like you to read it."

Her entries explained events from three years earlier.

"I had just celebrated my tenth birthday and everything

seemed wonderful to me. We lived near Mumbai and Daddy had a really good job. Mommy stayed home to take care of us and we were a very happy family. . . .

"One afternoon, I remember coming home from school with Ruma. My dad's friend from next door was there. He told us that my mother was in the hospital and he would drive us to see her. When we arrived, my father told us our mother had suffered a stroke. When we were finally allowed to see our mother, she was tired and did not look well. The worst part was that she was unable to talk to us."

Two days into their mother's hospital stay, Alli and her sister were visiting their mother, and she stopped breathing. Machines beeped, and doctors and nurses rushed in to save her and then took her to the operating room. Nobody was exactly sure how the events had unfolded, but the surgeon had made a mistake attempting a tracheotomy—bad enough that her mother stopped breathing for a long period of time. There was little hope that she would get better.

Alli described visiting her mother: "I remember thinking each day we visited that my mother was paler and thinner. It was horrible to watch her slowly dying, getting a little closer to death each day. I didn't see my father much during that time. At first, he was always at the hospital, but eventually we didn't know where he was—he just was not around."

Eventually the stress put on her father became too great. One day he went out and did not come home. No one in Alli's family ever saw him again.

It was horrible to imagine anyone going through this tragedy, let alone a ten-year-old girl. I wished I hadn't pressed to find out about Alli's parents.

Her mother died after being in a coma for several weeks. Alli and her sister went to live with their closest relative, an aunt in the United States. Two years later, Ruma got married and they moved out of their aunt's house and into the community where my school is located.

Alli's last few entries began with a note to me: "My friends tell me that I am pretty and should have a boyfriend, but I am not interested in that. My dream is to work as hard as possible in middle school and high school, go on to college, and eventually medical school. I want to become an esteemed surgeon and then do all that I can to make sure that things like what happened to my mother do not happen to anyone else ever again."

I sat at my desk for a while and then placed the orange notebook with the others, and I thought about what I would say to Alli the next day.

## 49.

Our classroom was buzzing with anticipation days before our first-ever Ethnic Feast. Weeks before, invitations written in Bosnian had been hand-delivered to our teachers, staff, and invited guests. Elsa, our Bosnian cook (and mother of one of my students), was the only person who knew exactly what we were going to eat.

A mom of four boys, in her late forties, Elsa fled to the United States in the 1990s from war-torn Bosnia. But looking into her eyes, you see no hints of self-pity, anger, or resentment. She walks as proudly as any woman providing guidance to her boys.

"I am Bosnian," she told me while we shared a cup of richly thick Bosnian coffee. "We do not quit!" I was magnetically drawn to her steel-like personality, strength, and quest for life. Her shapely, slight frame holds a woman with inspiring determination. The callused fingers and protruding veins in her hands reflect a woman who has scratched and clawed her way out of refugee camps to a new life in an intimidating country far from the homeland she loves.

We left a whole lamb, butchered and wrapped in cellophane, waiting at a local church in the walk-in cooler until roasting time. My students, our principal, and I laughed at the thought of the staunch "church ladies" opening the cooler door to find this headless, bloody, grotesque carcass sharing space in their sacred cooler. A sign reading "Be careful or this may happen to you!" was hung from its neck. I was quite certain our bashful lamb would bring new life to the church kitchen.

Together, Elsa and I began the adventure to find Bosnian ingredients in our mostly Scandinavian community. After buying all the needed items, we went to our school to see how feast day might unfold. We went through the details of where she would cook. I pointed to the area outside where the men would roast the lamb. I explained to her the role our students would play.

"Your son Jovica will be dressed in a very handsome tuxedo and wearing shiny shoes. He will greet and escort his teachers to their seats," I explained. I role-played her son's part as if it were really happening. When I turned around, her face was buried in her hands. Her shoulders shook uncontrollably, and tears fell from her eyes. Surprised, I cautiously asked if I had insulted her. After gathering herself, she looked at me softly and replied, "No! It's just that no one has ever celebrated my country before!"

In the stillness of that dark school hallway stood two women of different cultures who shared much more than either had imagined: a love and passion for children and respect and dignity for all people.

## 50.

I have always found beauty in the desert. Its beauty lured me to return to the reservation to teach and to live. I also find comfort in living in small rural towns where the population doesn't exceed twenty-five hundred, where the livestock usually outnumber the residents, where everyone is familiar, and where you run into people you know at the post office, convenience store, and church. I love living where people gather at the flea market on

Saturdays to sell, buy, or trade wares, and to eat traditional foods with family and friends.

Where I live, the houses vary in size, color, and shape. You will find a few houses clustered together and then miles of desert before you encounter the next. There are small pockets of federally subsidized housing in what is supposed to resemble a neighborhood. The traditional hogans of the elderly, with wood-burning stoves and dirt floors, stand next to the modern manufactured homes of the younger generation.

My high school is situated on a small reservation town in the desert. We are a tiny school of about three hundred students. We have one main building surrounded by a few portable classrooms. Some days you will find sheep, cows, or horses grazing on the periphery of our campus. Most days, the scene looks like a pristine painted landscape with its beauty reflected in the untamed wild brush and tumbleweeds.

But don't be fooled. We suffer from the same problems that exist in urban schools—domestic violence, alcohol and drug problems, gang fights, and deaths. All of these negatively affect a culture in which the elders prize "walking in beauty and harmony."

I didn't realize what a "frying pan" I had jumped into when I transferred to this school. Six weeks into the year, my truck was deliberately set on fire. I asked my students what I had done to be the target of their ire and dislike. T.J., a student in my first-period class, spoke up while his bros nodded their heads in agreement: "We don't like you. We ain't got no respect for you, and we ain't going to do nothin' in class for you."

Erick answered for the whole class: "The only reason you are here is for the money. All of you teachers come here for the money. You don't care for us."

"Yes, I do . . ." but Erick's smirk said it all.

I tried everything to engage them and to make learning fun, relevant, and interesting. I taught the state standards through culturally relevant materials, trying to show them that I respected them, their culture, and their history, but I still had no buy-in on the part of the students. They were hesitant and wary of this outsider. Too many people have been disrespectful of their culture, and too many have exploited it for their own gain.

Just when I was ready to throw in the towel, my kids reached a turning point. We studied genocide and people's ability to be resilient and to have hope when faced with adversity and overwhelming odds. We compared the stories of "The Long Walk," "The Death March," and "The Trail of Tears."

While studying the Death March, Isaiah, a special needs student, asked, "Why didn't the Jews go to their chapter houses and complain about their treatment?" This bought a discussion of the various governing bodies in each culture, and Isaiah probed further.

"Do the Jews belong to a tribe?"

"You're such a spaz," Nat replied. "They weren't natives. They were white people, stupid."

"You could say they were tribal people. They belong to the tribe of Israel." I tried to explain.

"Tribal people always get the shit end of the stick, don't they?" Isaiah said.

I had to laugh. "What Isaiah means is that minorities are often mistreated by the dominant culture."

"I liked Isaiah's take on it," Nat replied.

Students were discussing issues. They were talking to one another. They were accepting each other, and they were beginning to accept me.

These kids, this place: I'm right where I'm supposed to be, no doubt about it.

## 51

"Where are we going?" he asked.

"We're heading for the border." I replied.

Panic bounced back at me from Marcel's eyes as we drove. I held his stare. His was a fear I knew well.

Ten years ago, there was a knock on my classroom door. It was the night of my first day as a teacher. I was a missionary living on a small island in the Bahamas.

My principal—five-foot-four and no more than 115 pounds— stood at the door, hesitating. There was tension in her jaw as she said, "I have to ask your permission. I'm asking all the teachers who live in the house. The Bahamian government is rounding up illegal Haitian men, imprisoning them, and deporting them (by boat) back to Haiti. Some will run. Some will hide. Some will be shot. We need to hide them in our house. Is that okay?"

She had no fear. It was the right thing to do. She had such conviction, but I was filled with doubt. I shrugged my shoulders and muttered "sure." She left quickly before I could change my mind.

We hid five illegal Haitian men that night. They came at dusk. They left at dawn—silent, grateful for the safety we pro- vided. The next night five turned into twenty. We were up to one hundred within a week, five hundred by the end of the month. They hid in our house, our church, and our classrooms. We never heard a sound, but we knew they were there. Who else knew?

"It's better in the Bahamas" was a popular tourist slogan at the time. But better for whom—a Haitian, an illegal, an immi- grant? I too was an immigrant. Was it better for me—because I was white, educated, a schoolteacher, an American? It wasn't bet- ter. I was scared. I was only twenty-two, and I was breaking the law in a strange country. These people were strangers. They were powerless, hated, feared. They were treated with indifference, intolerance, a lack of humanity.

After several months, the Bahamian government developed a new strategy. They couldn't catch the men, so they went after the children. Police jeeps entered the school grounds, screeching to a halt. Armed officers pulled out rifles and headed for classrooms. Minutes later, schoolchildren filed out at gunpoint, scared and confused. The teachers stood by watching them leave, filing out so orderly as if it were a fire drill. They knew they would never see those children again.

I blinked my eyes, breaking my stare with Marcel and bringing myself back to the present. Confidently, I repeated, "We're making a run for the border." He'd just been denied a student visa—one we'd worked on for six months. The denial reasons—he was black, Haitian, and male. No appeal at the Embassy had worked. Marcel was trapped in Canada with no hope of being reunited with his sister—his only living relative. The last immigration officer suggested we "make a run for the border." With no other options, I decided to take her up on it.

As we approached the U.S. border, greeted by the "Welcome to the United States of America" sign (that arched over the immigration booths), I wasn't scared. Getting him back into the country was the only way to reunite him with his sister.

If caught, he faced deportation, and I faced prison. I said, "Three lanes are open—you pick one."

## 52.

Being in eighth grade has its difficulties: what to wear, how to walk, talk, and act. Eighth grade is a perpetual struggle to fit in. Marika, a fun, energetic, Hispanic girl, never really felt like an American. In her journal she wrote about how she always felt like an outsider in both the mainstream culture and the Hispanic community.

Marika felt that she had to shun her Hispanic heritage in order to accept American culture. She did whatever she thought she had to do in order to be like the American girls: She highlighted her hair, followed the latest fashion trends, listened to the same music. But she never felt totally accepted by her classmates, and at home she was facing intense pressure to maintain her Hispanic culture. Her parents accused Marika of being ashamed of her culture and said she was "becoming white." But their attempts to force Hispanic culture on her made her resist it more.

Reading her journal, I could relate to some of the frustrations Marika wrote about, such as how substitute teachers couldn't pronounce her name.

"Been there! Done that!" I would chuckle and write little notes of encouragement so she would know she wasn't alone. She seemed to like the feedback I gave her, always responding to my messages by writing a :) or an LOL.

One day Marika wrote in her journal about how excited she was to be auditioning for a major role in the school play. The role was playing opposite blond-haired, blue-eyed Ryan, one of the most popular boys in the school. She felt this could be her way "in" to a socially popular group. Marika did a fabulous job. She memorized her lines, spoke in a clear, expressive voice, and maintained eye contact throughout her audition. But the buzz around the staff room was that Ryan and Marika didn't "look *right* together."

The students were huddled around the board with the final list of roles. Marika separated herself from the group, and as she turned around our eyes met. I could tell right away that she didn't get the part. She knew why. She also knew that I knew why. Without saying a word, we both knew that the problem was her skin color. Our skin color. I didn't know what to say. She walked away.

I'm not sure why, but I never spoke to her about it. Maybe by talking about it, I was afraid that I would be acknowledging it, making it real. Maybe I had misread the situation, misread the look in her eyes. Maybe it would be less painful for her to simply not deal with it. I tried many arguments to convince myself, finally deciding it was easier to let it go.

A few days later, after a particularly difficult day, I sat at my desk staring at a stack of unread journals. I quickly looked through the pile to find Marika's. I wanted to read about how she had dealt with the experience. Perhaps it was just my guilt wanting to know that she was okay. She wrote about her feelings of disappointment, sadness, racism, and exclusion. Tears started welling up in my eyes as I read her words. She was not okay. She didn't understand. And I couldn't explain it to her. Not because I didn't want to, but because I didn't understand. That night I copied an entry from my personal journal onto a piece of paper:

*I will always be the "other" color for the rest of my life. It's not something I can change out of, like a pair of jeans. It is something I carry with me everywhere I go, for the whole world to see. Surrounding myself with white friends didn't insulate me from racial slurs and discrimination. Mrs. McCain, my third-grade teacher, told me that I wasn't the right color to be the Head Angel in the Christmas pageant. I was so angry! There were two of us who tried out for the role. Pretty little Lydia with her blond ponytail . . . and me, a dark-haired brown-skinned recent immigrant! Mrs. McCain knew that English wasn't my first language and she would have me read my lines over and over again waiting for me to skip or mispronounce a word. I didn't. I had stayed up late memorizing the words and practiced speaking in my loud voice. She even quietly offered me another role, but I was stubborn! I wanted to be the Head Angel, damn it! She was my first affirmation that I wasn't just the "other" color but that I was the "wrong" color. I was put into*

*a faceless position behind the stage. Behind the stage, away*
*from the viewing audience, where color didn't matter.*

The next day I slipped my note into Marika's journal before
handing it back to her.

"Thanks, Miss," she told me a few days later, giving my note
back to me.

"You're welcome, Marika. Did it help?" I asked.

But Marika didn't answer. She walked away. Her silence spoke
louder to me than the words she had left unsaid.

### 53.

My story is an American story; my history is American history.
But many Americans see my home only as a travel destination or
the birthplace of famous "Latino" actors and singers. My home
is Puerto Rico, and it is time that my fellow Americans understand their Caribbean neighbors.

In 1898, Puerto Rico became a colony of the United States.
From the time we became a colony, Puerto Ricans were required
to learn and speak English in school. But we refused to speak
English in our homes and at our markets—beyond the school
doors, we rebelled and spoke Spanish. Not until the 1950s were
we allowed to use our native language in our schools, but Puerto
Rican students are still required to take English courses each year.

Today, some private bilingual schools teach completely in English and use textbooks written in English; other private acade-
mies teach in Spanish but also use English-language textbooks.
My school has a combined program: both a bilingual group and
a Spanish-only group. Students are separated into these two programs in the third grade and continue in them until the eleventh
grade. As they enter the twelfth grade, the two groups are reunited.

For nine years my students were separated, and it was my task to reunite them in their last year of high school. I thought, "These Puerto Rican students were separated by language and curriculum, not culture or geography, so my task should be easy." It wasn't.

What I did not realize was that many of my students harbored prejudices, but they did not recognize their prejudices. Much more than simply preparing them for their next steps—college or career—my job also became the challenge of opening their eyes first to themselves and then to one another.

I used every technique I knew. I played the Line Game with them, hoping they would realize that whichever program they had spent the previous nine years studying, what they shared was much deeper and stronger than the differences they thought divided them.

"Go to the line if you had to turn off the alarm clock this morning more than three times," I called out.

Laughter filled the room as the line became crowded with still-sleepy students. The next challenge was a little tougher.

"Go to the line if you came to school in public transportation."

Only one student went to the line.

Then I hit them where I knew it would hurt.

"Go to the line if you have ever felt discrimination."

The silence and stillness hung heavily in the room until one by one they began to move, and soon every student was on the line. Once they noticed who was next to them in the line, they realized they have more in common than they had ever thought.

But this revelation would not become a breakthrough. A few weeks later I saw students who had studied in the regular curriculum throwing trash at students in the bilingual group and calling them names. This wasn't the first time. I knew I had more work to do.

"Do you consider yourselves racist?" I asked them after reading an essay called "El racismo en Puerto Rico" (The Racism in Puerto Rico), written by Nemesio R. Canales.

"No!" they answered immediately. "They are racist in the United States, but we are not racist in Puerto Rico," one student said.

"Let's talk about prejudice, then," I said. "What does 'prejudice' mean?"

"Making judgments," said one student.

"Ignorance," said another.

"Thinking I know somebody only from what I see on the outside," said a third.

"Do you consider yourself stupid or ignorant?" I asked.

"No!" they answered.

"Then why do you act with prejudice against your classmates? The only difference between you is the classes you have taken in school."

Their faces started to change. Their faces, once happy, became serious and ashamed.

Finally, they got it.

You don't have to look different to be prejudiced. You just have to feel different. My Puerto Rican American students came together after that, but I know it will not be the last time they feel the pain of discrimination.

## 54.

*"We should be able to wear the confederate flag. . . . It shows pride for Dixie Land. People always say they're offended. But only the blacks should be and if they want to throw a fit they can go back to Africa and eat out of their own garbage cans."*

The sentences scorched the page. I drew in the familiar yet unpleasant smell of cow manure through my open window. I teach in a farming community where many students work in the fields after school or milk cows before coming to class.

As I closed the composition book, I noticed the Confederate flag blazoned across the cover. *How could he do this to me?*

Joe, like too many, fights to feel validated. Every day during prep period I pulled a desk up beside him, trying to prompt him to make sense of his reading. I helped him dig deep into memories of fishing, hunting, or four-wheeling, to look for writing ideas. I shared my struggles as a slow reader. I wanted him to see me as a person.

In the midst of a unit on tolerance, my class read *Night*, by Elie Wiesel. A Holocaust survivor had been a guest speaker. I connected this history to recent-day racism. Was Joe not listening? Or was he listening and now seeing if I was? Joe had a learning disability, supported by little motivation from home, but that was not all I knew about Joe. During our meetings he told me about camping trips with his favorite uncle. His real father worked the night shift and then drank himself into a stupor regularly. Joe rarely tried at school, but he dedicated himself to rebuilding his truck. I took interest, trying to bridge the gap between us.

Now this. I felt flushed as I reached for the phone to get Joe down to my room immediately. Then I stopped. I couldn't throw that away by berating him. I needed to listen before preaching.

He sauntered into the room, adjusting his camouflage hat, and sat next to me. His cowboy boots tapped the floor. I fiddled with my pencil.

"I read your notebook entry. I have always considered you to be a fair-minded person so I was shocked when you wrote something so bigoted." I spoke calmly and looked him in the eyes. His smirk disappeared. Joe told me how his respected uncle talked about people that are different. He also told me he had never met an African American person. After listening, I talked to Joe about how my experiences shaped me. I told him about making friends from different backgrounds in my urban upbringing, and how I was forced to learn to build bridges between differences, just as I was asking of him.

We talked about *Night* and the Holocaust. I desperately tried to appeal to his essential humanity. I asked him how a friend of mine might have felt if he had read this. He shrugged and glanced away.

"Joe, look at me." I needed him to understand that I believed in him. "Bigoted remarks are against my core beliefs. I have always been respectful to you, and I expect that you do the same. I know you are capable of this. You are a hardworking and fair person." He nodded and left the room.

Later that month I asked the class to write about a significant event in their lives.

> *Dear Ms.,*
>
> *After reading the book* Night, *learning about the Holocaust, and talking about how they connect to things today, it has made me think. Maybe I should get to know some people first before saying they are all the same or saying something bad about them.*

Although his writing was still laden with deeply rooted stereotypes and misinformation, Joe's words created an opening. After that, we certainly had many days when we took steps backward, but progress was made. I believe that his exposure to new perspectives through books that convey passionate ideals and our conversation about tolerance developed a bit of genuine empathy. That image of a ballpoint Confederate flag etched into a composition book now serves as a reminder of the painful and challenging conversations needed to create the stepping-stones to help me make a difference in my students' lives.

## 55

"Today we're going to learn where stories come from."

My shaky hand set the needle down on the record spinning on the dilapidated turntable.

*Jesse James was a lad who killed many a man, he robbed the
    Glendale train.*
*He stole from the rich to give to the poor, he'd a hand and a
    heart and a brain.*

The high-pitched, nasal voice and twanging guitar of this traditional American folk song sounded as if they came from a tin can far away—but ears pricked up, mouths stopped in midair, boots tapped on the wooden floor. Then for the first time, my classroom was silent.

"Could ya play that agin, Mr. Booth?"

Yep, an outlaw taught them where stories come from. It was *their* story. Raised in lawless mountains where—as I'd been warned—folks shot at schoolteachers' tires and, nurtured on poverty, superstition, and the fine art of coon huntin', they'd seen their share of natural wonders and unnatural acts. They had a hand, heart, and brain, all right. What they needed was a voice.

Perennially all had failed the state writing test, so we wrote interactive journals daily. Devin couldn't spell or write coherent sentences, but it turned out he had a lot to say about life up on the back creeks. Once I'd written in his journal asking, "Devin, would you rather trail ride or go hunting?"

After a forty-five-minute struggle with the barbed wire of language, erasing till he wore holes in the page, he handed me his entry. From the smudges and scrawls, a voice emerged:

*I would like to reader ride than be hunt . . . When you can ride
in the wood and fulds and roads. The best thing about ride is*

*natest [nature] it is cool and the smul of the air and when the
baby amials are run around . . . baby deer are like baby horse
they stay close to their mom.*

At last in eighth grade, age fifteen going on fifty, he'd found
something he liked about school besides "givin' teachers a
cussin'." Writing made school suddenly bearable. Everyone remarked how it had changed him. Even Chickenbone the custo-
dian said so. So who'd a-thought the Fourteenth Amendment
would make him backslide?

Teaching civics was tricky. To begin with, they didn't know
much about history. "Who was the first American president?" I
asked. They were none too sure.

After some serious catching up, we came to the Bill of Rights.
They certainly had no squabbles with their right to bear arms or
with any unalienable freedom. Their motto: "Live free or kiss
off." But they proffered a whole nother credo for civil rights.

When I showed a video about Martin Luther King Jr., Devin
muttered, "Send 'em all *back* to Africa."

"Pardon?" But I'd heard.

"I *said*: They don't belong in my country."

"Devin, they're Americans now with . . ."

"No, they ain't Americans. They're *niggers*."

It was trial by fire. I looked at my two black students. Sharrell
glared at me; Deante looked calmly bemused. The rest were ready
for a showdown. One helluva teachable moment, but what the
hell could I do? You never throw kerosene on fire. I'd grown up
where schools shut down rather than integrate. I knew better.

I needed to find a path through the briars of racism. The path
I found was a book. Within days I put copies of *Sounder* in their
hands. Accidentally on purpose I neglected to tell my students
what it was about.

Page one introduced Sounder, the coondog. *That* got their
undivided attention. But something else struck a deeper chord: a
father unduly punished for stealing a ham to feed his family. My

students didn't need me to explain black sharecroppers' anomie; desperation was their daily bread, too. They knew days missing fathers, food, and future. So word by word, beginning to end, they were verily hooked. *Sounder* had treed them, so to speak. Now I'd reteach civil rights.

"Send 'em all back to Africa" flared again.

"All? What about the family in *Sounder*? C'mon, you liked *them.*"

Hank, cheek pregnant with chewin' tobacco, stammered, "But-but-but, Mr. Booth, *they's* diffrint."

Heads nodded. Had they begun to free the tolerance in themselves? Does tolerance begin with exceptions to our beliefs about *all*?

Not for Devin. Tolerance only fired his spite. He'd worked so hard writing his journal, now he took to scrawling on the bathroom wall, "Mr. Booth is a . . ." A thorn stuck my heart.

Come December he disappeared. When I went searching for him *way*, way up on the back creeks, it began to snow, the long-awaited first snowfall. Nobody shot at my tires that Saturday but I saw with my own eyes the strange freedom up there and could see where stories come from in Appalachia.

### 56.

Natasha was the type of girl who believed that everyone was entitled to her opinion. She didn't talk with you but at you. She talked to everyone as if she was in a different country where she didn't know the language. She would just talk slower and louder as if she assumed everyone else was stupid.

One particular Friday morning, I was asking the class about their impending weekend—birthday parties, who was invited, who wasn't, whose grandma was coming for a visit . . . the usual stuff.

Natasha raised her hand to share something with the class. She never raised her hand when she wanted to talk, so I was curious regarding her sudden grasp of classroom rules. She gave me a sly little look before she proceeded to rip me from my comfortable little routine.

"Mr. Hood, what do you think about the new law that was passed allowing gay people to get married?"

Uh-oh. How do I deal with this potential minefield? I didn't want to act as if I was afraid of the topic, so I did what any self-respecting teacher would do when faced with a problem like this; I deflected the question back to her.

"What do you think about the new law?"

Big mistake.

"I think that gay people are disgusting. They should all be killed. We don't need the government to pass a law telling me that it's legal. It's a sin. We should all live by God's laws. All we need is the Ten Commandments."

I had worked at fostering a sense of tolerance within the classroom. I was mindful of all the cultures and backgrounds of my students, quick to mention and highlight all the religious festivals and celebrations, not just the Christian ones, while remaining neutral in all matters of faith. Up to this point in the year, I had not been baited into a discussion regarding religion. That was about to change.

"The Ten Commandments?" I repeated the last thing that she said as a way to calm myself down.

"The Ten Commandments?" I repeated, this time without as much emotion.

"Yep, the Ten Commandments. That's what I said."

She could see that she had me reeling, and she was going for the throat.

I wanted her to see that although she professed to be tolerant and full of love for her fellow classmates, she couldn't have said anything more hateful.

"Okay" I said. "Name them."

"What?" Natasha said.

"Well, if you want us all to live by God's laws, by the Ten Commandments, you should be able to name all of them. Shouldn't you?"

Natasha remained defiant. "Fine! That's easy. One, thou shall not kill. Two, thou shall not steal. Three, thou shall not cheat on your wife or husband. Four, thou shall not lie. Five . . . ah Five, Thou shall respect your mom and dad . . . Six . . . Six, ah Six . . . Thou shall . . ."

It started as a low, almost inaudible vibration, but soon it grew stronger as more and more students were stifling a laugh. The class held on for as long as they could but finally gave in. An explosion of laughter erupted.

Natasha was getting angry now, really angry. I calmly, without any outward display of victory, asked the class to stop. Natasha's eyes were smoldering.

I shrugged my shoulders. "If you are going to say something as provocative as that, don't you think that you should be able to name at least seven of the commandments?"

The class laughed again, and this time Natasha smiled, almost in spite of herself.

She said, breaking into a chuckle, "I am still entitled to my opinion."

I countered, "I think that's the point. Make sure that when you have an opinion, it's your own and not something you've heard someone say. You need to think about what comes out of your mouth. You can't unring a bell."

The class resumed the Friday morning routine, but I was only half listening. I was replaying the incident in my head, preparing for the phone call that I felt sure would be coming from Natasha's mother. But then my thoughts turned to the students who might be struggling with their sexual orientation and wondering, "Why is it okay to hate me for what I can't control, for what I feel?" And now, with Natasha's unwitting help, I hoped I had shown my students, straight or gay, atheistic or born again, the futility of blind faith.

## 57.

"Hi, Enrique." I paused during my lesson as the young man walked into my room with a hall pass from another teacher's class. "Where are you supposed to be?"

"Bathroom," he said.

"Oh, well, we still don't have urinals here," I said and winked at him. The other students laughed, and he gave me his familiar boyish grin. The class settled down and refocused. Enrique took a seat and listened attentively as I continued. A few minutes wouldn't hurt him. It wasn't like he was going back to class anyway.

Enrique is a fun kid to have around, although most of his teachers may disagree. He's smart, funny, and likable. The problem is that he's not motivated to do much of anything with these talents. He spends most of his time wandering the halls, ditching class, doing whatever he can to avoid work. And he's usually in trouble, but as long as he is in my room, I know he's not causing trouble anywhere else.

Suddenly, Enrique left my room only to return again with some books, sit down, and begin to work, which was unusual. It wasn't long before his teacher came into my room looking for him. He barely acknowledged her and shrugged her off. Finally, she said to him, "I'll talk to you when you are ready to listen." She looked at me, threw up her hands, and left.

I approached him casually and whispered over his shoulder, "Enrique, you should really go back to class so you don't get into trouble." However, as I knelt down to talk to him, I saw a tear well up in his eye. He wouldn't look at me. He quietly whispered back, "It's just that it doesn't matter because my mom's sending me back to Mexico." A single tear ran down his face even though he tried to hold it back.

"Enrique, what's going on?" I asked with deep concern.

"I got in some trouble with the police. My mom and I have been fighting ever since, and she's sick of it. She wants to send me to live with my dad in Mexico," he said with his head hung low.

"But you don't even know your dad," I said, as my heart sank. I couldn't imagine him going to live with a complete stranger.

"I know and I don't want to go, but she doesn't want me here anymore. She says I get into too much trouble," he explained somberly.

I remembered when Enrique wrote in his biography that his father was dead. I knew this wasn't true. When I'd asked him about it, he'd said, "It's just easier than the truth." So here was this kid who was about to be sent to a father he has never known and a man he resents for leaving him and his mother. Of course he wasn't interested in going to class!

As the other students and I comforted Enrique, another student entered the classroom in tears. "My boyfriend just broke up with me," she sniffled. As her friend and I consoled her, I wondered what was going on. What in hell had I done to open the floodgates?

"Wow! Where is all this coming from? What is going on here?" I finally asked out loud.

"Miss, this is where we can talk about what's going on. Our friends are here and you're here. We know you'll listen and let us be ourselves," one of the girls explained.

It should have been obvious. This was home base. Everyone thought Enrique was just skipping class again, but when I took the time to listen to him, I found there was more to it. If I hadn't stopped what I was doing and listened to him, he would have been gone in a few days and no one would have known where he went or why.

## 58

As a counselor in a working-class community, I work with teens considered "at-risk" or "underprivileged." I call them "invisible." They do just enough to scrape by in their day-to-day lives without being noticed. I recognize these kids because not so long ago I was one of them. I told myself that I was the only one who could help them, the only one who could truly see these kids. I was wrong.

Maya was a struggling teen girl. When I met her, Maya had been living with a school administrator for seven months because she had no place else to go. She'd spent Thanksgiving night last year in juvenile detention following a conflict with her mother. The way Maya tells it, the argument had been resolved and the police were literally walking out the door when her mother called them back and told them Maya had hit her. Maya was taken to "juvy." The next day, while most teen girls were out shopping for Christmas presents with their mothers, Maya was desperately racking her brain to think of someone she could call because her mom refused to pick her up. The one name she came up with was this administrator, who dropped her own holiday plans in order to come through for Maya. Over the next seven months, Maya continued to struggle with her mom. She was repeatedly taken back in only to be kicked out a few days or weeks later when she'd fail to live up to her mother's expectations.

Maya was referred to me for assistance transitioning to adulthood as she neared graduation. In talking with her about her goals, it became apparent that she craved structure and consistency; the military seemed like a natural fit. She was motivated and excited at the thought of planning her life in a military career. Meetings with the recruiter went well, and Maya was ready to enlist. The only step remaining was a simple background check. She was rejected because of the "assault" charge.

"Plan B" was to become a nurse. She was accepted into a nursing assistant program only to find out that the "assault" charge again barred her from enrolling. She was beginning to lose hope, but again she persevered and decided to go in a third direction with a hospitality program through Job Corps. This time her own behavior choices sabotaged her success.

Maya had been at the Job Corps campus for about two months when she called me, saying that she'd gotten into a fight and been kicked out. She started the conversation talking tough and blaming everyone else. Soon I heard the fear and distress in her voice as she realized she didn't have anywhere else to go and had likely ruined her best chance for success. She heard fear in my voice too, as I came to those same conclusions. The next day we sat down and had a heart-to-heart talk. That's when she dropped the bombshell: "I'm HIV-positive."

I didn't know where to begin—an eighteen-year-old girl with no health insurance, no income, and no support with a life-threatening, chronic, and often fatal illness. As I sat back and attempted to wrap my head around all this, I looked at her face. What I saw startled me. I saw acceptance, even relief in her eyes. The secret? Her personal burden had now finally been lifted, and she could get on with her life.

That's when the lightbulb went off for me. A lot of the invisible kids that I work with feel the same way. They spend life believing that terrible things will happen to them and *should* happen to them. I try to change that mind-set and tell them, "You *don't* deserve this, so stop accepting it." Maya was ready to take control of her life. She was able to separate the negative experiences that she didn't have any control over from those that she did, and to see the positives in her life. She stopped waiting for the worst to happen and now looked forward to the future.

About six months have passed since that conversation. She has found an apartment and stable employment, as well as a healthy relationship with someone who knows about her HIV status and loves her for who she is. More important, she has found a way to accept and love herself for who she is. She's no longer invisible.

## 59.

Although some days are better than others, most of them are filled with anticipation, revelation, and regurgitation. Regardless, my goal is the same each day: for the kids to gain more knowledge of "self" through a variety of exercises, including the study of meaningful literature, and journaling. Today it happened.

I decided to start with the Line Game. I pushed the desks back and ran a line of tape down the classroom floor. I asked the students to line up on either side of the tape. I began making safe statements like "Step to the line if you have one brother or sister." Then I progressed to tougher ideas with "Step to the line if you have ever been homeless." Six kids stepped forward. My heart sank. The next thought was tough to articulate: "Step to the line if you have ever witnessed a shooting." Nine students came to the line. Then I added, "Step to the line if you've ever lost someone to gang violence." I could not believe that twelve of my students stepped forward. This was the second week of school, and I knew more about these teenagers than I ever knew about my students last year, even with the journals. We continued until I prompted them to "Step to the line if you've ever been shot or you've shot someone." I had taken a big risk.

Kim stepped to the line and totally broke down. She had appeared frail and troubled from the beginning, sitting quietly in the back row, almost nondescript. Immediately, her peers surrounded her in an attempt to offer comfort with "It's all right. We're your friends. We understand."

Shiedah asked, "Can we write in our journals, please?"

Elated with her enthusiasm, I responded, "By all means. Write your reactions to the Line Game and anything else you wish to reflect upon."

The students all returned to their seats and began journaling. Some of the responses were written in their typical mundane hieroglyphics. Others students talked about their genuine emotional reactions. Only one stood out: Kim, who had pulled the trigger and had never revealed this to anyone before. She tearfully scribbled the words "petrified, scared and lapse of concern for myself." The last to leave the room at the end of the period, she asked if we could talk at the conclusion of the day. Naturally, I welcomed the opportunity and assured her I would not open her journal until then.

At 3 p.m., she came into my room. Without uttering a word, she stepped to her class's box and pulled out her journal with determination and began to read: "My stepfather has been abusing me sexually for years. One night he walked into my bedroom while my mother was working. I pulled out a gun, aimed, and shot him in the chest." I listened intently as she elaborated, pausing only to catch her breath. When she was finished, she stared at me and asked, "What's going to happen to me now?"

I rose from my chair, stared for a moment, then embraced her, saying, "I have to report this, but it's going to be all right and I'll be with you through it all."

When she had her hearing, five months later, I was by her side.

### 60.

"Good morning," the visitor said, walking into my classroom.

I responded in kind and wondered why he was there. It was highly unlike him to show up in my classroom. The principal had been there only one time before today, and that was when the drug dog was doing a check. He motioned for me to join him outside the room.

"Finish working on your peer editing," I said to my students. "I'll be right back."

"It's Mary," he said quickly. "I'm going to need to bring her up to the office. She was doing drugs in the girl's bathroom before school. To be honest, this is the last straw. She has too long a history of drug and alcohol use here."

"Any chance? You know how hard I have been working with her, and this morning she even came in to check on her grades. That's a breakthrough and you know it."

He gave me a look that said what he didn't say. *No. She's gone.*

I opened my classroom door and asked Mary to join me and to bring her things. I could see her face change as she walked toward me. I made a motion for her to sit down so I could talk with her briefly before she left with the principal.

"Remember, I believe in you. You need to go with the principal now, and he's going to ask you some questions. Be honest, and don't let what happens stop the good work that you have been doing."

Standing up and slowly turning, she was looking at me with hopelessness in her eyes. I stood there watching her as she walked down the corridor away from me. I prayed that somehow she would be back. Reality shook me out of my dream as I heard noise coming from my room.

"Okay, now let's get back to work," I exclaimed, walking back into my room.

Walking from table group to table group and looking at my students' peer edit comments on their personal narratives, I couldn't help but think of Mary and how she too had a story, one that she had written about without fail in her journal— about her hopes, dreams, fears, and mistakes. I wondered if this mistake would be the catalyst that would change her, that final step to either move her out of her abyss or sink her completely. I was jolted back to the classroom by the ringing of the passing bell. Students packed up their books and headed out the door.

"Don't forget, tonight's a rewrite on your personal narrative, and read the next three chapters in *Zlata's Diary* for tomorrow's discussion," I shouted over the rumbling engine headed out my door. Then I headed out the door, grabbing my keys as I bee-lined to the office to check on Mary.

He was standing there to head me off.

"Come into my office."

"Not good?" I asked, but I had my answer. I could feel my heart break.

It wasn't the principal who stopped me but the school counselor. Together we had been working with Mary, trying to help her through some rough times. Mary's journal was filled with emotional abuse, drug use, sexual experimentation, and more. I walked in and sat down. We looked at each other, and there behind the door, two grown men shed a tear for a child who was not their own.

Our silence was broken as his cell phone buzzed. He pushed the silence button. The world was not allowed in just then. We talked about the little steps with Mary this year; we comforted each other, knowing that every day longer with us had helped her. She should have been gone several times over, but we had been able to persuade the powers that be for one more "second" chance. This time, she was dealing drugs, which violated her contract to stay. As I left the counselor's office, the police were taking her away, a young girl walking handcuffed like something out of *Cops*.

"I'm sorry, I'm sorry I disappointed you," Mary said.

A couple months went by, and I got a call from Mary. She wanted to let me know that she was enrolled in a new school, had been receiving counseling, and had been clean for twenty-one days. She said it was hard but not as hard as the tests I gave.

### 61.

"Why isn't he here?" I'm becoming frantic. "Matt, can you call his cell, please?"

"He told me yesterday that he would be here on time and that he would stay the entire day," Matt said.

He's chronically tardy and wealthy, and family members are willing to dispense excuses. But, bottom line: I miss my kid.

He cannot read beyond the third-grade level. He is fourteen years old and four feet tall, and he has never left his rural Vermont hometown. He hangs with "friends" twice his age, has tried smoking cigarettes, and chews tobacco on the town green. Are his actions a cry for attention, or do they scream "fuck you" to all of us? Is he saying "I don't need anyone" or "I need someone so badly"?

I work in an amazing program. It is located in a schoolhouse built in 1877. It houses a Ladies Workout Express, a Boys and Girls Club, a ballet studio, and the alternative education program that I direct. Its handsome and traditional community appeal runs contrary to the reputation of the alternative program students it houses. The students are considered "druggies," though none of them touch the stuff. They are called "stupid," though they are extremely gifted. They are looked down on as the "ones who couldn't hack it." The truth is they are in my program because the pace, the cookie cutter mold, the drama, and the memories of failure associated with the mainstream environment cause anxiety and fear. These feelings can be debilitating to any middle school student trying to find his or her way, but to the particular students I work with, they are both a challenge and a threat. The combination often proves volatile. And when my students are criticized—called druggies or stupid or accused of not being able to hack it—their reaction brings them to my program.

So, my troubled and absent student hates the system. He hates his family. He hates being confined. I get it. But how can I facilitate change when he is never at school? I want so much to reach this one kid, but I also have seven others, all with completely different needs and abilities. This occupation is only successful when treated as a labor of love, and love requires vigilance.

Finally, Matt reaches him and hands me the phone.

"Jeremiah, I am driving to your house and picking you up right now," I say. "I have so many exciting things to show you."

He knows how I get this goofy, giddy grin when I am excited about something, so that even in his worst moods I can steal a smile from him.

We start at the beginning. We get a base of measurement to grow from. He needs constant praise and encouragement. He is learning how to read at fourteen. We work and work and work. He tries and succeeds and then tries and withdraws, and then he's absent again for sometimes weeks or a month at a time.

I wonder if he is scared to be successful. I wonder if he finds comfort in what he perceives to be true. I know it is in him, but once I pull it out, how can I ensure that he triumphs, that he prevails?

He has no family support. He says he has no reason to go to college. I decide that I will be the one in his life who encourages him, pushes him to live up to his potential, and reveals to him the inherent joy of personal achievement. I will be the positive person in his life so that he will never be able to say there was never someone who cared for him, wanted the best for him, and worked so hard to show him how truly special he is.

My favorite questions from him are "Why do I have to know this?" and "How will this help me?"

We begin at the beginning, building our base.

I tell him, "Those are perfect questions."

Then we march, step-by-step, toward the answers.

## 62.

My classroom is unexpectedly lax for a detention center. I let them have some freedoms but at the same time they realize that I am in charge and I say when enough is enough. My classroom is also full of humor. These guys have enough on their plates, and a little laughter never hurt anyone. We joke back and forth, and no one ever gets insulted because we know how far we can push each other.

This morning I was late to class after struggling with a cantankerous copy machine that is a little less than top of the line.

"Whoa, Miss M!"

The voice of Danny the class clown came booming through the classroom. Danny was the one student who turned every day into a Battle of the Wits. I would always win the battle by stating: "Danny, once and for all . . . I refuse to have a Battle of the Wits with an unarmed person. It just isn't fair, man!" He would laugh and offer his typical response: "Whatever."

"What's wrong, Dan?" I asked. His reply was sure to be funny.

"Do you ever wash your face, Miss M?"

I gave Danny a weird look that meant, *What do you mean do I ever wash my face? What a stupid thing to say to me!*

"Ummm, yeah, I wash my face. Do you ever wash yours, hot shot?" I thought I had him this time.

"Well, Miss M, all I can say is that I wash mine a heck of a lot better than you wash yours."

He turned the mirror of my overhead projector toward the ceiling, and a roar of laughter came pouring through the room. Four finger-size black streaks lay across my forehead. I looked at my hands and noticed the ink that was left on them from my earlier battle with the copy machine. I rolled my eyes and sat down defeated but soon began laughing with the class.

"All right, Dan, you got me. But savor the flavor, pal."

That morning, class was a lost cause, but I didn't mind. I knew that when the pressure was on, my kids would get their work done. I had nothing but trust in my students—and I still do, even after they leave the center. As a teacher at the detention center, I am not allowed to have contact with them once they are released, but I never stop thinking about them. Danny had so much potential, and he literally was raised in detention centers. He was a good kid and had so much going for him, but he needed to have someone around who would help him on his journey, someone who would make him listen. Never a day goes by that I do not think of him and pray that he is all right.

I see my kids who come into my classroom so far behind their peers—sixteen-year-olds who are at a first-grade reading level, a senior in high school who is still struggling with an eighth-grade mathematics course. These kids do not need any special education services, and I can't help wondering how they fell through the cracks. Did the teachers really let them go by the wayside in order to focus on students that "got it"? Did my students—Danny is only one—just stop going to school and turn to the streets because that is what they understood and what understood them? It breaks my heart to think that they could be so much farther ahead but because no one wanted to take the time for them they were left far behind.

I can honestly say that I am content with the impact I have on my students. I realize that not every student is all the better for having known Miss M, but I know that I have at least reached one student and that is all that matters. I feel in my heart that I have left a lasting impression on my students, just as much as they have left one on me.

## 63.

*Hey, lady!*

In this instant, my inner voice eerily resembles that of Jerry Lewis, and I am more annoyed by its attempt to begin a conversation than amused.

"Not now," I think as I continue to discuss Nathaniel Hawthorne's use of the color pink in his short story "Young Goodman Brown." But the inner self is persistent and will not be ignored. The voice of the goofy comedian is quickly overshadowed by a low, steady rumble.

A wave of heat and nausea moves through my body as the

color drains from my face and a flash of panic sets in. "Did they hear it?" I wonder. Surely there is some mercy in this universe, and this classroom full of eighth graders did not hear the gas pocket in my stomach trying to communicate with me.

I count down from ten in my head as my student explains what the color white usually represents. *Ten* . . . "Purity" . . . *nine, eight* . . . "God" . . . *seven, six, five* . . . "Goodness" . . . *four, three, two* . . .

Before my brain can even start to process *one*, there is an exasperating pain in my stomach. The GPS of gastroenterology reminds me that I am OFF TRACK and must exit to the nearest restroom.

Shit! Shit! Shit!

I am running like Wilma Rudolph down the hallway. This is called the "poopy sprint," and I am a gold medalist.

When I return to my classroom, my students ask if I am okay. I reply honestly. "Yeah. I'm good. Just a Crohn's moment." They understand.

My first year teaching, I had a group of girls approach me on one of my particular big-belly days (I gauge them in pregnancy months, and this one was a second trimester day) and ask if I was indeed pregnant.

"Huh?" I asked.

"Well, you know, Miss, your stomach looks huge."

I'm thinking, "Wow—no tact." Then I began telling them the reason my stomach was so bloated. Initially, they were uninterested, wanting a simple "yes" or "no" response to the pregnancy inquiry. But as I began explaining my diet restrictions, suddenly they wanted to know more. This became one of those teachable moments, and I went with it. I told them about my treatments, surgeries, symptoms, and the effects of Crohn's disease.

I was bombarded with questions.

"Does it hurt?"

*Sometimes* . . .

"Do you have a scar?"

*Yes.*

"Can I see it?"

*No.*

"Is it contagious?"

*No.*

"I mean can we catch it? Can you give it to us?"

*I'm pretty sure that's the definition of contagious . . . and again, no, I cannot give it to you.*

"Are you gonna die?"

*Everyone dies.*

"No, Miss. I mean, is this gonna kill you?"

*I hope not.*

And in what seemed like seconds I was faced with my own mortality and the real effects of my disease. My *dis-ease*. My discomfort. It's funny to me how I call it that now. For so long I wanted no part of it. I mean, no one wants any part of a chronic disease, but even as I received monthly injections of an experimental treatment, I was in denial. I could not believe that I had an actual diagnosis. I had been healthy all my life, an athlete, and suddenly people were poking and prodding me, telling me how to eat, how to live. I was devastated.

There are days when I physically don't feel that I can get out of bed, but I do it. Days when I feel that I spend more time in the bathroom stall than in my classroom, but I'm there. They have to know that there are people in this world who believe in them enough to show up every day. These kids have to learn about commitment, dedication, setting high expectations for yourself and meeting them. I'm proud to show them how.

## 64.

As I neared the end of the first semester of my second year, I realized that recently I have spent lots of time thinking about Mr. Manook, my high school art teacher. Mr. Manook was scared of blood, and he taught Alaska Native Art, which included the use of sharp carving tools and classes of twenty to thirty high-schoolers. It was only a matter of time, then, before he passed out.

The day he fainted there were few who hadn't heard the story, but we reveled in telling it over and over. The boys responsible for the prank had molded an index finger out of clay and painted it realistically. They also mixed some red latex paint with a little water to thin it out just enough to be believable. During class, one boy stuck his index finger into a hole in one of the art tables, stuck a carving tool in the hole where his finger "ended," placed the molded finger on the other side of the blade, poured some of the paint around the hole, and frantically called to Mr. Manook. Upon seeing the "blood" seeping from the severed finger, Mr. Manook fainted. We couldn't believe the success of the joke, and Mr. Manook took it all in stride.

There are times when I feel myself trying to emulate him and take everything in stride. I look at some of my students, and I wonder how he put up with so many squirrelly, irresponsible teenagers and made them into the opposite. Then it hits me: I'm not Mr. Manook. A twinge hits my heart when I think this, and at times tears well up in my eyes. It's not so much that I struggle with situations that seemed easy to him, or that I somehow think I should be as good as he was but I'm not, it's that he died in 2001 at the age of forty-four. The importance of remembering him is to answer one simple question: How did he get so much done in such a short amount of time?

I'm slowly but surely figuring out some of his tricks. One is that I have to be honest with my students and myself each and every day I walk through my classroom door. Mr. Manook once told someone close to me who had recently been the driver in a near-fatal car accident that he had to slow down. Mr. Manook paid attention, he could see the situation for what it was, and he had the strength to come out and say it. This is one with which I have struggled. It's difficult, sometimes, to not fall into clichés and it's-gonna-be-okays. How can I tell a kid whose mother is about to get out of jail that their relationship might not improve? How about the one whose father just left them? The one whose mother is fighting cancer? The one whose parents stole and read her journal and then took everything out of her room because they didn't like what she had written? Sometimes I can feel my heart beating as I put my pen to their paper.

What I consider to be the most important trick is to believe in my students and always give them a "second" chance, even if it's their third, fourth, maybe even fifth chance. So many kids walked into Mr. Manook's room having already decided they were failures, yet left knowing they were fully capable as students and as individuals. Like any teacher, I face innumerable frustrations every day. Every now and again, though, I'm reminded that my kids face those same challenges. This year alone, I've had a student whose parents divorced, three students who have lost close family members, many whose fathers have been deployed to a war zone, two who have been facing time in a detention center, and more students with absent parents than I sometimes care to acknowledge.

I look at my kids, and usually I see who they are, right then and there. I'm learning, though, to see who they will become.

## 65.

The obnoxious, vibrating sound of my cell phone reverberated through the metal drawer of my standard-issue teacher's desk. Only one person could possibly be calling me at 10:30 on a Wednesday morning.

"Hi, honey, it's me," said my wife in between breaths. She sounded as if she had just completed her morning jog. "I'm pretty sure my water just broke."

The rest of her words were unrecognizable as I began to formulate my game plan for the birth of our daughter. I hung up the phone and raced back to my desk in search of the car keys, while my fourth-grade students stared intently. The math assignment I had just given them sat untouched on their desks. Their eyes followed my every move.

It wasn't long before they began spewing rapid-fire questions. *Mr. Cameron, how much did she weigh? What did you name her? When are you coming back?*

The fourth-grade firing squad was about to reload when they were suddenly interrupted by a commanding voice from the back of the room.

"Guys, leave Mr. C alone," said Jason in a very mature tone. "He doesn't need to worry about us; his wife needs him right now."

I had to look again to be sure that Jason was actually the one who uttered these words. Typically, his comments were followed by a one-way pass to the principal's office.

I never imagined how the birth of my daughter would forever change me as a teacher. From the moment my students entered the classroom on my first day back from paternity leave, I saw them no longer as students but rather as sons and daughters of parents just like myself.

As the students took their seats, I gazed at Jason. As usual, his face was planted firmly on his desk, and the journal he was supposed to be writing in was tucked away under a stack of papers.

"Jason, it's good to see you again," I whispered as I knelt down beside his desk. "Could you please reflect in your journal about the importance of family?"

"I hate this journal, and besides, I have nothing to write. This is stupid." He had marked a giant X across his paper.

The lightbulb began to illuminate. Jason's unwillingness to write in a journal, particularly about this topic, must stem from the fact that his father is not currently in his life. He was missing an essential piece of his family's foundation: a father. I was the one who was temporarily filling that void.

Each day when I return home from school, I walk through the front door, happily proclaiming, "Daddy's here." My daughter runs to me in anticipation of a gentle hug or a warm kiss, because she knows her father is home. When I open the door to Room 10 and witness the range of emotions on my students' faces, I become a father again. A father to every Jason who needs someone to love him, respect him, or just listen to him. As a teacher of ten years, I've become a better father. As a father of one year, I've become an even better teacher.

## 66.

I held my breath as my husband opened our credit card bill. He scanned each purchase as I continued to stir the pot on the stove. He sighed as he put the bill on the table and asked: "Why is there a charge for two hundred dollars to the university on here? Who is it for this time? When are you going to draw the line between being their mother and their teacher?"

As steam from the pot swirled above the stove, I recalled the faces of my former and present students. There was Lexie, who recently lost her mother; there was Perry, who was expelled for selling drugs on campus; there was Mona, who recently confided in me that her dad had threatened to kill her; there was Shea, who was unable to live at home and became a couch-jumper.

"How in hell are you going to support a baby!" Those words must have felt like a slap in the face to Shea. Here it was, the end of Shea's junior year, and she was pregnant. I reacted more as a mother would than as a teacher should.

Nine months later, I watched the nurses clean, weigh, and check over Shea's beautiful baby boy. Silently, I wished that life would not be as chaotic for this baby as it had been for his mother. Shea's mother walked up and stood beside me and said, "Thank you for being here and for being there."

I saw her mother again several weeks later. I was standing on the porch of a house down the street from Shea's, watching firemen work to extinguish the flames engulfing her home. It was a damp, cold morning so the smoke from the fire enveloped us as we stood nearby. Despite the intense heat we could feel from the smoldering embers that were once Shea's house, there was a chill that reached our very souls. As she cried, I embraced Shea and her son. Over her shoulder, I saw her mother stumbling around from another night of heavy drinking. I pulled Shea tighter.

I spent the rest of that day trying to secure temporary housing for the family. I made phone calls, but because none of the adults in the family would test clean for drugs or alcohol, charitable shelter programs would not allow them into their program. The Red Cross paid for two hotel rooms for three nights so our time was limited. Shea, her baby, and I went shopping for the bare necessities to help her get by. As we placed the diapers, baby lotion, baby food, formula, and wipes on the checkout counter, Shea asked me, "Why do you do this? You are just my teacher."

As if my mind had a rewind button, I watched the last four years of Shea's life as my student replay in my head. From the first semester that she sat in my classroom, I knew that she had a fighting chance to succeed, and I knew that I had to help her.

A few months later, I picked Shea up early. We were at the dorm by 9 a.m. "I can't believe it! I can't believe I'm going to college!" Shea's excitement couldn't hide her nervousness. We located her room and put things on her bed before heading out to register for orientation. The students were participating in programs separate from their parents, so when it came time for them to separate, I told Shea, "I'm really proud of you. You can do this, you know. You have the power to change your world." With that, she hugged me, joined the other students, and walked to the next building. Turning toward my left, I stood there, watching her as long as I could. Then, turning toward my right, I watched the parents. I turned around and slowly walked to my car and headed home. That very moment was worth every penny of the $200 I'd spent.

## 67.

Over a year of negotiations ended yesterday when our union settled with the district for a 1 percent raise. The raise is so small that the increase in each paycheck won't fill my gas tank halfway.

I have always known why I am in this profession—for the kids and because it's what I am meant to do. But this raise offends our dignity as professionals. It is insulting to receive less than a dollar a day increase to be a mother, a therapist, a confessor, a nurse, a role model, and a drill sergeant.

Even on days like today, it's easy to reassure myself by looking at my kids that this is what I was meant to do, no matter how much I get paid. It was Marcus and the many other voices that I heard today that reminded me that it really isn't about the numbers behind the dollar sign. I realized that no matter what the terms of our contract, I do this out of love and necessity.

Marcus, a boy who thinks he's a man, has failed at school. He gets kicked out of classes for fighting, sleeping, and telling his teachers where to stick it. In his first few months of high school, his behavior record is longer than many seniors'. I knew from the moment I saw him that all the good things about being a kid were missing from his life.

The first day he walked into my classroom, he needed everyone to think he was unattached, that he didn't give a shit. Yet he was so deliberately seeking attention and approval from every set of eyes. His hair was in neatly wrapped cornrows that ran down the back of his neck. His jeans were at least five sizes too big, his shoes were sparkling white, and his shirt hung down to his knees. In his world, he had it going on.

Every time he spoke, he wanted to get a laugh from a peer. He was the star of his own show.

"Can I be Romeo?" he asked when we started reading *Romeo and Juliet,* " 'Cause you know I'm a ladies' man! I am all *over* that part!"

However, when we started reading aloud an adapted version of the play, Marcus could hardly sound out basic words. No one laughed at him because he has a reputation for being really tough, but he didn't volunteer the next day for the part of Romeo.

As school has continued, parts of Marcus have disappeared right before my eyes. His swagger is a little less confident, his hair frizzy and unkempt, and his shoes a little dirtier. He has been bragging to the class that he was kicked out of his aunt's: his last-resort home. He is living on the couches of friends, neighbors, and acquaintances. Homeless, he has run out of places to run.

"My 'hood is filled with music, from the voices busting rhymes to the booming depths of the speakers," he read from his journal, volunteering for the first time and surprising all of us with his insight. His voice was confident, walking the line between being an adult and a child.

"Last year, I was beaten up bad because some kid wanted my tennis shoes and my jersey. I fought back and kept my clothes," he read.

As he stood tall and proud in the back corner of the room, he articulated the fear young people have of being out too late or being on the wrong corner at the wrong time. It is his reality, and he was speaking from his heart about things he knew.

Most important, he, of all kids, wanted to share his story. When I asked my ninth graders to pass their papers forward, he quietly asked me if it was okay that he used *'hood* instead of *neighborhood,* and then he stood up to read his description in front of our class. The other kids were silent as they listened to their story coming from Marcus's mouth.

There were looks of understanding and sorrow on the faces of these kids. Kids who have been quiet all year couldn't wait for their turn to share their own stories. Marcus made it okay to talk about the reality that many of these kids live every day.

When I worked in the business world, I dreaded waking up to sit in my cubicle doing work that didn't have any meaning to me. I was never proud that my professional goal was to make more money for billion-dollar companies. I have come to terms with the fact that I will never be rich. I've always known this, but I needed a reminder of why I do what I do.

It's Marcus. I teach for him.

## 68.

As a first-year teacher, I thought I wasn't prepared for what was to come. When we got outside the classroom, Kirk immediately broke down in uncontrollable tears. He told me that he was tired of moving from foster homes to group homes and that enough was enough. I didn't know what to say. Kirk had always seemed so privileged and happy. He opened up to me, and I felt compelled to try to ease his pain. I mustered up all the professional development training I could and began to explain how everything would be all right and offered to send him to the counselor. I knew in my heart that all he heard was "Whomp, whomp, blah, blah, blah." I could see it in his eyes and in the way his shoulders heaved with each sob. As if he was reading my mind, he said, "I'm tired of talking to people who just don't understand." For a moment, I forgot I was his teacher. I said, "Oh, I know how you feel," only to be cut off by his frustrated outburst of "You stand here with your perfect little life like you really know how I feel. You ain't never walked in my shoes!"

It seemed as if an eternity passed. I knew I had to be a woman of my word and show him that I knew exactly how he felt. Damn, it was time for me to share my own foster care experience. There was no turning back now.

"Kirk, I was around your age when my world finally fell apart. I remember my mom saying that she was leaving us for a better life and that we were not a part of it. Man, there were five of us. I remember wondering how a mother could just get up and leave her kids. I didn't know what we were supposed to do; all I knew was the pain of being separated from my sister and brothers. I experienced the horrors of living from one foster home to the next. Kirk, I went through four foster homes and an orphanage during my junior and senior years in high school. Trust me, I know how you feel."

He didn't say a word.

I told Kirk that just like him, at one time I found myself at a bending point. I knew we had an irrevocable bond when he stopped crying. He whispered, "Why did you say bending and not breaking?" Trying to mask my emotions, I felt tears welling in my eyes as I explained that a social worker who really cared about me once told me that I could bend as low as I wanted just as long as I didn't let people or circumstances break me. Kirk then blindsided me with a hug and a smile.

Not long after that, I went home and found my old high school address book and dialed the number for my last social worker. When the voice on the other end picked up, it took every inch of me to not cry. This was the only person who believed me when I reported being mistreated in various foster homes. I gathered myself and slowly said, "I know you might not remember me but this is . . ." I didn't even get the second syllable of my name out because she sniffled and finished not only my first name but my last name too. Her next reply was, "Sweetie, I have always wondered what became of you. The last I heard, you were in college somewhere in another state." I filled her in on my daughter and my new profession, and I told her that I even still had the little ceramic Bible with the Lord's Prayer written on it that she gave me way back then. I asked how she was doing, and she proudly exclaimed, "I just retired after thirty years of being a social worker with the state's department of social services. Of those thirty years, I *only* had three foster children go to college. Of those three children, only *one* of them graduated, you."

## 69.

"You'll see." That was all my professor said and was probably all he could say.

"You'll see." That's it. That was his answer to a question posed by a small, mousy-looking girl in the front row. It was the last class of the semester and my last class before heading out into the world of student-teaching. Our English methods professor was giving us some final advice. He warned us that no matter how well we thought we were prepared, we would always run into something in the classroom that would baffle us to no end. He asked for any other questions, and Small and Mousy raised her hand.

"Like what?" she asked.

"You'll see."

Now almost four years from that day, I can think back on all my "You'll see" moments, and it makes me laugh and cry and get angry. Some things have happened that I don't think I would have believed if I hadn't seen them with my own eyes. My non-teacher friends think I am making up half of my stories. I do not lie and I do not embellish. They are all heart-breakingly, gut-bustingly true.

There was the time a colleague of mine told a student he could not go to the restroom because the student was not finished with his work. The student proceeded to pull a pop bottle from his backpack and filled it right in the middle of class. True story.

In my own classes, I have had students with all kinds of emotional baggage, and whatever they bring with them stops them from relaxing and trusting anyone, especially a boring English teacher who always wants to talk about reading and writing. I have tried to reason with them. I've tried yelling. I thought I would never find a way to reach some of these kids. Then something happens that can break down any barriers and make all the frustrations seem not so important.

On a warm summer morning, about three weeks after school ended for the year, I woke up and turned on the news. The newscaster was telling of a fatal accident the night before that involved a teenager. I didn't really think anything of it. I went about my day, and a few hours later I got around to checking my e-mail. In my inbox was an e-mail from a student who had just graduated.

"Mr. A! Did you hear about Ray? He died in a car accident last night."

I sat in stunned silence for a while and finally made myself call around to confirm the news. It was true, and the funeral was in a few days. I decided to go, but I knew it would be difficult because Ray and I had developed a bond. He was a bit of an underachiever and was more interested in playing video games than in learning about Shakespeare or dangling modifiers, but he was a good kid. In fact he was liked by everyone. He transcended any racial or socioeconomic boundaries there may have been, and he got along with everyone. His desk had been right next to my teacher desk, and I spent the whole year joking around with him and trying to convince him that he could really do anything he wanted if he would actually try. I like to think he started to get it toward the end of the year as graduation approached.

As the service began, I found myself sitting in the overflow section of the funeral home and looking around at all of my current and former students in attendance. It broke my heart to see all of them in such pain, and my lip started to bleed as I bit it to keep from crying. I wasn't mourning only the loss of Ray. I was mourning for all these young kids who had to go through something so difficult at such a young age. I looked around that room at all the faces of the kids whom I had sent to the hall, all the kids I had given a detention, all the kids who will surely make me prematurely gray, and I saw the sorrow in their faces. And that was about the time that I lost it. I didn't care if they saw me cry. I didn't want to be the stoic teacher anymore. I wanted to be human, and humans cry in times of great sorrow. So I did.

After the service I was milling around the foyer of the funeral home, making small talk with a few of the other teachers in attendance. As we walked out, a student who I thought never cared for anyone but himself came up to me with tears in his eyes and put his hand on my shoulder. He told me he appreciated me coming. He told me it would be all right. Right then we both saw each other in a new light.

Occasionally, friends and acquaintances will ask me why I do what I do. They reckon it must be for the summers off. They want to know why I am going through all this work and spending extra hours at school and money out of my own pocket on the "problem" kids in my classes. They want to know if it is all worth it. I can only answer them one way.

"You'll see."

## 70.

"Colored chalk," I thought, "that's how I'll get them to see the components of an essay." And what a beautiful box of colored chalk I bought. It was more like a box of Crayolas, with chalk in magenta, sky blue, lilac, chartreuse, and azure.

Getting students focused after lunch was always a little tougher than during the other block periods. That they were in their own worlds and ignoring me didn't come as much of a surprise. But one group of six was being extra squirrelly. They were spring-semester juniors who would simply not quit their hysterical laughter. I tried separating them by moving seats, to no avail. I was still transparent, and their attention to one another was undiminished. Their classmates started looking at me like, "All right, already; just get on with it. Just start."

I proudly plucked the brightest pieces of chalk from the box. I accepted cooperative topical suggestions and composed on the board from student input, color coding their sentences as we constructed. But the group didn't quit laughing. They were actually chiding me, pointing at what was on the board, and waving their fingers in the air as though they were individual conductors of separate orchestras. They started singing the Rolling Stones song "She's a Rainbow": "She comes in colors everywhere." I bit a hole in my tongue; I wasn't giving up. I didn't care how far they took this; I was giving it everything I had. They would grasp it if we could just finish it. Other students were nodding their heads, like, Okay, I'm seeing it. But not the group. Tears were streaming down their cheeks from their hilarity. What was going on? I succumbed to sarcasm.

"*What?* Are you going to tell me that the cafeteria is spicing up the food with magic mushrooms?"

It worked—complete and total silence for about thirty seconds. Then they exploded and got even weirder. I had sworn not to give in to this unforgivably disruptive behavior, but it was time to fold. I strolled to the board and set the chalk in the tray. I grabbed an unoccupied student desk, turned it to face the students, sat in the desk, and calmly said, "It looks, students, as if we will be focusing on colors today. Describe to me, painting with words, some of the colors in your world." After all, narrative detail is an intrinsic component of what we were trying to build into the body paragraphs of the essay.

Amazingly enough, and much to my surprise, every student participated in a collaborative conversation about the colors around us. The period ended without essays, but also without bedlam.

The first day of school a year and a half later, Stanley, one of the hecklers, walked into my classroom holding a box. It was a box made out of exotic woods, which he told me were blond ash, ebony, and African mahogany. It was filled with red pencils, erasers, whiteout, and Chicklets gum—items he thought a teacher might appreciate. I ran my hands over the highly polished box and thanked him.

Stanley said he had made the box for me because he wanted to express his appreciation.

"For what?" I asked.

"I was too afraid to come to you until after I graduated. That day that you asked us if we were on magic mushrooms, because we couldn't control our laughter? We knew you were frustrated. What you didn't know was how close to the mark you were. Except, we weren't on mushrooms. We were tripping on acid."

## 71.

"Yo, Will. Can you help me with my poem?" Ace asks. I glance at the clock. It's 7:25. My board meeting starts at 7:30. I know that my responsibility should be the meeting because I am now a board member, but my real passion is cultivating relationships with the students. I haven't spoken with Ace since last spring. I'm in the middle of a divorce and in the throes of an Ivy League graduate school program. I ditch the meeting.

"Sure thing, man. Let's go to work. We've got an hour."

I pull out a notebook from my binder filled to capacity with five years' worth of poems by students. The names on the papers and the words of those poems flood my mind with voices and faces of students past.

"Ace, it's good to be back here. I've missed you guys."

"We've missed you, too, Will. Why don't you come back as a staff member again?" Ace wants an answer. Though I want to come back, I know that I can't. I have to work on other parts of my life right now. However, I know that I have to be real with Ace about this. No bullshit will do.

"Believe me, man, I miss you guys. This house is my home. I've got a lot of craziness going down right now. I would be a terrible staff member if I were here. It wouldn't be fair to any of us. At least I can still be here some as a board member."

Ace doesn't hesitate to let me hear it.

"Naw, Will, man, you need to be here as a staff member. We miss you. You were always around us."

I manage to hold back the tears. The conversation turns back to the poem.

"All right, Will, I've been thinking about this poem for a while. I just haven't been able to write it. I need your help."

"Okay. I'm here. Do you need an idea for a poem?"

I don't even know why I asked Ace the question. As an artist who constantly paints and draws, Ace is always full of creative ideas. I just need to reach out and offer my help.

"No. I need you to write down my words as I think aloud."

"Okay. I'm ready." I fold back the cover of the notebook and take a seat on an old pool table donated to the house a couple of years back. Ace thinks for a moment as he saunters back and forth. "Title it 'Father, Where Art Thou?' "

I know Ace's father has never really been in his life. Ace doesn't even know him. I feel lucky. Ace is opening up to me. I listen.

Ace slowly looks up, then begins: "Sometimes, I wonder, are you in eternal slumber? Why ponder if I haven't seen you since I was younger?" It rolls off his tongue.

"Damn son! Hold on. That's deep."

Ace laughs. I write furiously.

He continues: "I asked for you, then my sister, too. My mother said you were through."

I stop him.

"So, how is your mom? Is she coming to the house to make some of that good Dominican rice and beans?"

"She has left the country."

"I'm sorry to hear that."

He keeps on spitting rhymes.

"Damn! I wish you were here to see how much your boy grew! If it's not too much to ask, I'll forgive your past."

"That's decent, son!"

He continues, "I know that years have passed. Your face in my mind is blurry. But, at least, your memory I carry."

Ace pauses for a moment, then intones, "Guess what? Right now, I'm a little hairy." My grip on the pencil relaxes, and I guffaw. Ace always manages to inject some humor into the most serious of moments.

He continues: "My sister plans to marry when she gets thirty. My mother moved to another country. Where have you been all of these years?"

Ace pauses. I can tell that he's going in for the lyrical kill now: "If I see you, I wouldn't know if I should cry in tears or run out of fear. At least one thing will remain true: Father, I miss you."

"Daaammnn!"

"Will, will you write something in Spanish at the bottom?" Ace asks.

"Definitely. You just have to spell it for me."

Ace chuckles.

"B-e-n-d-i-c-i-ó-n."

"What's that mean?"

"Blessing."

"P-a-p-i."

"What's that mean?"

"Daddy."

"Blessing Daddy?"

"Yes."

Blessings. I hold Ace's poem. I pick up my binder. Full of poems. Full of blessings. I add Ace's to the count.

## 72

The ragged and tired look on Mom's face says it all at the parent-teacher conference. She had to request to leave early from her twelve-hour-a-day downtown hotel cleaning job to talk about the future. We communicate through a translator, although her facial expressions show her attempts to follow my words.

Her daughter Carla has been struggling despite working hard. Carla's parents came from Mexico when she was five, forcing her to master a new language in addition to the same new skills all students are expected to acquire in public schools. Seven years later, Carla's language and math skills are progressing significantly slower than her peers'. Last year Carla still struggled to read English, and she spent a summer in school trying to make up for years of lost time. By all indications she will not pass the state test, the measure used to grade our school and district. And in front of me are Mom's tired eyes, a look I have seen before in other parents. Her hope is in her daughter, who wishes to show her mom success. How do you say, "She is still struggling," to a hopeful parent and a willing child?

We decide that Carla should come in and work with me one on one. Normally I would be hesitant to surrender time, as the twelve hours I spend teaching, planning, grading, and meeting parents and other teachers take a toll on my life. But Carla is eager to work and show her parents why they came to the United States. Everyone is putting their hope in me.

Carla ends up coming in the next few weeks and starts to record her thoughts and progress in a journal. She writes about living up to her parents' dreams. I respond after reflecting on parental pressure: "Your dreams count too, and what you do will please your parents." Eventually, Carla's dedication permeates efforts in math and science. I informally discuss Carla's progress with the other teachers and learn that others also give extra time. It reassures me that I am not alone in this battle.

The standardized test is on the horizon. The test doesn't track hard work, dedication, or the background of a student. It produces a cold, hard, nonforgiving number. One day as I address the class, I hide the fact that the message is for Carla: "Don't measure your self-worth on numbers. Some of the most successful people did not necessarily test well." Later I tell Carla I am not concerned about her scores and am proud of her improvements. As she hears this, she looks down and meekly says, "Thank you." Still, deep down we both know some community members, and even some other staff members, make assumptions about teaching and learning based on the numbers. When the local paper plays up test scores as if the numbers could tell people everything about a school or a district, I realize how much of a losing battle I fight.

During testing, Carla struggles. Her lips are curled and she has wrinkles like a forty-year-old on her forehead. Desperately, she asks me what a word means, to which I respond, "By test rules I cannot tell you." I am annoyed for sounding like a robot, but the mandated proctor test training offers dire consequences for saying anything else. She closes her eyes as she goes back to the test.

But I am resilient and have tricks up my sleeve. I, along with some other teachers, decide to strike back against standardized testing. At the end of the year, we invite Carla's parents to the awards assembly. Her parents stand amazed as they realize the next awardee is their daughter. They are proud; there is almost a tear in her mom's tired eyes. My stoic armor has been damaged, and I try to keep my usual unemotional teaching face from showing feelings.

Later, I reflect on Carla's future. I want someone else to realize her potential and kindheartedness and nurture that. Or will they see her as a number, someone who struggles to grasp the English language and judge her?

## 73

As my fall class filed in, I took note of all my new Resource students. There were sixteen of them from seven middle schools. They were noisy, rude, and challenging. Most didn't want to be here. But one student stood out from all the rest. David was larger than life. Only fifteen years old but six feet three inches tall and weighing 275 pounds, he was the largest kid in my small, portable classroom. As I called the roll, the other students were yelling at the top of their lungs, but David sat quietly. I had students with various levels of need. Julie was semiparalyzed; Ryan and Art had super-ADHD (they were excessively hyperactive); Teresa was always angry; Matt was high-level autistic; and Kevin, Anthony, and Ken had parole officers because of various crimes. But David appeared to be as serene as the Dalai Lama himself.

David sometimes stayed after class to talk. He raised his hand to answer questions. He talked quietly and with composure. While Ryan, Art, and Teresa yelled and expressed their anger, David ignored all the noise and confusion and tried to learn.

When Halloween rolled around, I started taking pictures of the kids. My students dressed up as witches, ghosts, Dracula, and other characters. David simply wore a rubber monkey mask. I made a massive wall collage with the pictures, which was a hit because the kids loved looking at themselves.

One day I was sick, and a substitute filled in for me. Ryan had gone to school with David from grammar school all the way to my ninth-grade class, and he knew how to press all of David's buttons. Ryan teased David until, at the breaking point, David picked up a table and threw it across the room, missing other students by inches. It took three monitors to subdue him. He was suspended for five days even though this was his first disciplinary problem. At that point I should have looked more closely at David's special-ed file, but being inexperienced I did not. I came back from being sick, and David came back from suspension. Life returned to "normal."

Then one day, in the middle of class, David stood up suddenly and collapsed into a violent grand mal seizure. He woke up groggy as if nothing had happened. Now I had to look at his file. Apparently when he was much younger, his father beat his head against the wall until he had seizures. He was taken away from his father and went to live with his grandparents. He was put on medication to control the seizures, but it didn't always work.

In his second and third years of high school, David seemed to have more seizures. He became enraged easily and much more often. He began hurling desks again, one time narrowly missing Julie's head and breaking an overhead projector. He became harder to calm down. Our gentle giant was taking a turn for the worse. David's father had put into play a vicious turn of events, and I was afraid of how it would turn out.

In his senior year, David and some of the other students helped me move my classroom across campus. We needed his strength. The move went well, and David seemed to be settling down again. Then, on his way home after school, David had a seizure in the crosswalk next to a campus police officer. He knocked her down. She called for backup, thinking he was attacking her. He was handcuffed and taken to the police station. There was a meeting. It was decided to reduce his time at school. He would take an extra year to graduate.

Except for periodic seizures, David's life moved on toward graduation. I talked to his grandparents frequently. They were very proud of his achievement. He graduated with a diploma. At graduation I took a picture of him in his robes and put it on my picture wall next to his Halloween picture. He gave me a big hug after the ceremony.

Periodically his grandparents brought him to my class to say "hi." Things were going well for David. Sometimes his grandparents called to update me on how he was doing. He got a job.

One day, a year after he graduated, I got a call from David's grandmother. She was crying so hard I could hardly understand her. She said that David had died and she thought I should know because I had been so close to him. Apparently, he had been at the YMCA pool, sitting on the edge and talking to two girls. They left him to go talk to their mother. When they came back, he was gone. They looked all around for David, and then saw him in the pool. At first they thought he was swimming. Then they noticed he wasn't moving. He had had a seizure, slipped into the pool, and drowned. Our gentle giant had crossed over, and I will always miss him.

I was told when I started teaching Resource that many of my students, upon graduation (if they made it), would end up in one of three categories. They would get a low-level job, they would turn to crime, or they would die. Ever hopeful, I never believed that. Fortunately, David is the only student I've lost in thirteen years of teaching. His pictures are on my wall, and he is always looking down on my new students as they roll in every fall.

## 74.

I hate January. In Alaska, it's a cruel month, and there is no Christmas to ease its passing. The cold and the dark begin to eat at you, and there is little reprieve from the wind storms, the snow storms, the below-zero temperatures.

This particular morning I'm running a little late. My feet crunch the snow-packed earth as I scurry toward the front door. And even though I'm bundled for the January weather, the air is thick and biting and it makes its way through my clothing, licks my face, and burns my lungs. The only consolation in these dark and cold mornings is that when there are no clouds to insulate the air and the moon comes for a visit and the stars shine bright in the night sky, the northern lights can be seen dancing and crackling across the sky.

But my mind is somewhere else this morning. I am to meet a student, Charity, before school to go over what she missed last week. I'm worried about her. Her grades are drastically falling. She often doesn't show up at school anymore, and if she does, it is during fifth or sixth hour. Charity is only a freshman. She is one of the many students in her class whom the counselors have targeted as at-risk. The problem lately is trying to motivate her to do something.

I suspect Charity suffers from depression. I've told the counselors about my concern and they've tried many times to contact her parents for intervention, but no one returns their calls.

I gave Charity a notebook to show that I care. A notebook— like that is going to be the answer to Charity's problems. I told her that my therapy is writing and maybe, just maybe, putting her story on paper will help her heal and dream and look to her future for comfort. Charity has always told me she wants to go to college to become a psychologist. I remind her every time I see her to stick to that dream. My inscription for her journal: "Shine on, you crazy diamond."

Fifth hour, Charity walks into my classroom.

"Hey, Mr. Nelson. Sorry 'bout not making it to school this mornin'," Charity says, her light brown hair covering her eyes.

"I'm worried about you, Charity. This isn't about my class. It's about your life and helping you."

"I know, I know. But my life's a mess. My mom, my sister, and I got evicted from our apartment. We don't got no money so my mom wants me to watch my little sister while she works. That's why I don't come to school, and all I really wanna do is sleep so I can forget about everything."

"Charity, I'm sorry. I know that doesn't help anything, but I'm here for you. My door is always open."

"Thanks," Charity sighs. Then, suddenly, tears start to fall. I grab some tissue and put my arm around Charity, and we both sit there.

What do you say?

When students like Charity tell me that they've never known their biological fathers or that their mothers are recovering addicts or that they can't go to school because Mom has to work and they have to take care of their brothers or sisters, I go silent. How can teenagers concentrate on the themes of *One Flew over the Cuckoo's Nest* when they are taking care of their siblings or if their dad doesn't come home?

After I console Charity, she hands me the journal that I gave to her. It's completely full.

"Mr. Nelson," she says. "I took your advice and began to write out my thoughts."

And with that Charity hands me her journal and leaves. It's filled with her life. A life scarred by experiences she shouldn't know at her age:

> Now I realize I finally figured it out. I'm always writing about love and how I can't find it or why I need it, but now I realize it's my parents. Every kid needs a parent. Someone who loves them and will listen to stupid things, tuck them into bed, read them stories. I never had that. Maybe I did, but it was never enough. I woke up to screams and loud bangs, cursing, tears, and holes in the wall. Every day in my house is a new thrill, a new thought in the back of my head that says something is gonna go wrong. No kid needs to go through that. I guess a parent's love is irreplaceable and me looking for someone who respects me is me looking for my parents. I know that I'm missing something and it hurts.

I place Charity's journal in my backpack, bundle up once again to brace myself against the weather. It's dark outside, and clouds are covering the moon. I breathe in deep the taste of winter. As it burns down my throat and into my lungs, I brace myself and take the warmth of Charity's words toward home.

## 75

"Can I ask you a question?"

The chat window appears as I'm working my way through a pile of subpar essays.

"You just did, but go ahead and ask another one."

"It might not be appropriate."

I've grown accustomed to these questions. My online availability gives my students the cover they seek to ask the questions they can't bring themselves to ask in class, or to share the life events they can't find the words to relay in class. Usually, the topic is love—especially, the unrequited love reserved for the difficult journey through adolescence.

"How about you let me decide whether or not it's appropriate," I suggest.

"You sure?"

"I am."

"Um, are you gay?"

Shit.

The cursor blinks on my computer screen, mockingly. The essays don't seem so bad anymore.

Somewhere, on the other side of the city, a fourteen-year-old girl has asked *the* question.

In class, students have always broached the subject in a way that gives me an out: "Do you have a girlfriend?" I've always been ready with an adept sidestep. "I don't have time to date anyone; I'm with you guys all the time."

I feel resentment growing somewhere between my own adolescent memories and my adult logic.

I love being a teacher. I love the look on my students' faces when something in their brains moves to make room for a new thought. I love watching a heated class discussion in which the class loudmouth starts firmly rooted in an unquestioned belief and walks out of the room truly questioning what he believes and why.

An affirmative answer means I am no longer singularly a teacher. I work arduously to gain my students' trust and respect, and I resent even the possibility that an affirmative answer would create distance between us.

This is to say nothing of my unwillingness to be a poster teacher.

The cursor continues to mock.

As damning as an affirmative answer may be, I think of what it would have meant to have anyone in my life as I was growing up to show me that all the things the other guys said about people like me weren't true. I wasn't weak or small or abnormal. What it would have meant to have someone show me that this part of me that felt so huge and burdensome was only a part of me and needn't feel burdensome at all. If the research is to be believed and two-thirds of all teen suicide attempts are made by teens who identify themselves as queer, would an affirmative answer make the difference to a student searching for the seemingly intangible hope of normalcy? I remember the hopeless emptiness that crept in to my own teendom.

I look back to the screen and realize a new question has appeared: "You there?"

"Yes," I reply, but it's too late.

"The person you are messaging has gone offline."

# DISILLUSIONMENT

At some point, every teacher thinks they've hit rock bottom. There are many days when we all want to curl up in a ball and just give up. Failure may not be an option, but it is always there, looming, waiting to strike down even the most seasoned teacher.

On some days, I simply wanted to throw my hands in the air and quit. Yup, even I've been there. If I could have measured my own meltdowns with the Freedom Writers on a Richter scale, the printout often would have registered a 10.0. But I guess that's what you get when you have condescending administrators who have forgotten what it is like to be in a classroom, disgruntled parents to be called after school, and 150 essays to read before 7 a.m. Stressful? I think so. Those days were never a pretty sight. I sometimes grumbled on the phone with my father for hours, but, thankfully, after a good pep talk, I always found myself back in the classroom the next day. I knew that I had to show up for my students. I couldn't give up on them because so many others already had.

The stories in this section are painful. They hurt because they are honest, they are real, and there is nothing we can do to change these teachers' experiences. But there's still hope. These teachers talk about the daily battles that their students must endure, while others share the disillusionment inherent in high-stakes testing environments. The heart of a teacher is exceptionally resilient, so in the face of these adversities, they learn to push on.

## 76

KC's '70s muscle-car muscle shirt announces, "One size doesn't fit all." Over six feet tall and broad, poured into his well-worn shirt, Wrangler jeans, and Carhartt coat, with a ball cap perched just so, KC has the biggest, most compassionate heart you could ask for in a kid. Proud to be a cowboy, a "hick" like other cousins and "double cousins" before him, KC moves and talks with a slow, deliberate drawl. His grandma calls him "My turtle." "Casey Jones, you better watch your speed" doesn't fit here. KC is a resource student in my beginning drawing class. He works hard—he has to, to keep up. He processes slowly, moves methodically. Partially disabled wrists fused from a childhood injury make fine motor movements a chore.

KC is most engaged when he is drawing muscle cars and monster trucks. KC *loves* muscle cars. "The Super Bee is my all-time favorite car," he discloses openly, simply. KC loves everything about muscle cars. He can tell you more about differences in engines and lifters and wheels and about what he is going to do when he gets his than you can spend precious time listening. KC will be a meticulous mechanic, a hardworking, dedicated employee like his family members before him.

A test question on a world-civics exam asked, "What was the impact from the United States' Depression on the British economy?" KC answered simply, "Pretty damn bad."

KC's cousin was killed in a car crash recently. After KC announced to a group of us educators that he would be going to her funeral, and we gave our "I'm sorry" condolences, KC paused a moment and said, "Ya know, I can throw a knife clean through a tree."

KC didn't pass his reading and writing state competency tests; nor did he pass his reading and writing state core tests. KC worked his hardest, did his best, but didn't pass.

We hope that he rolls with it and doesn't let the failure get to him, as it has gotten to others before him.

We hope that through hard work in his classes that he will successfully pass . . . but to what end? KC is already a hard worker with a commitment to his goals and values. He will be an excellent employee and a contributing community member. He is likely to "Go forth and serve." But he may not pass the test—the mandated test.

We know our students, our students' stories. Yet we give these mandated tests to them. We have to—it's the law. Judgment is cast on a single test score—"high stakes." But we teachers hope for our student's successes beyond a passing score. We hope for a more civil society.

## 77.

"Miss Snow, not another test! We just took a test two weeks ago! What is the test about, anyway?"

"This one is to test your reading ability," I said.

"So what were the other tests for?"

"Those were to measure what you know in other subjects."

You name it. They test the students on it. Questions keep coming up in my mind: "What is all this testing doing to my students?" "Will the questions even be relatable to my students?"

I began to take a hard look at my students' situations during testing time. Ricky: Eleven years old, goal was to be a Latin King Gang member. The day of the state standardized test, Ricky fought with his mother and was taken to school by police escort. Anna: Ten years old, goal was to be a single mother with children. Anna never knew her father, but on the day of testing, her mother dropped her off to reside with him permanently. Doug: Twelve years old, star athlete, reading at a preschool level. The week of testing Doug was absent because he knew he couldn't read any of the assessment. As I administer the exam, I think to myself, "How in the world can these students concentrate on this test after the morning they've had?"

More depressing, the questions on the examination do not address my students' experiences and surroundings. For example, one question has students write about a time when they went to another country. Many of my students haven't had the opportunity to travel outside our city.

But the bottom line is simple according to the news on the state and national levels: Get the percentages up. Do I have less money? Deal with it. Fewer materials? Deal with it. A growing English-language-learner population? Deal with it. And that's exactly what I have done.

Using creative methods to spark students' attention, I make sense of frustrating testing practices. It is not an easy task to get students to forget about their daily trials, if only for a moment, and to concentrate on an assessment that will determine their futures along with schools' funding and practices. Trying to make standardized tests relatable is also a daunting task. It takes time and understanding to go beyond the curriculum and reach the students. Who would have thought that something as simple as Fruit Loops could inspire vocabulary growth and usage?

"What's the Fruit Loops for?" Ricky asked when I distributed cupcake holders full of Fruit Loops.

"It is for a vocabulary game that we will play together to help you increase your knowledge of unfamiliar words."

"I don't know why we have to do this. We won't use these words anymore anyway. These are school words that I don't need."

"Then we need to change that," I said.

In that one simple and easy game, I got my students to learn new words and actually use them in their daily dialogue and writing. They translated our game into a kind of code. "Hey, Miss Snow, you are sauntering to the door." I couldn't help but smile at the sound of the word. The testing practices still remain a challenge for my students and me, but I continue to seek out ways to reach them in spite of everything that is going on in their lives.

Ricky's thoughts about the testing practices still ring in my head.

"When are we going to be done with all this testing?"

"Well, I have to administer these tests throughout the year to meet the requirements on the state and national level."

"Are these tests going to get us into college?"

"They are to see if you can remember the standards and to see where you are."

"Why don't they just ask you what we are doing? You know what we can do."

"These assessments compare you to other students around the country."

"So why can't they just ask us without using these stupid, confusing questions? If they don't get us ready for college and just make us frustrated, why are we using them? They never ask about things that we know about. It seems as though they were set up to put us down or something."

I am speechless and run out of answers for Ricky. I see him fight back tears as he sees the test. Frustration mounts on his face.

"I always get nervous and upset every time I take these tests. I am just so tired of testing."

## 78.

The room was filled with bodies, shoulder to shoulder, and with the musk of pubescent energy. No one knew where to sit.

"Good, Javonne is absent. I'm sitting in his desk."

"That girl's in my seat. Where am I supposed to sit?"

"Get the fuck outta my seat!"

There were simply too many bodies in the room—more than thirty freshmen in a small beige room that barely fit the twenty-six desks I had. The room felt like a detention center minus the

armed guards. Students had to drag in desks from a cl'
across the hall. Other students grabbed chairs and claimed op.
space on a cluttered table.

Feeling overwhelmed and defeated, I felt tears begin to well
in my eyes as I asked the class for the hundredth time to please
give me their attention. No such luck. I felt the tears flooding as
I bolted out of the classroom. Four students immediately charged
after me, but I snapped at them to get back into the classroom.
Passing students in the hallway as I searched for the solitude of
the teacher's bathroom, I shielded my face, hoping they didn't
notice my flushed cheeks and streaming tears. Once inside I
crumpled down onto the floor and just let it out—wailing until
no more noise came out. In this exhausted silence I heard two
students outside the door.

"I heard some kids made a teacher cry," one boy proudly said.

"Yeah, you know that hot teacher across from Ms. Roberts?
She just ran out of the room crying," the other boy added matter-
of-factly. Apparently news spread fast around here.

After a quick blow of my nose with a wad of scratchy public
school–grade toilet paper and a glance at my puffy, bloodshot
eyes in the mirror, I realized there was no way I was going back
to that room—at least not that day.

A few doors down, my colleague worked busily at her computer. At the sight of my swollen eyes, she ran up and gave me
an empathetic hug. As I rehashed my overwhelming frustration
about teaching a new course with absolutely no curriculum or
resources in a classroom that had been irresponsibly overcrowded
with at-risk teenagers, my assistant principal came in with her
walkie-talkie in hand ready to "put out the fire."

"What did they do to you?" she asked with anger and concern.

"What do you mean? Specifically?" I responded as I heaved a
deep breath and slowly stopped crying.

"Did they physically hurt you or do something that needs a
referral?"

"Oh, no, no. No one did anything like that," I said, not really sure how to explain why I had had a meltdown. "I just can't do this—I can't take this anymore. There are too many of them, and no one will listen. I don't want to be here anymore."

She simply told me to go back to my room when the bell rang and to speak with my principal, who had been covering my abandoned class the entire period.

"Don't take this the wrong way," he said, "but I would've never taken you for a crier."

This was all he had to say? This was it? How about, "I am sorry that we expect you to teach in an environment that not only sets up your students for failure but you as well?" How about, "We are going to fix this problem so that you and your students have the opportunity to be successful in this new class that we've ironically named 'Strategies for Success'?"

But instead, he left the room, telling me that he could not promise that anything would change.

### 79.

"Be quiet!" "Sit down!" This is all I seem to be saying lately.

This class is horrible; in fact most of my classes this year are horrible. The bell rings, but these kids continue to act as if they are outside at recess. I hurry and take roll and get the class started, hoping maybe they will get the message and calm down. Quickly I walk to my desk, and I notice Lily has her head down on her desk.

My eyes are drawn to this small girl who is practically curled up on the desk. She sits in silence while everyone else acts crazy, throwing paper airplanes, drawing on the board, and having all sorts of personal conversations. I raise my voice in order to give the assignment so I can immediately go over to Lily.

"Are you all right?"

"No," she says as a tear slides down her cheek. "Can I talk to you in the hall?"

I look around the room. I am concerned that if I say "yes" these kids are going to be left unattended and, with the way they are acting, something will go wrong. Yet, I nod "yes" and follow Lily out into the hall.

We walk into the empty, quiet hall, and she begins shaking and pacing.

"My friend was killed this weekend. Another friend was killed several months ago. My baby died in my arms. My stepdad tried to rape me, and my mom doesn't believe me. I have so much anger built up. All I want to do is run away!"

This small-framed, seemingly innocent girl has suddenly turned into a panther, scared and defensive. No one comes into the hall, and no one passes my door. What am I supposed to say? What did she want me to say, or even expect me to say? I am not a licensed counselor. I'm not her mother. I barely know this girl. We have been in school only a few weeks.

I want to reach out and hug her, but I know that could be deemed inappropriate. I do my best to comfort her—some "teacher" words of wisdom and encouragement and a pat on the back. After a while, she seemed to calm down.

"Why don't you go wash your face and join us back in class," I said.

I reenter my "zoo" and attempt to teach my lesson, to those few who care. I find my eyes wandering over to Lily.

As the end-of-the-day bell rings, Lily gets up and then lingers for just a few moments. I catch her eye and smile and say, "I'll be here if you need someone to talk to, or just listen." She nods. She believes these words, more than I do.

I am forced to put an end to any thoughts of how to help Lily and to put aside my day as my own children, a preschooler and a third grader, come racing down the hall to my room.

"Mom, I played with Play-Doh today!"

"Look, Mom, I got an A on my spelling test and a smiley face for conduct!"

How has this happened? How does a girl like Lily go from being as innocent as my own children to having enormous grown-up problems at fifteen? How can I make a difference so my own children will not have to be faced with these same problems, questions, or frustrations? I kneel down, hold out my arms, and readily accept my children's hugs.

## 80.

*Proprius erudio magister.* Unlike most other species, which keep their classification throughout their lifetime, half of those who earn the classification "special-education teacher" give it up for another. Only a few are able to keep this distinguished title, which holds a certain honor within their "specialized" circle but not outside it. The *proprius erudio magister* is often viewed as a glorified aid by staff, teachers, and students. It's tough being the ugly duckling of education. Not everyone is cut out for it.

No day in school sums up the life of a *proprius erudio magister* better than the first day of school when the staff goes over test scores. It always starts out the same. The principal starts talking about how scores improved from the year before and everyone should applaud themselves for their efforts. Then the desegregation of data begins. First pops up the regular education test scores. You get a few hoots and hollers from the staff. There is always some ridiculously high percentage like 90-something percent that passed. Then the principal moves on to the *proprius erudio* scores.

For a *proprius erudio magister* this is the one time you have all eyes focused on you. Most people love that kind of attention, but not in a situation like this. It is like winning an ugly contest. You already know what's coming. The principal begins to explain how the school would have made annual progress if not for these scores. The whispers, snickers, and sneers start. The principal says that the teachers worked really hard with these students and that they made great strides. But you know the principal, like everyone else, is thinking, "Why can't a *proprius erudio magister* do their job?"

At the start of new classes, teachers ask, "Who is in your class this year?" It is an innocent enough question, and you hope that each student will start the year with a clean slate, but that is not often the case. Instead, it's a way to identify the troublemakers and lost causes that teachers want no part of. Teachers label these students the "unteachables."

Though constantly shunned, you're supposed to perform miracles: Raise scores 70 points in a year. Increase their reading level by three grades. Make sure they can pass algebra even though they are fourteen and still cannot do basic arithmetic. Make ADHD students sit at a desk throughout a one-and-a-half-hour class. On top of all of this, you're supposed to perform these miracles with limited tools. Sometimes you don't even have your own classroom and need to borrow space throughout the day. You're given workbooks that do not interest you or your students. You're supposed to assign novels that use language they don't understand, and tell stories that don't apply to their lives in any way. The task may seem impossible, and no regular education class would be expected to cope with these circumstances.

The life and pressure of a *proprius erudio magister* and an *ordinarius erudio magister* are entirely different. A *proprius erudio magister* is the teacher who makes the biggest difference on a group of specialized students. Instead of hoping that the students take away one piece of information from a day's lesson, a special educator hopes to teach many lessons a day that are remembered. So let half of all teachers try to be *proprius erudio magisters* and then leave for greener pastures. But for the ones that strive to be master teachers, the impact of a good lesson is worth much more than the acceptance of colleagues.

## 81

I have just finished printing out an Individualized Education Plan (IEP). Ema is a senior who enjoys photography, dance, and her iPod. She arrived at high school with little expectation to graduate. Her family told her she was likely to end up like her aunt: drop out, have babies, and do drugs. Ema plans to wear the cap and gown, but as the weeks go by she grows uncertain. School work is difficult. Words jumble off the page, text appears to make little sense, and her interest begins to evaporate. Reading aloud is okay in small classes, where the risk is low, but overwhelming in a large class of thirty-two. Keeping track of who's who, what they did, where they did it, and why is hard enough, but then comes the analyzing. Why did their action matter? Compare this action with previous action, and determine a pattern. What was the first action? Ema must go back and read it again and again. The longer the text, the greater the challenge.

High school is difficult for many students, but for the dyslexic student, high school can be mountain climbing in flip-flops or swimming relays in steel-toed boots with a ten-pound brick as a paddle board.

What makes dyslexia so difficult to live with is its invisible presence. It does not show up in lab work or show itself in a wheelchair. For many teachers what is not visible is not believable. Few students work harder at mastering synonyms, homonyms, spelling, and reading comprehension than dyslexic students. Yet the only certainty they receive in the text of the English language is that the letters constantly shift and the numbers routinely flip.

With an annual IEP written and distributed for the third time to all five of Ema's teachers, with modifications clearly identified, Ema's tolerance and her belief in adults is tested again. Ema again comes to me, her special education teacher and her case manager, asking, "Why don't teachers read and follow the modification page of my IEP?"

An Individualized Education Plan is designed to level the playing field, to give what is needed to students who need it when they need it. Half of my day is spent teaching Resource English classes to students with an IEP in reading and writing. The other half is spent advocating the needs of my caseload students (not necessarily students in my English class) to each of their six general education teachers and conferencing individually with students about how they think their modifications are working in each of their classes. With a caseload of twenty-seven students, each having six classes to confer about in a sixty-minute period, given four times a week, I am forever a day late and a dollar short with paperwork. My frustration multiplies when I must pull out individual students from their general education classes to hold consultations, then hold additional conversations with teachers not complying with the IEP, and in the worst cases, turn in to administration the names of chronic IEP violators. This tips my own scale of tolerance in a downward spiral.

Ema is no exception. Routinely I hear student frustration: "Why aren't teachers required to learn about dyslexia before they are allowed to become a teacher?" "It's the same every year, six teachers every year and the only one who knows about dyslexia is my special education teacher."

I ponder Ema's question and the comments of so many IEP students. Why aren't schools training teachers about dyslexia and attention-deficit hyperactivity disorder (ADHD) at the same rate they are training teachers about raising reading, writing, and math scores? I am both saddened and ashamed of the answer. I am sad because I know that the state exit exam required to graduate from high school is driving the train of professional development in all public schools throughout America. I am ashamed because I must somehow find the words to explain to Ema and others that my profession of twenty-six years does not validate the need for IEP students to have all six of their teachers become aware of and understand the origin and impact dyslexia and ADHD have on learning in the classroom. Once again I must find the words to empower Ema, to help her see that she is not alone.

Dyslexia appears in advanced-placement, college-bound families as well as families of Resource and developmentally delayed students. Dyslexia and ADHD do not discriminate by IQ, race, or gender, nor do they choose addresses by zip code or area prefix. It is not shame that helps us navigate dyslexia or ADHD, but education that allows us to manage and thrive with it. As an English teacher with all IEP students, I use audio books to aid in decoding and DVDs to provide a visual learning tool, I play the Line Game for survey taking, I hold oral debates in lieu of essay writing, and I honor illustrative note taking. But the real challenge is to build hope in Ema and others to stay the course, not give up, not drop out of school in spite of the speed bumps, to be the first in their families to graduate and achieve a high school diploma.

It is always my pleasure to host adult dyslexic and ADHD speakers in my classroom. Some are former students. These people include a successful TV host, long-haul truck driver, receptionist, longshoreman, teacher, business owner, salesman, and artist. Each of them has said that high school was the most turbulent of times for them as persons with dyslexia or ADHD. They describe life after high school as more accommodating and less at odds with their own learning styles. They note that life after high school allows for building on strengths rather than hammering on deficits.

The bell rings. My students fly out the door to their downtime, to their feel-good-doing-it tasks in life—auto detailing, welding, rebuilding engines, cooking, landscaping, carpentry. I think back to the beginning of the school day, to seeing Ema, Ana, Sam, and Michelle in the hallway. I started the day with the Pledge of Allegiance to the American flag. I end my day with an ongoing pledge to Ema and other students to give them hope to hang on to, to acknowledge their being, and to honor their heroic efforts to graduate from high school.

## 82.

The dreaded fourth-period bell rang, and I ran to the Time-out Room (TOR) to fulfill my daily duty period. Hoping that the room would not be bursting at the seams, I said a little prayer to myself as I walked through the door. The TOR is a very small, dreary room, cold or hot, depending on the season, that houses all "In School Suspension" students in my relatively small district. A different teacher proctors the TOR each period of the school day. I have proctored the TOR for the last four years, because I am one of the few special education teachers and most of the students in the TOR are classified in some kind of special education category.

As I crossed the threshold, I saw the negative answer to my prayer. Almost every desk was full, and all of the repeat offenders were present. Hector, Ruiz, Heriberto, and Miguel all greeted me with a friendly "Hi, Mrs. Leigh," although they knew that even their greeting was against the "no talking" policy.

Mr. Estrada gave me the daily rundown of which students had already been kicked out, which were with the school resource officer, and which might be on their way out the door. I settled into my desk facing the students and logged into the computer, hoping that I might be able to get some work done. Before my screen saver even loaded, I knew that it was going to be a very long fourth period.

"Hector, you know you can't sleep in here," I softly reminded the large gang-color-wearing teenage boy who sat in front of me.

"What the fuck, Mrs. Leigh! I'm tired. I was up all night last night."

I did not ask why he was up all night for fear of the response I would receive. The in-house phone rang two or three times, informing me that several other students were on their way to my room, already filled to capacity. As they arrived, I signed them into the log book just as they would be monitored if they were in juvenile detention: name, age, grade, incident that caused them to be sent to the TOR, and length of stay.

About twenty-five to thirty students sit in that tiny room all day, some three or four days a week for offenses as minor as cutting administrative detention or as severe as breaking into school property or brandishing their weapon of choice. The entire day is a waste of time. It's a meaningless power struggle that the teachers are forced to inflict on the students.

The fact that these same students will no doubt return for another day after another disciplinary infraction is proof that this system does not work. Isn't there a *better* way to do this?

"Heads up! Hoodies down! Wake up! Don't you have any work to do? I see you sending text messages. Put the phone away, please."

They aren't listening to me. Even *I'm* not listening to me. What kind of change do we really expect? Apparently none. Finally the bell rings to release us all from this in-school prison for another day. There must be a better way.

"See you tomorrow, Mrs. Leigh."

"Yeah. See you."

## 83.

It was the middle of second quarter, and Keola had been a no-show since the first day of school. Suddenly, like a tropical storm hitting the islands without warning, Keola showed up.

"Who the hell are you?" he asked, eyeing me up and down.

"I'm your teacher," I said quickly.

Keola stared at me for a while and finally said, "Are you serious? You can't be my teacher. You look hella young!"

In my second year of teaching, I was considered fresh meat by the students and inexperienced by the other teachers. I quickly realized that teaching was a journey, not a destination. It would be long and strenuous but definitely worthwhile. So I endured.

Although he didn't know it, Keola and I had a lot in common. He was from the West Side and always looked out for his homies. He was the second eldest of four and was the go-to person in his family. He made friends easily and became well known among his peers as a leader. I could see he was a good kid with a bright future, only he didn't think so.

I knew Keola was in a gang, so one day when he ran into the classroom and started yelling, "Everybody get down," I feared the worst. We all ducked under our desks, and I shouted, "What's going on?"

Keola crawled toward me and whispered, "Be quiet, they're coming."

Immediately, two campus walkers appeared at the front door. They were out of breath and looked pissed. I stood and asked what the commotion was all about.

"We're here for Keola," one said. "We gotta take him in."

Keola jumped up and said, "What now, man? I didn't do anything!"

This was a typical day in the life of Keola in my classroom. At first he seemed threatening and disinterested in his schoolwork. He often threatened to burn my class down because of the many books given out to read. Then one day, he decided to be a part of the process instead of working against it. Reading was his worst nightmare until he picked up a copy of The Freedom Writers Diary. He started reading it and was mesmerized by the stories written by teenagers his age. Able to relate to many of the stories in the book, Keola began writing his own stories. Every day he opened up a little more, sharing another piece of his life. Keola worked hard in class and maintained high marks on class assignments. He worked even harder at being a positive person in the classroom, because life outside the four walls was anything but. While battling to stay on top of his studies, he struggled to carry the weight of his family.

Keola lived a hard life. He grew up in a low-income housing project, with hardly any food to eat or money for daily necessities. He was raised by a single, alcoholic mother. His father was serving time in prison, and his older brother was a well-known drug dealer in their neighborhood. Keola's younger brother was a notorious bully in his middle school. Teachers, administrators, and students were afraid of him. But his little sister was his pride and joy. She was the youngest in the family, and no kid dared mess with her. She was the only good thing in his life, and he was going to protect her.

With no food at home, Keola bargained with me to bring him breakfast and snacks in exchange for his time and effort in class. And it worked, at least for a little while. He worked hard to complete his assignments and was an excellent speaker and team leader. He got along with his peers and was comfortable enough to share many of his personal experiences so that others would not fall victim to his circumstances. His face always lit up when he talked about playing football. He even played on the varsity team for a while, but it was short-lived because he rarely attended practices. Keola opened up about the burden of caring for his mom and family.

But at the end of third quarter, Keola started missing school. It began with a few tardies; then he would cut out halfway through the session. He then started ditching the entire day. Not long afterward, he simply stopped showing up. Things looked really bad when he missed an entire week of school. No phone call, no note, and no reason. Keola was nowhere to be found, and none of his friends knew where he was.

Then suddenly, like the Kona trade winds that blow from the south, Keola showed up. He reeked of alcohol and was obviously high on pakalolo (pot). I didn't know what to do. I called the department chair and informed him of the situation. We found Keola knocked out on the couch. I also found a half-full bottle of vodka in his backpack. I took the bottle, emptied it in the sink, and threw the bottle away. Keola finally woke up and began to cry. He kept saying, "It's too late! It's too late! There's nothing you can do to help me." He said he had to take care of things his way.

That was the last day I saw Keola. He never returned to class. He dropped out of school and went back to his life on the streets. I was devastated because I thought that he would make it, that he would be the exception in his family. Through the good and the bad, I wanted Keola to make it. But he didn't.

## 84.

"Hey, you see Shaud on the news this morning?"

I play dumb. "No, Shaud who? What happened?"

Of course I had seen the news that morning. That was just my luck. The one day I get up early enough to sit around, eat some Smart Start, and take in what is happening in the world around me, I see Shaud, a former student, on the news. I wasn't certain it was him. The security camera image from what appeared to be a cheap hotel was pretty grainy. What I could see, without any doubt, was two young men jumping an older couple as they walked in the side entrance of a hotel. The perpetrator that knocked the elderly woman down to the ground before wrenching the purse from her grasp appeared to be Shaud. What a great way to start the day.

Shaud had left my school maybe a month earlier. Just like the other kids, he ended up at my school through the juvenile court system. I remember him strutting into class his first day. On campus, his reputation had preceded him. Many students from the same area know or know of each other from the outs—their lives outside our school. Shaud was too smart to be a problem; he would simply sit, doodle, and glance at the clock a few times a day during his first few weeks of class with us. Then it happened. One day I was a little late getting into my room from the hallway. The bell rang, and class was supposed to be under way. When I walked into the classroom, Shaud was up "teaching" what we had learned the previous day. The students were engaged and participating; it all seemed very natural. After that class, he approached me, asking about lessons for the next day and then offering how he could be involved. Eventually, Shaud was pretty much teaching entire lessons himself, leading discussions, fielding questions, asking questions of "his" students. He was no longer part of the classroom, it was his class, he had taken complete ownership, and the other students loved it.

I still didn't want to admit it was him I'd seen this morning; it had to be someone else. Driving to school, I started thinking about how to react to questions from my students. Most of them wouldn't have taken the time to watch the news in the morning even if it were an option for them. I knew the rumors would be circling, though. Kids would be on the prowl to get the real scoop on the latest gossip. What would I do? Admit defeat? Remind them that as hard as they work, they still go home to the same neighborhood, the same family, and the same friends? Admit to these kids who want to make a change in their lives that it probably won't ever happen? "Yeah, Shaud really screwed up. The same kid most of you guys looked up to failed himself, his family, and you by choosing to be a victim of his environment. You might as well give up now and stay locked up." I couldn't tell them that.

It's so hard to focus on the successes of my students when their failures are on display for all the world to see. Sometimes it makes me question why I even bother to put time and effort into my students when all I hear about is how much they fuck up the second they walk out the door. You definitely don't see stories headlining the morning news about a juvenile delinquent picking himself up after hitting bottom, deciding he is the only one who can really change who he is, then doing it, as so many kids have. You would have to dig to uncover a story about an under-privileged, abused kid like my former student Kory, who is graduating from his independent living program and has earned enough college credits to be heading into his sophomore year. Those stories don't make the morning news.

Maybe it has come time for me to decide what kind of teacher I intend to be. I could assume the path of so many other teachers who have given up on kids. So many in this profession appear to have forgotten, or have chosen to ignore, why they became teachers in the first place. You can have the best lesson plans and attend all of the latest seminars to be on the cutting edge of education, but if you don't care about kids it doesn't matter. Have I already happened upon this junction? I wonder why we tend to focus on the bad and ignore all the good our students accomplish. Would it make a difference if the morning news covered Kory's graduation rather than Shaud's assault? It would make a difference to me.

Maybe that's what happens to teachers. You know those teachers who seem to really enjoy yelling at kids or trying to assert some power over them? I suppose they have been dragged down by the negative aura that seems to surround the teaching profession and those kids. There must have been a point when they decided to surrender. One moment must have come upon them when it became easier to turn their backs rather than help those kids.

## 85.

It was 3:35 p.m. and in walked Dalton to serve the detention I had assigned to him earlier in the week for sleeping in class.

"Well, surprise, surprise!" I said. "I didn't think you would actually show up. I was just heading out the door. Sit down for a minute, though, and let's have a talk." Dalton casually strolled in and sank into one of the desks close to mine. "Why are you always so tired in my class?" Before he could answer, I asked, "Do you sleep in all of your classes, or just mine?"

Dalton had an answer for everything when he didn't want to give an answer. "Basically," he said. He paused for a few minutes, hoping that I would leave him alone. But I continued to look at him intently.

"No teacher has ever given me the time of day, Ms. Carl. I don't see why you're wasting yours."

"You being here tells me something. I know you wouldn't just come for detention because I scheduled it for you."

We had this common look that we exchanged in class every time I called him out on his behavior or lack of work: I knew that he wanted me to be a support for him but he couldn't show it in class because that would ruin his image. And he knew that I knew this.

"Ms. Carl, I'm not like all the other prep boys and beauty queens in your class. That's why I can't stand it here and why I keep to myself and don't want to do anything. They just don't know what it's like to be me."

"But you don't know what it's like to be them either. You are assuming they've all had it easy."

"Nah, but they ain't had it like me. You know what I write in my journal? You asked me the other day if that stuff was true, and I lied to you. Told you I like to make up stories about things I see going on in the world, but all that shit's true in my world. You know what, ever since I can remember as a kid *both* of my parents have been hooked on crack. Both!"

This was only my second year of teaching, and I had done a pretty good job of staying neutral regarding my kids' lives outside of school, but Dalton's words were threatening to derail me. He went on.

"My mom's just got two kids, me and my brother, but my dad's got six and the other four all by different women he was with while he was still with my mom. I don't want to be like that, Ms. Carl. I mean, my dad's a good guy and all. I even stay with him sometimes, but it was real hard when I was younger. All I remember about my childhood is drama. I remember drugs on the table right in front of me when I would be watching cartoons. Mom took my brother and me and left eventually. She's straightened herself out a lot."

*Breathe.* I remembered hearing this over and over in my head. How does a fifteen-year-old kid deal with all of the mess he just laid in front of me? How does an adult deal with it? And why hasn't someone helped him with any of this stuff? Surely, I wasn't the only person he ever allowed into his world. What was I supposed to say? He saved me from the indecision.

"So, I'm tired because I have to work late. I try to help my mom out. She lost her job a few weeks ago."

"Well, why are you working so late? You can only work so many hours if you are a minor."

He paused and looked at the clock and out the window. "I know my time ain't up, but I gotta go, Ms. Carl. I just wanted you to know that it's not you. And I'll try harder to stay awake and do my work."

Sighing heavily, I got up when he did and walked him to the door of my classroom. I knew that he had just laid a huge burden on me, but I worried about letting him go. I later found out that Dalton's late-night job was selling drugs. I realized I was beginning to ask too many questions.

That was in the middle of his freshman year, and after this Dalton made it a point to seek me out after school—sometimes for advice or just as someone to talk to. I spent a great deal of time that year trying to help him muddle through all that was going on with his life in and out of school.

He should have graduated this year, but he didn't. After freshman year, Dalton dropped out. A little over a year ago, he came to see me and caught me up on everything he was and was not doing with himself. He assured me that he was going to GED classes. (I later learned that he wasn't when I ran into a former girlfriend of his at the grocery store.) It felt good to see him and know that he still trusted me as a person he could talk to. When he left that day, I was almost in tears.

"I want you to know how much I respect you," he said as I walked him to the door of my classroom. "You've always been there for me, Ms. Carl. Even more than my own family. And you *never* gave up on me. Even when *I* gave up on me. You will always be my favorite teacher because of that." I was speechless. He looked me in the eye, beamed that little smile that I had grown to love, and gave me a giant hug. "I'll keep in touch, but I just wanted to say thanks." Then he left, and I haven't seen him since.

I still worry about Dalton and wonder if he is on the right track. I worry that he might still be selling drugs and losing that side of him that I know he wanted to keep alive—the side that was hurt so long ago when people abandoned him. I also worry that maybe he doesn't have anyone to talk to.

It should be enough to know that I have a lasting effect on my students as Dalton said I did, but for some reason it's not. Sometimes it's hard to let go.

## 86.

I have always cheered for the underdog. I have been a teacher for more than twenty-five years. I taught in the same schools my sons attended from their elementary through their high school years. As I saw my classes come in the first days of school, I looked for the kids who were picked on or who were very quiet and shy. I encouraged them more than the others kids, but that didn't mean that I didn't care about the others.

I felt like the protector of the flock. Many of the unlikely heroes had problems in class, mostly because they lacked support from home. My sons didn't lack support at home because they lived with their mother part of the time and the rest of the time with me. Ike, my eldest son, was strong and healthy. My younger son, Michael, was a true underdog. He'd had a brain tumor since birth. It caused him to have epileptic seizures, and his right arm did not develop normally. But Michael had the heart of a champion, and I tried my best to encourage him in whatever he did.

Michael and his friends were labeled "losers and misfits" by the athletic director. Many of them did not play football and other contact sports. But I knew that most of these kids could run, so I invited them to become part of a new cross-country running team. Many of them joined.

Two of my boys were brothers who came from a broken home and had run-ins with the law. Another boy, Miguel, was labeled "special needs." The truth was he was embarrassed to speak because he mumbled. One father brought me his son Ramiro because the boy was a very big kid and the parent wanted him to be part of something in school. Another boy came from a violent home—the father was abusive to his wife and severely beat the boy's brothers and sisters. Luis wanted to be a gangster; one asthmatic boy, Jessie, was too small to play in other sports. And then there was my son Michael. These kids became the Warriors Cross Country Team, an unlikely group of champions.

The Warriors wanted to prove to the athletic director that they could be winners, but they did not start out as winners. In their first meet, they finished dead last. Because the trail was very dusty, they finished the race covered in dirt from head to toe. They looked like a bunch of coal miners. We all laughed together because there was no water to wash the dirt off and we had to go eat looking like that. They told me that would be the last time they would finish last.

First, things in school started to turn around for them. I knew that many of them had problems in their classes. I encouraged them to help each other out because without good grades they could not stay on the team. When Ike, my eldest son, quit soccer, it was his decision. It later bothered me that I didn't encourage him to stay, *like I would've done with the Warriors.*

The team became a family. The kids played and ate together. They encouraged one another, not just at the meets but in class too. Five runners received sixth-week honors. As for the results at the meets, the Warriors were all finishing in the top and were winning meets at their level. I told them that they needed a new challenge: to compete against larger schools. At first, they weren't too sure about the idea, but when my special-ed student Miguel spoke out, everybody just stopped and watched him.

"Hey guys, we are good," Miguel said. "We come from a small school, but I know we can beat any of them."

He wanted to show everyone that the Warriors were just as good as teams at the bigger schools that had successful running programs, and the Warriors showed everyone at their first big-school meet that they were as good as any team in the region. They competed against two hundred other schools and won. Miguel won the three-mile race against the best. Mark and Cande also placed in the top ten in the region. Eventually all the Warriors got to the state meet. All those boys, the "losers and misfits," had accomplished more than they were ever expected to achieve in school and then on the field. But, as Frank Sinatra might say, the best was yet to come.

Very few schools knew anything about this group of kids. They looked out of place because they did not have matching warm-up suits and they joked around with each other. Their biggest concern was where they were going to eat after a meet. Well, the gods of running and their own will to succeed got them the Texas State Cross Country Championship. They placed in the top four slots in the meet. They became state champions. Michael did not participate because he came down with bronchitis, but he was there cheering everyone on. Most of their parents cried because they recognized what their kids had accomplished.

One evening, many years later, Ike came to the house. He was upset and drunk. His mother had been calling me, for a while, worried about him. I started to lecture him, just as I had been doing ever since he graduated from high school. He was the strong one. As he stood there, he started to cry. He told me something that shook me hard. He said, "Dad, how come you never encouraged me as much you encourage the other kids? You never believed in me like you did them!" I didn't know what to say. I hugged him hard, maybe for the first time. It tore my insides because he was right. I saved the sons of others and may have lost one of my own.

## 87.

I pull into the snowy, slick parking lot at the detention center. Shit, late again. I hate winter. I hate snow. Only a week and a half until Christmas break.

As I walk into the classroom, I look at the expectant faces of my students. I love my students. I love them even though most of them are little hellions and they get to shower only at night, so by the time I get them in the morning they smell like rotten eggs are lodged in their armpits! I love teaching them. I love making them feel important, even if it is only for fifty minutes in a classroom setting, I know I am making a difference.

Mario will not look at me this morning. His head is down on his desk, which is unusual for one of my brightest students.

"Mario, what's up, man?" I ask. "Still tired?"

He won't respond, and the other students shake their heads at me and mouth the word "no," indicating to leave him alone.

"Mario, look at me. What is going on? Did you get bad news from your P.O.?"

Mario finally raises his head, looks at me with swollen eyes, and says, "Man, fuck my P.O., and fuck everyone else."

This is not like Mario at all. He is usually cheerful, funny, and very optimistic.

"What happened, Mario?" I ask.

"Miss, the ICE (Immigration and Customs Enforcement) came to my parents' work yesterday in a raid and took my parents. They didn't show up to visit me last night, so I called home. My neighbor answered our phone and said they had both been arrested and taken in a van, and no one knows where they are. She was staying with my four little brothers and sisters 'cause I don't have any family here to take them."

Mario begins to cry. "I could hear my brothers and sisters in the background. They were all crying. I talked to my little brother, who is seven, and he was crying so hard, I couldn't understand why. When he finally calmed down, he cried that he missed Mom and Dad. He cried that he didn't want them to go away. He cried that he was never going to see them again. He cried because he is seven years old with three younger brothers and sisters, with no family to take care of them, and no idea about the future. Will the family be broken up and put in foster care? What about Christmas? I don't know where my parents are. They could be back in Mexico for all I know. Will we ever see them again? This is so fucked up, Miss!"

I sit down. I have to. For once, I'm at a loss for words.

"What's going to happen to me?" Mario continues. "What's gonna happen to my brothers and sisters? Miss, can you please find out where my parents are? Can you please?" he begs.

I don't know how to even begin to try to find out what happened. How could someone do this to these kids? I know his parents are here illegally, but they are hardworking people, just trying to make a better life for their kids.

"Mario, I don't know where they are, but I will try to find out," I say.

"Miss, I'm scared, I don't know what to do. I miss my mom."

I don't know if you have ever seen a sixteen-year-old boy sob, but I never want to see it again. Mario is sobbing for his parents, he is sobbing for his little brothers and sisters, he is sobbing for the uncertainty of their lives. Standing there, helpless to help him, just as uncertain as he is about his future in this country, I can't even give him a hug because of the stupid laws in this place. I literally stand there, crying with him and the rest of the macho young men in the class.

Merry fricking Christmas, Mario.

## 88.

"Join the Guard if you want to kill towel-heads!"

*What? Surely the sergeant said something else. . . . I must have misheard him. . . . No, he said those exact words.* Like a CD skipping and grinding out the same repetitive beat, my mind annoyingly repeats those words. A cold shiver overtakes me. I have worked so hard to teach my students not to prejudge by sharing my personal, painful stories of the effects of making assumptions. None of my students are laughing; the recruiter is maliciously grinning. Some of the students turn their eyes to me, awaiting a response.

"Thank you, Sergeant, for your time and speaking with us today." It is all I can say.

My kids leave for their next class. I sit at my desk and replay in my mind the words he spoke. One minute left before the tardy bell. No time to mull over it now. I focus on my next class lesson.

I was born a Muslim and raised in America. My life in the South has been a struggle to balance culture with desires and dreams, tradition and expectations with individuality. Memories of kids in school calling me "cow-worshipper," asking me enraging, embarrassing questions like "Where's your dot?" and "So what are you?" all began to surface.

Shortly after 9/11, a Sikh businessman in Mesa, Arizona, was murdered in front of his gas station because he resembled a "towel-head." Five years later, in the confines of my classroom, anger, racial prejudice, and rage still consume this representative from the Army National Guard. His words continue to feed the fire with fear, hatred, and revenge. That night, my mind races.

Sleep deserts me. The next day, I decide I must talk with my students.

"The word 'towel-head' used by the sergeant to describe Middle Easterners is very offensive to me. It is no different than calling an African American a 'nigger' or a Caucasian a 'honky.' I was shocked, but it was my mistake in *not* pointing out how degrading and ignorant that word actually is."

"Didn't he know your background?" one student asks. Half black and half white, she understands exactly how stereotypes have a negative impact on people of all ages.

"I guess not, but that shouldn't matter. We must refer to groups of people as people and not use slanderous words. While people may look like a certain ethnic group, they may actually be something completely different. We should not make assumptions because, in the end, all blood runs red. We are all human, and we should treat each other with kindness and respect."

Most of my students are supportive. Some aren't fazed by how upset I am. Could they be chuckling on the inside at the sergeant's remark? Are they pleased to see their teacher deeply hurt by an insensitive comment? One student approaches me after class.

"I'm gonna join the military after high school, but I don't think like that. I respect people and my country, too. My parents were also immigrants just like yours." She wraps her arms around me and softly says, "I'm sorry."

"Thank you." It is all I can say. I needed to hear those words from her.

She looks me straight in the eyes, smiles, grabs her books, tosses her long brown hair over her shoulder, and says, "See ya tomorrow!" The next swarm of students arriving drowns out the clink-clink of her JROTC shoes. Despite the masks they attempt to wear, my students are great humans with unbelievable hearts.

I am still ashamed. But I am glad I spoke to my students about the situation and the effects of it. My hope is that they will stand up when faced with injustice within their own lives, and handle any adversity with dignity and integrity.

Dr. Martin Luther King Jr. once said, "Our lives begin to end the day we become silent about things that matter."

I will no longer be silent.

## 89.

I remembered my dream vividly. I was arriving at school early, as usual, at about 6:15 a.m. The sun was only beginning to peek. As I pulled in, I noticed my car was the only one in the deserted lot, the first eager teacher of the day. I quieted the engine, gathered my supplies, and opened my door. That's when I noticed them. The entire lot was full of men in white sheets carrying torches. The schoolyard was lined with crosses, burning. The masked men were chanting, over and over, "Go home! We don't want your kind here!" They were getting closer; I knew that the Grand Dragon was there with them. I felt his beady eyes upon me, just as they had been on the residents of this small town for so many years. I could feel the heat from their flames on my cheeks. As the warmth began to penetrate my skin, that's when I always woke up.

When I started teaching *The Freedom Writers Diary* in my English class, I never anticipated the controversy that would ensue. I knew that even though my students were from "White Town," USA, they could benefit from this book just as I had. Even though this town is known for KKK marches and rallies as recent as the late '80s, and "traditional" white family values are what is often taught, I knew my students could find themselves within the pages of this book.

A day after handing out the books and beginning our unit, I received an e-mail from an angry parent: "This book is inappropriate for our students. There is sex and violence and profanity.

It is not acceptable for my son to read, nor do I believe it should be taught, period. I will be going above your head to see that it is removed from the hands of all of your students." This mother insisted that the molestation pieces were "titillating" and said she felt that this "smut" did not belong in the hands of our children. She equated *The Freedom Writers Diary* with *Hustler* magazine and called it pornography.

But in the classroom, kids who usually BS their way through everything were actually engaged. I finally had them hooked. So I tried to reassure this parent, letting her know what the goals and objectives were, what I hoped each kid would take away from reading the book, and what the benefits of reading it would be. I offered her son an alternative choice, as was district practice, but she insisted that she was going to take this matter beyond me.

The public criticism began with a short e-mail from a parent and wound its way through the city. The principal demanded I remove the book from my students' hands, but my students objected.

"Why do we have to put the books down if we bought them ourselves?" stormed one of my students.

"I'm not sure myself," I responded.

The controversy dragged on. A community member submitted my name to the FBI for giving pornography to minors. I wonder how many public school teachers have an FBI file for teaching a book?

Adults within the community continued to blog, admonishing me both as an educator and as a person. "She should be fired!" wrote one blogger. "Did you see what she was wearing that day?" wrote another. "She just wants to corrupt our kids." And they went on and on.

When I think back to those nightmares, I still shake. I know the KKK is alive and well; a faction of the Klan came after me and my job through the media and through my administration. At the time, I didn't know what to do. I couldn't just sit there and let this happen and let my students see me do nothing. Packing my bags and leaving, as this group of community members wanted me to, was not an option. I was not going to let my students see me back away from this fight.

That evening, as I was beginning to feel the nightmare come again, something changed. As the men in hoods approached my car, I shouted back, "I'm not going anywhere!" That was the message I wanted to leave my students.

## 90.

Music flows through my blood. It's in my genes. My father was a gifted tenor who could bring the house down, melt your heart, or put a tear in your eye whenever anyone asked him to sing. I wanted to have that affect on people, too. I wanted to spark goose bumps in audiences who paid to forget about life and problems for a while as I belted Broadway show tunes in theaters across the country. But I was not blessed with perfect pitch. Instead of blending in, I often stuck out. When my parents dropped me off at college, I was already marching to the beat of a different drummer. So it came as no surprise that when I made the front page, above-the-fold headlines last year it was not because I had transposed myself into a golden-apple English teacher. My notoriety resulted from the cacophony I created while sitting at my desk one day watching my students read.

"Excuse me. Aren't you the teacher from Kennedy High who got fired for letting your students read that book?" asked the nice-looking young man in Wal-Mart as I pushed my cart down the candy aisle.

"Yes."

"I graduated from Kennedy last year and never had you as a teacher, but I thought what they did to you was horrible. You should be commended. I think what you did took a lot of courage, and I just wanted you to know I admire you and hope you're doing okay."

"Thank you. You're very kind." And before I reached my car, I was crying once again.

That happens a lot. It happens at restaurants and drive-throughs, libraries and ATMs, grocery stores and gas stations. Each time I am caught off guard, touched by the kindness of strangers, and when I come home, I cry. Other times I don't make it home or even to the parking lot. These are times when I bump into a student I had in class. The worst one happened on New Year's Eve.

My daughter wanted to spend some of her Christmas money at her favorite teen girl clothing store. I didn't know Charise worked there. She saw me and ran over, and the first thing out of her mouth was, "Mrs. Carpenter! Are you coming back second semester?"

"I don't know."

"Do you *think* you might come back? Do you know *when* you might come back?"

"No, and I'm not supposed to talk about it because it is a legal matter pending my dismissal hearing. But you can tell me about yourself and how things are going. Do you like the sub?"

"He's okay. He's nice and all, but it's just not the same."

"Well, tell me about . . . ," and I proceeded to ask about various students from her class of twenty-one juniors.

One by one she told me, "No, she transferred. No, he moved back with his mom. I don't know; she just stopped coming." Until finally, "Really Mrs. Carpenter, on the last day when we took the final, there were only like nine students in the class."

I told my daughter I left something in the car, bolted for the door, and emerged into the cold night air like some diva from act 3. My aria was composed of dry heaves and a woeful moan followed by waves of anger as I pounded my car and kicked the tires. I wailed to an empty balcony, "You bastards! What have you done? Those kids were wanting to succeed and you ruined it. I will fight this! I will fight to prevent this from ever happening again."

Ten months later, the opera continues. Despite the hundreds of calls, e-mails, and letters the Kennedy School Board received from around the world on my behalf, the board suspended me for a year and a half without pay. My crime: insubordination.

After waiting three months for the top dogs at central office to approve a book not in the eleventh-grade curriculum, when the permission slips came in and my principal gave her consent, I handed 150 students their own copies of *The Freedom Writers Diary*, an American bestseller purchased by a corporate sponsor that I had brought on board in August. The reading began. Students read in my class, in study halls, in the corridors, and in school suspension stalls. When the top dogs finally said "no," it was too late. My students didn't want to stop reading. I tried to collect the books, but they refused to give them back. And that cost me $95,000—seventeen months of unemployment, for which I cannot collect any unemployment because technically I'm not unemployed.

The financial loss is not what hurts the most. Neither is the continual reminder from strangers in my community that what happened was so unfair. I can even accept being shunned in public by my former colleagues, ostracized by my peers because their floundering conductor fears his orchestra will dismantle should they tune in to my interpretation of the score he has tried to rewrite. What haunts me daily is the silencing of my students.

When they removed me from my classroom, my students were enraged. I was forbidden to contact them, but they sought answers. Teachers, counselors, and administrators gave them none. It was a legal matter they couldn't discuss. My students wrote letters to the school newspaper supporting me. None were printed. "If they published the opinions of the students, they would only be presenting one side of the controversy, and that would not be fair," reported the paper's faculty adviser.

For twenty-seven years, I worked to instill in my students the power of words—how skill and deliberate consideration create voices that make a difference. I wanted them to read a book, a beautiful testimony to drowning out discord from their environments and rising above misconduct by practicing tolerance and creating harmony in a chaotic world that doesn't want to blend together. Instead, what they pieced together from this unfinished symphony was a lesson that many of my "kind" of student knows all too well. It's impossible to make music if you don't have the instruments. There is no hope of harmonizing, if you can't even sing.

## 91.

There is a name for educators, and it has nothing to do with books or classrooms. It's sunshine.

As soon as my students arrive, I greet them: "Good morning. Are you ready for a great day?" There's the bubbly student body president, who immediately mirrors my grin. Our boy genius can only nod above his teetering, larger-than-a-small-country science project. My favorite, the girl who's not yet fully awake, shoots me a look that says, "Seriously. You're this cheery at this hour?" I know she'll thank me later. The smiles, the potent shots of optimism, and their hugs are my favorite ways to start the students' days and my own.

But this morning was different. We did not pull in to see the school bus or cheerful children. The day turned gloomy. Hate robbed our hope, scrawled all over the building. "Mama, what does that say?" my first grader said, showing off his reading skills as he sounded out "w-h-i-t-e p-o-w-e-r."

"Nothing, sweetie. Someone is just trying to be mean."

I pushed the clouds aside and forced the sun to shine. I saw Mona, who always manages to bring a smile to my face. "Get out my way, little kid," she grumbled as she made her way through the elementary building. "What are you wearing?" she disapprovingly asked one of the teachers. No matter what she said, though, I could never be upset with her. I knew that behind the rough exterior was a gentleness she showed only when she thought no one was looking. She would soon be reading to the same kid she had just brusquely told to move.

Months later, as I sat in the lobby, I thought back to that day—to the hate, to Mona, and to the sunshine that prevailed. Seconds later, my world shook.

BOOM!

With my two young children next to me, the sound from outside sent a shudder down my spine. The Nazi images and hate words spray-painted on our building and trees were all too fresh in my mind.

Now there is another crisis. I know we are not a random target. I do not know what to do in these vital moments. Secure the kids or run outside to make sure no one is injured?

The swastikas on the trees had begun to fade, but the pain they caused still burns deep. I frantically make my way to the basketball courts. As I rush by the playground, I remember seeing the students swinging up toward the clouds just a few hours earlier and hearing their laughter all the way in my office. It was that special laughter, the kind heard only on playgrounds where students play innocently.

The pure-acid explosion did not cause any serious physical injuries when it came crashing down toward the girls who were wrapping up basketball practice; but the emotional damage was far more detrimental. Mona was there, and now she was not so tough. She trembled as she watched the basketball roll off the court.

As a Muslim administrator, I must go beyond slapping on a Band-Aid to discovering the injury beneath. I know, more times than not, it is related to the scarf my student wears around her face or the decision by another to greet each dawn with a prayer. Just a few moments earlier Mona had scored a three-pointer and was screaming in victory. She now sits beneath a tree, crying. I rush over and remind her of the strength she has within. "We are who we are, Mona, and nothing shakes us." I comfort her, all the while fighting back my own tears. "You are so strong, and I know you are going to do great things one day. Do not let this faze you."

Against all odds, Mona proudly wears her scarf, treats her parents with the respect most children do not learn until they have had kids of their own, and strives to make a difference in the world and for all of its creatures.

My role is to teach my students that we must do our best no matter what challenges we face, be they grueling math tests and AP essays, or swastikas and acid blasts. We may grow weary of showing the world that we are not terrorists—not the ones throwing makeshift bombs at a basketball court full of girls—and we must persevere until we have undone each and every stereotype. That is our personal struggle, our personal jihad. We are all human beings who want what is best for our kids and our communities. That happens only when we become our best.

I tell the world what I tell my students: Bring it on. My sunshine never disappears. As an educator, as a principal, and as a mother, my personal jihad is the same: I will do whatever I can to light your path.

### 92.

I did not want to see my beloved soldier go. With tears in my eyes and pain in my soul, I watched the man I had fallen in love with walk out the door. We refused to say good-bye and opted to leave things at "I'll see you soon." God had brought this man and me together, and war was now going to separate us for months—or, God forbid, forever. All I could do now was leave things in the hands of fate that Rich would come back home safe to me.

Before Rich's deployment, I never truly understood what many of my students were going through when a parent or loved one went off to war. I teach in a military town, and everywhere you go there are constant reminders that families have a loved one missing from their dinner tables, or that a child is tucked into bed every night without getting a good-night kiss from Mom or Dad.

Sarah, one of my second graders, came running into my classroom with tears streaming down her face. Her daddy was going off to war. I gave Sarah a big hug and told her that Daddy would be home soon enough. I held her tiny body until I sensed she was ready to let go.

To help Sarah deal with the loss, we periodically sent her father handmade cards. Sarah worked tirelessly to try to make her masterpieces of glitter and construction paper as nearly perfect as possible for him. She could envision her father showing off her card with great pride to the rest of the guys in the unit. Sarah asked me, "Ms. S, do you think he will love it?"

"Yes, Sarah, I do. As long as he knows you made this card especially for him, he will love and cherish it."

Night time is when I miss Rich the most. When the kids are in bed and silence engulfs the house, I miss him. I miss the little conversations about bills or the day's events before turning in. I miss knowing when I turn over in bed the warmth of his skin will be there to meet mine. When I'm at work, I can immerse myself in my job and in my students. There are lessons to be made and papers to be graded. There are questions to be asked and answers to be given.

Sarah's daddy came home for R & R after a couple of months of being away. It was Halloween, and I was having a party for my students. Sarah's father arrived. He couldn't have been older than twenty-five, and his thin build made him appear younger. Sarah was constantly holding his hand or draped around his neck as if she feared that if she let go for a moment he might vanish into thin air. He thanked all the children in class for the care package they had sent. He gave them all hugs. It was as if he was trying to desperately forget where he would be returning in just a few short weeks.

Rich's image flashed on the computer screen. I was as excited as Sarah was with her daddy that Halloween afternoon. It had been four months since I'd actually seen Rich's face. He looked a little tired and worn out, but overall it was my Rich. My tears began to flow. They were tears of relief, not tears of sorrow, and my heart was filled with joy, seeing for myself that he was safe and okay. We talked for an entire hour, but the time flickered by quickly. Before I knew it, it was time to let go. Our conversation ended with "Be safe. I miss you. Talk to you soon."

Sarah, I finally get it now. I understand. We share a bond, a bond that few know about or truly understand. The ones who leave us live every day to come back home, and we live every day waiting for their safe return.

## 93.

I might be undatable.

It's a shame, really. I'm not unattractive. I'm a college graduate. I'm a good listener. I'm not even opposed to long walks on the beach.

Unfortunately, I'm also a teacher.

I elect not to share the news with my current date. He seems to be having such a good time, and I don't want to ruin it.

We've talked about the weather so far. It's unseasonably warm or cool or something, and we both agree it's a sure sign of global climate shift. We've commented on the décor of the restaurant— its use of warm colors and hard woods. Deep stuff.

When the conversation—engrossing as it is—hits a lull, I ask what he does. He inhales slightly—this is the moment my date has been waiting for.

He talks about his job, how long he's been there, how he

came to choose accounting or anesthesiology or composting, and then he does the polite, gentlemanly thing. He asks about my job.

I feel that I should apologize for my response in advance. As much as he enjoys accounting, anesthesiology, or composting, I'm going to love my work more. I start to talk about the kid in class who would not shut up today and how he's a great kid but always trying to get attention through inappropriate means and I've had several conferences with his parents but nothing seems to be working but I'm not giving up because the kid is so smart and funny when he's not being a pain in the ass.

My date masticates his crepe and meditates on my answers. He makes an effort to engage: "So, you teach in the city?" And his question has that slightly wonderstruck tone as if he imagines me strapping on Kevlar as I prepare to teach poetry.

"Yes," I answer. Then, without the slightest provocation and in the interest of full disclosure, I say, "I teach at this great magnet school."

"Oh," he replies, sipping red wine. But he doesn't really mean "oh"—not just "oh," anyway. He means it in that way that might be one of the last socially acceptable ways to say, "Well, then, you don't have to teach the brown children."

"Prick," I'll think, but "Yeah" will come out of my mouth.

He thinks my "yeah" is answering his "oh," but the "yeah" really answers my initial fears. If it is difficult for a single parent of a lone child to find a partner and settle down, then I'm going to have a doozy of time finding someone willing to welcome me and my 120 children into his life.

My composting accountant anesthesiologist says something like "My sister is a nurse."

"Oh, yeah," is all I can think of to answer his attempt at bridging the divide between his balance sheets and my flagging homework return rate.

I wish someone had told me I was supposed to pair off in college, while I was surrounded by people who knew me before I began to teach. I flash to the numerous weddings I've attended over the last year and realize they've all been of couples who met each other in college. Clearly, I missed the filing deadline.

The check arrives, and Date insists on paying. I begin to argue but eventually give in. I reconcile my defeat with my honor by telling myself he's paying in lieu of a second date. It's probably for the best, anyway—winter break is almost over, and I won't have any time to date.

## 94.

Michael waited four days before our wedding to say, "I don't want to get married. My mom and family aren't coming to the wedding, and I don't want to get married without their blessing."

Shaken, it took only moments for me to swing from sadness to extreme anger. Michael stirred a savageness in me that I didn't even know existed. My hands curled into tight fists, and I focused my aim to punch him dead in the eye. Were we not standing on the sacred ground of our church assembly, the outcome would have been far different. I gave him back the ring and quickly walked away.

We had a long history together, and as I walked away, I thought about all I was leaving behind: ten years of friendship and dating, including a two-year engagement. Michael was the only man that I trusted enough. A physically and emotionally wounded woman, I resented men when we first met. And even though I resisted him at first, we eventually became friends—a friendship that revived my belief in the integrity of men.

I don't know where Michael and I went wrong. I never thought he would lie to me; I never thought he would lead me on, convincing me that I was his future wife. He proposed to me on camera in front of family, friends, colleagues, and our students. The night before our breakup, Michael had professed his undying love in a poem at my bridal shower, where I was surrounded by my bridesmaids and sisters from our church who prayed over me and for the health of our coming matrimony. My father had spent thousands of dollars, hundreds of guests had been invited, airline tickets were purchased, and rooms were booked. So how did we get here, Michael calling the whole thing off and me ready to meet his refusal with violence?

I had it all planned out. By late August, I would have three things to celebrate. Three months of marriage to my college sweetheart, a fellow Freedom Writer teacher; the completion of my Freedom Writer Institute Training; and the commencement of an exciting teaching opportunity at a brand-new school. But little went as I planned. By July, my fiancé and I had broken up. In October, I resigned from the school, which refused to pay its teachers and closed in November. I lost a lot: my fiancé, my job, and amazing students and coworkers who had become like family.

My breakup was the most difficult. But if I'm honest, I must admit that I ignored warning signs. We weren't communicating, and we allowed work, friends, and family to take a front seat to our relationship. Although we were unquestionably divided, I wanted to know why Michael didn't fight to save our relationship and how he could cast aside, with only a few sentences, all we had worked to build.

I never got the answers that I was looking for. In April, at a Freedom Writer Teachers gathering, Michael and I had a civil conversation. We now lived in different states, and this was the first time we had spoken in months. Michael confessed that he should have told me sooner that he didn't want to marry me. He said he had a list of goals he wanted to achieve first, including financial security, attending graduate school, and weight loss. I told him none of that mattered to me. I would have married him if he was dirt poor because I believed that he was the one for me. I wanted Michael to admit that I just wasn't the one anymore and that his feelings had changed. But I realize that what he didn't say spoke volumes.

One of my greatest fears—losing Michael—was realized. I thought life without him would be unbearable. I didn't believe I could survive putting my all into something so precious only to see it fall apart. I knew that people close to us never approved of our relationship, and I feared looking foolish, as if they had been right all along. But I couldn't dwell on what others thought of my failed relationship. I had to focus on what really mattered: my own well-being. And although it was grueling, accepting the breakup didn't destroy me. Overcoming this fear is the conclusion to a long chapter in my life. Finally, it's time to embrace this moment and begin a new one.

## 95.

I feel completely naked. Usually I consider myself an effective communicator and speaker, but today I feel unfocused and unprepared. I briefly scramble through my notes, trying to focus my thoughts, but it is not working. I disregard my notes and try to wing it, but the results are the same. I cannot seem to put two sentences together. I stumble over the key points of my speech: passion, courage, and action. Nothing is coming out right, and I know my students sense that something is wrong. As sweat begins to pool in my palms and I make a halfhearted attempt to avoid eye contact with my students, it sets in. My shortcomings as a husband and father are affecting my confidence as a teacher. Today I find myself feeling like a hypocrite as I attempt to stress the importance of sacrifice and courage in their young lives. I desperately try to mask my cowardice, but I know that my students can see right through me like a wet piece of tissue paper.

My family looks to me for strength and for action. As I stand in front of my students, them waiting on my every word, I know I have not met the needs of the ones who need me the most. I bury myself in my work while neglecting my family responsibilities. It's not that I'm robbing my family of time. I do not stay late grading papers, and I am not on countless committees that require me to stay after school. No, what I do is rob my family of my emotional availability. When I get home, I am emotionally drained. All I want to do is to have my 210-pound body slowly sink into my sofa while I channel-surf, looking for sport talk shows on ESPN. I do not want to talk about anything that matters, I just want to *be*. One would think that having been married for almost ten years I would know how this would go over with my wife. But doesn't she understand that I talk all day? The last thing I want to do when I get home is to have an in-depth conversation about how much money we put on the credit cards this month or how my four- and seven-year-olds misbehaved in Home Depot.

I can feel my chest tighten and the vein starting to pop up on the side of my head as my wife vents to me about her day. I want some fucking peace and quiet, is that too much to ask for? Have I not earned it? My kids are waiting for Daddy to get home so they can go swimming or play baseball.

To be honest, most times I look for any excuse to stay plopped in front of the television (which, by the way, is not considered to be a romantic evening by most women). Daddy has a headache or Daddy has a lot of papers to look over is what I usually say. Does anyone else in my family realize how many lives I saved today at work? The problem is that the kids at work are so needy that it's easy to be the hero in their lives. It is easy to validate myself through my profession. I need to be the hero of my own story. I need to preserve the lives of my wife and my own kids. No wonder my wife grows resentful of everything I do outside our home.

Accomplishments at work mean very little to her because of what I give or do not give my own family. What is wrong with me? I know what I must do, but I simply don't act. Where is the passion and courage needed to foster a healthy marriage? If this were one of my students in a similar situation, I would jump his ass and insist that he "step up" and do the right thing. Maybe I should start taking my own advice. I feel so ashamed on this day, not only as a teacher but as a man. I feel bound by my apathy most times; it's like jogging in quicksand. I want to be a good king that fights for the hearts of those left in his charge. I want to be that good king for my students as well as for my own kids. I want to be that good king who talks the talk and walks the walk. Today I do not feel like a good king; maybe tomorrow, but not today.

## 96.

*47, XY + marker*! It looked like some odd kind of code used for communication purposes between military personnel. "What does it mean?" I asked Dr. Broome. She looked at me like an old mother owl gazing on her baby chick before coaxing it into flight; then she began to explain the specific details of the results of my abnormal genetics blood test. My wife and I were looking for answers. This was the second time she miscarried in the last two years. I lost my baby twins. That ultrasound image of those two lifeless bodies in her womb still haunts my dreams. I still have not recovered from that day because I have so desperately wanted to become a dad.

As I sat in front of Dr. Broome, so many feelings and thoughts flashed across my mind. Was there something in my DNA that would forever rob me of the joys of watching a smaller version of myself jump into the wilds of life? Maybe I was just dying? Or maybe I was developing a genetic illness like Parkinson's, cancer, or MS? For the last few weeks I had been secretly coughing up small amounts of blood every morning in the shower. I was always tired and low on energy. I had begun having muscular spasms and trembling in my right hand that had become very noticeable to my students. I had been in and out of the E.R.

many times in the last two months. What the hell was wrong with me?

Dr. Broome calmly explained that I had a rare genetic makeup: I carried an additional piece of a gene. I have 47 chromosomes, while everyone else has 46. Most people who carry additional chromosomes in their bodies suffer from severe Down syndrome, or any number of severe facial or physical deformities. Because I did not exhibit any of the classic conditions, she thought it was most likely a familial gene, kind of like a genetic fingerprint passed on from father to son. She told me that all my family members would need to undergo the same test. If my father and brother tested positive, then the anomaly was highly unlikely to cause any problems with any pregnancy that my wife and I would attempt in the future. If the anomaly came from my mother's side of the family, then running further tests would be almost impossible because my mother had no ties to her biological family. There would be no way to test another maternal relative to see if this gene had caused any infertility, physical deformities, or mental impairments in family members on my mother's side.

Dr. Broome also mentioned the possibility that I was the sole carrier of this genetic anomaly in my family. When she said this, I was completely stunned. My life felt as if it had been completely derailed. All of our plans to build a family were fading into the distant horizon. My wife reached out and held my hand. She squeezed it tightly, offering her unwavering support in silence. Dr. Broome gave me the phone numbers to set up appointments for my family.

I walked out of that office feeling as if I was bearing the weight of two failed pregnancies and the lives of three little babies on my shoulders. My wife tried to assure me that everything was going to be fine. She tried to be a rock for me the way good wives are supposed to. She now held me the way I held her the first time we knew our first child's life had come to an end. I felt so lost and angry now. My wife deserves to have a family. She deserves better than this. I feel that I have cheated her out of this dream. She has given me so much as a wife, and I have returned so little as a husband.

The next day during my first-period class, one of my girls, Veronica, asked me how I was doing. I must have been wearing my emotions on my sleeve that morning because she knew that I wasn't being myself. I knew I would be unable to work if I did not get this weight off my chest, so I got up from my desk and walked to the front of the room. My students knew the background of my story, so I told them what had happened at the doctor's appointment. As I spoke, I could feel myself begin to break down into uncontrollable sobs. They all sat there quietly and listened until I finished. Many of my girls and some of my boys cried along with me. I think it shocked them to see a teacher be so genuine and real with them.

One of my girls, Maria, finally asked, "So does that mean you might never have kids?"

I responded by saying, "I don't know, but I think that this is all taking place because God has another plan in mind for me right now. Maybe you were meant to fill the void of those children that I have so longed to have. Maybe God is telling me I already have a family, you."

## 97.

There he is, the young man I have raised for seventeen years. I have not seen him for weeks except for a few moments. He's in our driveway stripping down to his boxers to put on his clean clothes to avoid spending another minute in our house, his home. Silent tears stream down my face as I watch my son from my bedroom window, at a loss as to what options I have following his fierce display of disgust toward me.

"I'm not coming home!" Matt harshly declared as he filled his suitcases with both clean and dirty clothes. In a frantic search

he calls out, "Where's my blue case?" My heart is eased some-
what knowing that he is still speaking to me, even if his back is
turned.

"What case?" I ask.

"The one with Dad's coin," he hollers over his shoulder,
avoiding eye contact.

My husband died suddenly ten years ago. I had to keep the
family going and didn't realize that burying my grief was dam-
aging to me and my family until I reached out while dating. I
shared my soul with another man. My disclosure drove him
away. My buried emotions resurfaced when he, too, left abruptly.

"I can't live here with you. This doesn't even feel like my
house anymore." Matt's fist punches a hole in his bedroom wall
with his words of anger.

"This is your home and will be your home for as long as I live
here," I say. But there are no words at this point to change Matt's
mind. Our home is the same structure it has always been. The
truth is it still lacks the loving father we once held in both happy
and sad times. For years I attempted to shield my son from this
painful reality, leaving a communication crevasse so distant that
we were no longer able to talk.

I watch from my window as Matt's friend rumbles away in
his truck. My son is gone. I have been abandoned again. I am all
alone. I couldn't let go of my late husband. I refused to lose my
son. In my refusal my son felt smothered by me. I struggled with
grief for as long as my mind said I needed to. I told myself I was
over the loss of my late husband. I lied to myself when I said my
heart was no longer broken. I believed myself, but my son did
not believe me.

A few months before, I began changing our house—the home
that had remained the same even through the ending of a second
marriage. I let go of the last of my late husband's stuff. I used the
eastern practice of feng shui to renew the energy of our home,
placing crystals and other sacred items in strategic locations and
getting rid of things no longer needed. Our abandoned feelings

were forced to the surface with the physical letting go of the reminders of the past. I refused to believe that the torrent of emotions expressed by my son stemmed from my own grief, not his. After all, it was his fist that created the holes in our walls, not mine. Unbeknownst to me, my being was controlled by my fear of abandonment.

The more Matt and I tangled in rage, the more I thought *he* needed help to face the loss of his dad, not me. I had grieved fully, so I thought. Several weeks after Matt left home, he agreed to go to counseling with hopes of getting his car back. I was done with my grief. I provided responses the counselor wanted to hear to prove that it was Matt who needed the weekly sessions, not me. But my heart knew otherwise.

We met several times with a licensed psychiatrist. But not until we met with an intuitive counselor did things begin to shift between Matt and me. This counselor had dealt with enough of her own stuff that she quickly saw through my facade. My heart knew that it didn't matter what the loss—death, divorce, or otherwise—it hurt like hell. But for years my mind covered the hurt by doing what others wanted, needed, or expected. My "doing" served me well, and I earned the label "gifted classroom teacher"—another mask covering the ongoing pain of abandonment.

Now, as I faced the thought of losing my own son, the fear of endless abandonment was becoming my reality. I was losing my son only weeks after moving my college-age daughter into her first apartment. When she said, "It's official now. I'm finally moved out," her words sealed shut my biggest fear—that soon I would be all alone.

As Matt and I sat in the counselor's office in the presence of crystals and the delicate sounds of nature, she spoke out loud *in front of my son* what my heart had known all along: "You've got deep sorrow in your heart center. You've got to let go of your late husband. Your fear and control are driving your son away."

Matt and I walked to the car in silence after that life-changing session. When I closed the driver's-side door, I openly shared aloud for the first time words about my grief process with my son: "Damn, I thought I was done dealing with my grief."

## 98.

"Mom, I know what I want to be when I grow up!" I shouted as I sat in my car reveling in this grand epiphany. But before I could reveal my answer, my mom calmly replied, "A teacher." Stunned into silence for moment, I finally asked, "How did you know?" She merely said, "I'm your mother; I know it's what you were created to do."

Throughout our lives, Mom and I shared many similar conversations, each with its own unique brand of revelation. I remember learning through these talks how much her past and my future seemed to be intertwined. She was raised in a convent with wicked nuns and later in a foster home, where she was molested. I always wanted to be the voice she never had, and show the compassion to my students she never received. As I was finally beginning my teaching career, what better opportunity could I ask for than to have my mom become a living part of my dream?

My mom and I spent the summer painting and decorating my new classroom. I rearranged the desks at least twice a day, while my mom sorted books and supplies. We talked about the things I would say to the students when they walked into the room. She reminded me that many times all my new students would need to be successful was love. By the time school started, I felt confident the world was about to see a change. But I wasn't prepared for what the world was about to put in my way.

In the first months of school, Mom was an integral part of the lives of my elementary students. During her time in our classroom, it seemed that she could connect with some of my students on a level that I was not able to reach. She would patiently sit for thirty minutes and guide a student through a math paper that should have taken ten minutes. She fielded questions from my elementary school students like "Miss Gloria, were you a slave?" or "How come I don't have those blue lines in my skin like you do?" With this question, my head popped up as I anticipated what her answer would be. But, in her compassionate way, she touched Theresa's arm and said, "Well, my skin is not this pretty brown like yours, so my veins show through." These humorous yet meaningful conversations became a common part of our classroom, until the moment her health began to consume her time.

Although I continued to teach, in between my early-morning and late-night hospital visits, Mom's absence was evident in the classroom, and the guilt I felt for not being able to save her was, at most times, overwhelming. I tried to hide behind a veil of assuredness, but my students saw right through it. One day I walked into class, and Anthony noticed my eyes were red. He simply asked, "Ms. Barton, are you okay?" In that simple question I realized that as much as my students may need me, right now, I needed them. I began to cry. With a quavering voice, I said, "You know how Miss Gloria has not been able to visit lately? Well, she has been pretty sick and right now she is in the hospital. Her kidneys are not working, and the doctors are trying to fix them."

As I stood before my kids, fear set in. Had I gone too far? Did I tell them too much? Will I get parent phone calls tonight? Then, like signs intended to ease my mind, my students' hands began to rise one by one, and they shared stories of their loved ones who had suffered. Sharing with my students had a powerful, transforming effect on them as well as on me. We became a family, and in the weeks and months that followed, my students wrote poems and prayers and left on my desk drawings that had been done for my mom. There were banners that the students had coerced the art teacher into letting them make. Marie wrote a letter telling my mom that God had spoken to her and told her that my mom was going to get better.

My mom's health declined rapidly, and within six months of her last visit to my classroom, she was in the ICU on a ventilator. Our lives were once again intertwined, only now it was her future that was bringing up my past and the easy conversations we used to have. Long talks about family and life played in my head as if they were on a continuous running track. As I searched her eyes for the words she could not speak, I was met with emptiness and sorrow. I could never express in a few words what she meant to me and my students, but as I revisit the journal I kept while she was sick, I find this:

> *Dear Mom,*
>
> *It's the day before Mother's Day and two weeks since you died. I miss you so much! I have so many regrets, and no more time to fill them. I wish I would have spent more time with you. I just always thought you would be here forever. As I face my students, I am lost. You were my best friend, the reason I became a teacher, and the first person I wanted to call when you died.*

## 99.

I never suspected anything. I feel sick to my stomach. I go to the fire department and tell them I am from out of town and visiting a friend. They direct me to the address of—the suspect. I turn onto the street and see his truck in her driveway. My eight-year-old son sees her through the window and exclaims, "That's the lady who wrapped our Christmas presents."

*Has he been seeing her since last Christmas?!* I start shaking. I say to my daughter, "Will you . . . please . . . go . . . to the door, honey . . . and ask . . . Daddy to come . . . see Mommy?" He comes out of her house in a white sleeveless T-shirt and blue jeans holding an Orange Crush. With his other hand he points to me as I am rolling down the window and says matter-of-factly, "You had better not make a scene." The kids cry. This is the first time they hear this tone, these words. He never even looks at them in the backseat.

I watch him open her front door and go in. I pray that I don't throw up. We drive off slowly.

It's six months later. I greet my class, "Good morning, guys!"

"Hey, Ms. B." I turn toward the chalkboard as if I am thinking about the lesson. I pretend to look in my desk drawers. They wait. They sense something is wrong. They know about the trial, that he took my oldest daughter.

"Okay y'all, I need you to spend class time today writing. Choose something that happened over the weekend, maybe a best thing/worst thing kind of thing, okay?" My face is working overtime. My eyes tell a different story. They know it.

"Ms. B? Can you come here, please?" the new girl, Sara, asks.

I take a deep breath, hoping her question will require only a "yes" or a "no." I give her a half smile. It's the best I can do. She'll probably ask how long the assignment should be, something the kids have heard me explain a million times. She's cute, brown-skinned like cocoa, round cheeks. She wears a hat every day, a T-shirt, long-flowing skirt, and leather sandals or moccasins.

When I reach her, she leans on the bookshelf, giving me a look I can certainly understand. "I can't get my mom off my mind. I miss her."

"Where is she? What do you mean?"

"It's a long, bad-ass sad story. I was thinking about you missing your daughter. Sucks, huh?"

"Yeah, sure does." *Damnit, I need to keep it together. Listen. Focus.*

"Did your daughter see you Saturday?"

I shake my head, look at the floor. "No, she never showed.

She knows I am not going anywhere." I breathe. "Tell me why you miss your mom."

Sara starts talking: "Last Christmas . . ."

Right then, it feels as though a finger is pushing that way-too-familiar rewind button.

". . . my mom and me got into it again. 'Think you're better off without me?' . . . All that shit."

Sara bites her bottom lip and looks up to see if I'm listening.

"I made her cry fucking rivers. But being the self-centered ass-hole I am, I didn't give a shit."

*Why is she telling me this? I would die if any one of my children spoke like this about me.*

"It sounded like a crash, and I think my mom must have bro-ken something and she'll probably bitch at me about it. I don't go and see if she's all right because I don't want to hear any of her shit. Then she starts calling for me."

*I miss my daughter, making brownies, searching for her backpack. I miss that house.*

"I start to walk past the closet, and I see her lying on the floor. The gun is right there."

*His voice: "Katy, I swear to God if you don't stop spending money . . ." Gun? Did she just say . . . gun?*

"I start freaking the fuck out, crying. She's on the floor saying, 'God, please forgive me.' I get the phone and dial nine-one-one. The operator tells me to calm down. I scream for her to shut up!"

Sara sighs and says: "Yeah, Mom died."

I just sit there, staring right through her. Am I breathing? Talk about humbling. Sara helps me realize that when you lose people and dreams, you hold on to your hope even tighter. I reach for her hands, look her in the eye, and tell her: "I am so very sorry. I can only imagine how much you are hurting. I know you are missing your mom, and I know she is missing you. What your mom did was not your fault. You are lovable and special, and you will get through this. I am here for you."

I let loose a deep breath. I *hear* my own words. I too am lovable. What he did was not my fault.

This time I smile at Sara and the whole class with my whole heart.

## 100.

Moses was from Soweto, an outsider in my classroom. He wanted everyone to know that he was in charge, that he could solve all his problems by himself—with his knife if necessary. Moses was a quick stabber, so I kept my eye on him. I knew that giving up on him would support the apartheid system that created his frustration.

"Remember to review your notes on chapter eight," I reminded my students as the last bell rang. My voice drowned in the voices of fifty teenagers eager to get out of their school uniforms and to enjoy the weekend. No one seemed to care for my well-intentioned reminder. Like a swarm of bees they burst out into the busy hallways, pushing and shoving along the way.

I collected my books and put away my belongings, unaware of Moses, who was still slowly packing his book bag. Then I heard his raspy voice behind me: "Miss, take this." He handed me a nine-inch knife. My heart skipped a beat, but I did not reveal my fear. I gave him a puzzled look.

"I want to change. If I do not have it, I . . . uhmmm . . . will not fight anymore." He stuttered without looking at me. Although he was very shy, he commanded fear among his peers. I hesitated to take it.

"All right, I will keep it for you only if you promise not to get another one."

He looked me straight in the eye and without hesitation said, "I promise," and swiftly left.

I stood there staring at the empty room. It seemed dirtier

than usual, and the dusty floor was littered with crumpled papers full of unfinished thoughts. I felt the chill from the autumn wind coming from the broken windows. My eyes wandered to the back of the room, where Moses shared a small desk with three other students. I thought back to the day when, while proctoring an examination, I'd seen Moses with what looked like notes. When I approached him, he gave me a look that said, "You better stay away." When I moved closer, he reached under his desk, took out the nine-inch knife, and placed it carefully on the right side of his paper. I'd gotten the message loud and clear: "You stay out of my business and no one will be hurt." Later that day, I told my principal what had happened. He let me know that there were things not worth dying for, and a test is one of them!

To me, Moses embodied the anger and frustration resulting from apartheid. The slogan that had taken root in the struggle against the system, "Democracy now and education later," resonated with my students. The teachers, though all black, were overwhelmed or had given up long ago. The male teachers were the first to give up because their lives were in the most danger. I was young and small in stature and therefore not seen as a threat by students whose very existence depended on their prowess to defend themselves. I refused to give up, knowing that my inaction would only perpetuate the system we all reviled.

As I stood in the empty room, I picked up a crumpled paper; it felt fragile in my hands, like the uncertain futures of my students, who never had any reason to be hopeful. I turned back to my desk to collect my belongings. I was drawn back to the knife lying on my desk. I carefully collected it and stored it away in my drawer. As I left the room, the big chalkboard, the only teaching resource at my disposal, seemed to be staring at me mockingly.

That Saturday I got a call from Rita. "Miss, he is gone. They killed him," she whispered.

"Who is gone?" I asked, dreading the answer.

"Moses was killed this morning."

I felt as if the bottom of my stomach had dropped to the floor. I gasped for air.

Monday morning I did not know what to say to my students. We couldn't look one another in the eyes. Then a student stood up strong and tall and said, "We've got to stop the crazy killing."

She liberated us to mourn and find meaning in Moses's death. Our lives, my student was telling us, were intertwined. We all understood that if we did not work to improve our community, we were part of the problem. With raised fists, the students danced and chanted in unison, "Democracy now and education now!"

## 101.

Why does it bother me so much? I'm sitting there today, talking to a colleague who's complaining about how "uncomfortable" she felt in a workshop about white privilege. I hope I didn't come off too strong. My love for my people is often confused with anger toward others, but all I want is respect for my students and the lives they live. She felt as though she was being attacked because she is white. She felt she was being accused of things that she had nothing to do with. All eyes were on her and the weight of the world was on her shoulders as she heard accusation after accusation about how "white power" was to blame for all the wrongs in society. I understood how she felt, but that's the reality my students face every day in our schools, in their community, and everywhere they go.

As I began telling our story, I knew she'd appreciate my honesty if I found a way to express myself without losing sight that she was an ally, not an enemy. I let her know how easy she had it: "Whenever you get knots in your stomach, all you have to do is get up and leave the room. My kids and I, we can't just get up and disappear." When our blood boils, we are chained and forced to swallow comments about *our* families and *our* community. We contemplate ways to defend ourselves without sounding as if we're pulling the "race card." We're accused of being radicals if we speak up and sellouts if we're silent. This is a fine line many of us try to navigate every day.

She felt the need to voice her opinion this morning; we feel the need to scream at the top of our lungs every day. Tears formed in her eyes as I continued. I saw her heart start to unfold as she began to understand our pain. I told her that the same ripping feeling that she felt as she clenched her fingers into a fist this morning, my students and I experience every day. Her pain is mirrored in the daily lives of my students and me every time she feels the guilt of white privilege forced down her throat. The feelings she felt this morning, my students and I experience every single time we walk into a store, every time we watch a movie that portrays our people as servants and slaves, every time we hear a politician, Democrat or Republican, refer to our people as "illegal immigrants" and "aliens." It's the same feeling we feel when we're stopped on the street and asked for "papers," or when our families are torn apart by federal agents with *ICE* in their veins. I asked her to think about how we felt when women clutch their purses as if we're about to snatch them, or we hear racist comments in school about our people and our community. A blindfold was removed from her eyes, leaving her speechless. She began to understand how we feel every hour of every day. Yet we find a way to persevere, and her students find a way to make it to class every morning.

I tried to explain why some of her kids act out and some seem not to care about school. They're fed up or completely demoralized due to being under constant scrutiny, constant attack, or constant discomfort. Teachers might call them "unmotivated," "defiant," or "disruptive," but I asked her how she thought she'd feel if she lived their lives, if she looked through their eyes. I'd bet their world would burn in her mind and a new reality would arise.

I can only imagine how much damage is done to our students

in our classrooms every day. I think of what I have to deal with on and off my school campus and how easily my colleague's comfort zone was violated this morning. It's clear now that we need to be heard. Have we asked our students to tell us how they feel? Have we asked them if we've ever hurt them with the things we say in class? We can't be afraid to hear what a few courageous youth would tell us. Hopefully, we can become more sensitive and conscious of the impact we have on our students.

There are some things you just don't do, and I know they happen all the time. How dare we tell our kids they can't speak Spanish? How dare we tell our students they could do better than their parents? How dare we mispronounce their names? How dare we tell them not to be proud of who they are and raise their Mexicano flag? How dare we tell our students they've come *so far*—as if their existence began in 1492? How dare we say they're immigrants when their ancestors witnessed the first colonizers who set foot on *their* land?

If you ask me, "white America" and my friend need a reality check. We have to walk many miles in our kids' shoes if we ever want to be the best teachers for our students. Are we willing to? And if we're not, what does that say about our profession?

## 102.

"I pledge allegiance to the flag of the United States of America," drone the voices of my barely awake students. "And to the republic for which it stands, one nation, under God" *more like a nation divided by economics, education, the haves and the have-nots*, I think cynically, "indivisible, with liberty and justice for all." I scan the faces of my students, knowing that some of them have parents who are incarcerated and who would be more than willing to challenge the validity of such an assumption.

Each morning the school day starts with the principal calling all students and staff to rise to their feet for the Pledge of Allegiance. Only threats of having to write it out by hand rouse the students to stand, though with moans and groans and outright disinterest. The children go through the motions, mouth the words mechanically, and proceed to plop back into their seats the millisecond the last word is uttered.

How did these words instilled in all of us since kindergarten become so distasteful? The little ones in kindergarten are eager to display their aptitude and their pride at being able to mimic what the older kids take for granted. They have not yet been tarnished by the realities of life. To them Santa Claus still exists and the Easter Bunny brings chocolate eggs. But life has a way of tearing away the enthusiasm. In the elementary years, the dawning of a new reality begins to surface ever so slowly. They begin to hear things, a rumbling of discontent, the chimes of inequality. The rosy picture of life depicted in storybooks begins to fade.

"Why do we have to say this stupid pledge every day?" asks a defiant sixth grader.

"Anybody with any sense knows it ain't true."

"Isn't true."

"Whatever! My mom says there ain't—isn't—justice for all. Just ask my dad. He's going to be in jail for the next thirty-six months."

I think to myself this might make for a great writing assignment. As if reading my mind, a student chimes in, "You can write all you want. It isn't going to change a thing."

My students want to give me a reality check. The truth is that not all the faces before me are on the same playing field. In fact, some already expect that their life expectancy will be short. The prospects are dim, and as history would have it, by the time they are eighteen, it is likely they will be either dead or incarcerated. That's the reality.

My students are not interested in writing persuasive or informative essays. They want to write about their reality.

For Ricky, despite his dad's hope that an education will keep his son on the straight and narrow, the reality is that Ricky writes about visiting his dad in Detroit this month. He longs for the day when he can be reunited with his dad so he won't have to live under the watchful, constraining eye of his grandmother anymore.

Ricky's thoughts and his words are angry, filled with bitterness. He looks out at some of his peers and wonders why his life is so different from theirs. Reality for Ricky is harsh. He has only a fleeting memory of his birth mother, tarnished by the harsh and angry words his grandmother uses to describe her. Ricky's neighborhood is beleaguered with violence and crime. For Ricky's grandmother, her reality is that in all likelihood the neighborhood will claim her grandchild just as it claimed her son. His grandmother will strive with every last breath of her being to turn Ricky from the drugs, gangs, and violence that engulf them daily.

For Ricky, his only bastion may be a frail but no-nonsense, strong-willed grandmother, whose determination might be his only hope for survival. This woman of limited education and limited means who has weathered the injustices of her day vows not to see her only living grandchild become another statistic, another unfamiliar name that darkens the pages of the newspaper.

"I pledge allegiance to the flag of the United States of America . . ."

A grandmother, Ricky's grandmother, whose pledge of allegiance is only to him . . . "One nation, under God," reflects one solitary individual whose faith in the face of adversity is undeterred. "Indivisible, with liberty and justice for all," will be her mantra. Under her unalienable rights, Ricky will not be denied his liberty and justice as long as a breath is within her being!

While all the odds may seem stacked against him—drugs, gangs, and the streets—one lone, unlikely individual will be in Ricky's corner whether he likes it or not.

## 103

"What the hell was that about?" my students asked as they looked up from their catechisms. The nun from next door had flown into my classroom, looked around as if we had interrupted her morning prayers, and then flew back out. It wasn't the first time she had left her class to check on mine, to correct my misinterpreted teaching about the Church, or to scold my students for being too loud during small-group work. I was a first-year teacher, and she was my department chair, a woman who always made me feel bad about myself.

Only a few weeks into the school year, she instructed me to give a detention to one of my students who had broken the commandment "Thou shall not eat in class."

"Why?" I asked.

Anybody who knows what it's like to go to Catholic school knows that you never question authority, especially that of priests and nuns. It was just that I didn't see the boy eating in class, and I really didn't want to bear false witness against him and chastise him. I wondered why the teacher who saw him eating with her own eyes couldn't assign the punishment herself instead of doling out the responsibility to someone else. I felt that my department chair was forcing my hand to set an example for the rest of the students.

"Because he broke your rules," she said. She left me behind with a prisoner awaiting sentence, a jury of his fourteen- and fifteen-year-old peers, and a sin that, to her, warranted crucifixion.

I really didn't want to do it—it wasn't who I was as a teacher, first-year or not, to teach about Christian social justice and then do something like that. Deciding to teach a lesson in virtue, I let him go with a warning. I still don't know how she found out about it, but she came into my classroom the next morning with a detention slip for him and a scolding for me that stung like the metal edge of a ruler.

After that, she developed the habit of randomly closing my classroom door during the school day. In "teacher school," they had warned us to keep the door open when we were alone in a room with minors, in case somebody decided to get litigious. Actually, that open-door policy would have been great for her, allowing her to observe my classroom, to supplement my lessons with her more experienced point of view, and to support my classroom management—all of the good stuff in teaching. But that didn't happen after the incident with the detention. Instead, she instituted a shut-the-door policy, accompanied by criticism: She told me not to smile in front of my students, because smiling is a sign of weakness. She told me to stop letting my students call me by my last name only, because that was a sign of disrespect. She told me to cut off class discussions when my students got "too deep." And, she always added, my students were too loud, regardless of whether they were involved in large- or small-group work.

My administrators and colleagues played politics when I told them that I felt that I was getting picked on by my department chair. Each of them said that they couldn't see what was so plain to me—after all, she was a nun. But all of those small things throughout the school year made me question my vocation. Is this what it's like to be a teacher? What does it say about being a teacher if I have to endure that? Salvation came when my principal notified me that the school wasn't going to renew my teaching contract for the following year. Nearly ten months of never feeling good about myself came to an end.

At the last department meeting of the school year, my colleagues' eyes were finally opened. The nun asked us, "So, who's not coming back next year?" and then locked eyes with me. "Me," I said finally. But it was too late to start any kind of crusade.

On the last day of school, as I watched my students leave my classroom for the last time, she handed me a dented metal tin of biscuits, gave me a hug, and told me that she would say a rosary for me. I watched her leave, weeping on the inside for justice, for that proverbial bolt of lightning to shoot out of the sky. I suffered my last scourging at her hands and walked out of that private Catholic school, abused by my own religion and instilled with the belief that I did not belong anywhere in education.

## 104.

I sometimes fantasize about telling off my principal. I have known her since my career began, yet she has never realized everything that is wrong with our school. We are hypocrites, plain and simple. If I ever had my way, or was pushed hard enough, I think this is how it would go:

Before I walk out of here and quit this profession forever, there are some things you have to know. Your laziness and your lack of any discernible skill outside of the occasional yelling at students is a disgrace to this school. You give people like our assistant principal, who is afraid of teenagers, and your literacy coach, who hates all of us, so much power, and not because they want to help but because they crave it. Your assistant principal is an office rat who would rather sit in her air-conditioned hole than interact with students. It seems her greatest pleasure is observing her math department teachers and embarrassing them in front of their students. The fact that you have a young, energetic math department is a blessing that many schools would murder for, yet you allow this person to fracture that.

You allow our literacy coach, who is a teacher not an administrator, to run roughshod over your entire staff. Everything she has touched, and I know that you know this, has fallen apart. I understand that everyone makes mistakes. I have tried to take on responsibility here, and my weakness has always been that I feel I have to do things alone. Yet I will admit that this is a fault of mine, even though I can admit to people that I screwed things up, and I need help. Your literacy coach refuses that. Things are always our fault. She is perfect, and you never let her feel that she isn't. She speaks to us like peons, yet in spite of all of the complaints and the obvious detriment to the morale of your staff and your student body, who feel constantly picked on and disrespected by her, you continue to allow her to feel she is doing a good job.

I know you are overwhelmed, but this is what you signed up for. You became a principal, you created a school, and right now your school is a joke. You graduated students who spent a few hours with you the day before graduation writing papers, and somehow those students were able to make up twenty failed credits!? I understand you want to "move our students along," in your words, but at what cost? You know I would do anything, and have done anything, to help my students learn, even put myself in debt and spend hours into each weeknight here in my room, working on things I feel will help my students learn what they need to know. But I can't do that anymore—I can't. Something inside of me hurts when I think of what you have done, pushing our kids along like that.

Four years ago, our plan was not only to graduate our students but also to have them ready for life, for college. What does this show them, that the bottom line is more important? That our numbers mean more than their lives? That if they wait long enough, not work hard enough, they will get what they want? The students you "helped" graduate that night were on the verge of learning who they really were: cowards who would run away from what mattered, or young men and women who learned from their mistakes.

I know that in some respects you have treated me very well here. You have allowed me to try things that many administrators would not try. But you also have taken advantage of me. I created our student government. I created your first yearbook, your first play. I was able to get our school in the news for all of the right reasons. I cannot stand by and accept this anymore. I cannot accept *you* anymore. I gladly hand you my resignation, effective immediately. I would rather wait tables in a greasy-spoon restaurant than stand by and let you continue to use my talents to resuscitate a school that you seem bent on leaving on life support because it's easy for you to continue to simply get paid and not be a leader.

Well, I guess I can dream, can't I? I spent the whole spring and summer looking for a school that felt the same way I did. After over forty submissions to schools in my area of the country, only one responded, and the position was filled the next day without an interview. I feel doomed, that one day the scenario I imagined will happen, and I will have to leave teaching forever. I would feel good for a day, because everything that was stored up in me would be out, but I also would have lost my love.

## 105.

"What the fuck are you doing to my son? All of you better get your motherfucking hands off my son before I call the police. Who's fucking idea was it to hold Jaheim like that? You all have the security guard, two fucking teachers, and oh, here we go again with Mr. Moore. This means four grown, bad-ass motherfuckers are on my boy," said Jaheim's dad as he angrily limped into the classroom.

I never knew that I wanted to be a principal. Actually I never knew that I wanted to work with children. I pictured myself working on Wall Street, living in a loft in Manhattan, and working for IBM or some other computer-based company. During my last year in college, I had to conduct some volunteer work with a group of children at a Boys and Girls Club. The experience was okay, just something I had to complete for class. I had no idea I would actually be working with children as my career.

"Damn, I am about to fuck someone up. Mr. Moore, I need to see you." Jaheim's dad was six-foot-eight, weighed over 300 pounds, and carried a cane because of a drug-related incident. Not only was Jaheim's dad intimidating but his cane wasn't an ordinary dollar-store cane. It was an elaborately engraved wooden cane. It almost said, *I am too cool for a cane so I am going to have the bad-ass, most intimidating cane so when I come into a room people know not to mess with me.*

Jaheim had thrown chairs at kids, turned the teacher's desk over, and cussed everyone out, and when we came into the room to calm him down, he didn't even stop or blink an eye. It usually took four adults to restrain him, but he'd outlasted us.

"Do you want me to call your father to come up and speak with you about your behavior?" I asked. "You seem to be getting a little upset because you cannot eat lunch right now, but it isn't your class's lunchtime."

"I don't care, I want to eat now," Jaheim said, then quickly added, "I don't want you to call my father."

"Okay, let's take a walk, and I think I can find something to hold you over. But you need to calm down and get yourself together," I said, hoping my offer would help calm Jaheim down.

Jaheim was a kindergarten student who was indeed stronger than four grown adults when he was upset. He would get upset if he couldn't sharpen his pencil when he wanted to, if he couldn't get to the workstation that he wanted, or if he thought someone had looked at him the wrong way. In all my days and experience of being a teacher's assistant, teacher, coach, assistant principal, and principal, I never experienced so difficult a child and parent.

I didn't want Jaheim to be a special-ed student because we have too many young black boys in special education. I didn't want to call the police, despite the fact that Jaheim put kids' lives in danger once a week. I mean, I fought for that kid. I worked with the father and rarely suspended Jaheim because I knew that if he was home with his dad, he would be hustling with him. So he had to stay in school. In the two years I was an administrator, I never kicked him out. As I reflect on my actions, or lack thereof, maybe I was all wrong with that approach. After I transferred to another school, his father took him out of the school. But nobody knew where he went.

I still think of Jaheim today and wonder how a three-foot kindergarten student could have the strength of a grown man and why his father didn't trust the school or believe that his kid became violent at times. I think about him often and how Mrs. Doyle, his teacher, was such an amazing person to love him and start fresh with him every day after his whirlwind of terror. I spoke to Mrs. Doyle recently. She had heard that Jaheim is in an alternative and restrictive middle school because of his behavior.

I wonder what else I could've done to help him.

## 106.

"I quit."

That was what I'd said to the director of human resources, the school board, my principal, and myself. It was simple. I was really tired. Exhausted from fighting every little battle. Annoyed watching top administrators earn more money and have better benefits and retirement plans than teachers. I was tired of colleagues' intolerance, torturous to both students and staff. I was tired of relentless testing; federal mandates; loss of art, music, and sports programs; and ever-more test preparation. I was often the only teacher at school board meetings, twice a month, speaking out on these issues.

So I resigned. In early spring, the green form came to my school mailbox asking if I would be accepting the same assignment next year. I checked "No." I felt happy to do it, as if a load was lifted off my back and I was free. Free of the frustration, the defeated attitudes of credit-deficient high school students. Free from the bureaucracy. I felt fresh air enter my life.

In addition to being a teacher, I was a community organizer and activist. A weekly program for girls that I'd begun three years prior was about to get serious funding from a three-year grant. I planned on transitioning the girls advocate position and focusing on "community-based education." Forget the system. I'd be completely grassroots.

I turned in my resignation in early March, and I was excited about my new career.

At a Freedom Writer Teachers retreat, I shared my plans with everyone. Everyone was totally supportive. The weekend was productive, working on new activities, catching up on life, and laughing like crazy. I had great ideas and renewed vision during the ride to the airport to hop on the plane home.

At LAX, I ran into another teacher from my group, waiting for his flight. As he boarded his plane, he called back, "Good luck. How incredible you're not going to be teaching anymore!"

Then it hit me. I wasn't a teacher anymore. What would I say when people asked "What do you do?" What would I tell them? I couldn't say, "I'm a teacher." Right there in the airport, I had a serious identity crisis.

I thought of my amazing classroom library and how my cool, painstakingly collected books had inspired my students to read until I had to force them to stop reading to listen during class lectures. I thought about teaching human rights, revolutionary social movements, and U.S. history and government, and about what good readers and writers my students had become.

I always felt pretty happy every day when I got to school, no matter how groggy and pissed off I'd been waking up. Now, those happy mornings would be gone. I remembered all the great books and people's histories and work that had liberated my students' thinking and turned them into lifelong learners, critical of the popular culture that pervaded their lives.

As I boarded the plane, I started to cry. I cried the whole way home, even in the car as I drove out of the airport. I did not know what to do to make it stop. I called a friend and blurted out, "I think I am going to un-quit my job." He was quiet for a few seconds and then said calmly, "I was wondering why you even quit in the first place." As soon as the words were out of my mouth, I stopped crying. I *am* a teacher.

## 107.

"Ms. Wilson, Mrs. Matthews needs to see you in her office."

The disembodied voice came over the loudspeaker, and I turned to my friend, whose room I had taken refuge in, and asked, "How did they find me here? What if I just don't go?" Getting called to the principal's office is just as scary as a teacher as it was when I was a student, if not more, and this was a different kind of trouble. I knew exactly what they wanted: I was about to lose my job.

The meeting was quick and impersonal, but it was more face-time than I had gotten with my administrators for the entire year. A handshake with a "these are hard times, sign here, and thanks for all you did for the children," and that was it. I was officially unemployed. I managed not to break down into tears until I stumbled into Laurie's science room. She was a friend whose classroom was down the hall from mine. It was the first year for both of us at a new school, and we leaned heavily on each other for support, as we certainly didn't get any from the more seasoned faculty members or our trusty administrators. Our other friend, the algebra teacher Emily, was also in Laurie's classroom, and as soon as I walked in, they both jumped up to console me, as they too were awaiting their fate and immediately knew mine by the look on my face.

"I can't believe they let you go. Did you remind them exactly how much you have done for this school?" Laurie asked me as tears rolled down my face.

"I just don't understand how this happened. Didn't you have the highest test scores in the whole school? Did you get cut because of the budget, or did she fire you?" Emily asked. She had been my advocate and informal mentor for the year because she had dealt with many of the same issues that I had battled over the last nine months.

"I don't understand either," I sobbed into my hands as I tried to process what had just happened. "My kids did better on their writing test than any other eighth-grade class in the history of the school. And our writing camp was such a success. Almost the entire eighth grade showed up, and I created a partnership with the local university for college education students to volunteer at the next writing camp. And on top of that, I got all those prizes donated: footballs, bicycles, even computers. My kids were pen pals with another middle school across the country, and my journaling project was so successful that students actually *asked* to take their journals home over the Christmas break. I even managed to get a student sponsored for the field trip to Washington, D.C. I just don't understand. Was it personal? Did I get fired because they think I really did a bad job, or is it because they just didn't like me? Can administrators be this callous?" I wailed to Emily and Laurie.

It was a bad year for education in my district. The district was short almost $40 million, and teachers were losing their jobs left and right because of the budget shortfall. I had always thought that teaching was one of the safest professions out there; schools would always need teachers. And because of all the hard work I had put into my classes and my kids, I had assumed that I was relatively safe. Once I got the tears and the anger out of the way, reality set in. But the reality that I was confronted with was not that I was now unemployed, but that I wasn't a teacher anymore. Teaching was my profession, my passion. My entire identity was anchored in my job. Teaching wasn't just something I did; it was who I was and everything I believed in. I hadn't thought I would be spending my summer looking for a new job, and I definitely hadn't thought I would be looking for a new career. Teaching was supposed to be a career that was safe. All I ever heard in school was how "in demand" teachers were and that you could get a job teaching anywhere. All the surrounding counties were on a hiring freeze, and even if I was able to find a position in another district, I knew my principal would refuse to support me by giving me a recommendation. At thirty years old, I have finally figured out who I am, what my talents are, and where my passions lay, but losing my job called all that into question. Can I still call myself a teacher if I don't have a classroom?

## 108.

Why do so many teachers leave their jobs after just a few years? Is it the long hours, the daily stress, the responsibility heaved onto one's shoulders all at once? Sometimes, teachers leave their jobs because they've become scapegoats for their schools' shortfalls, another excuse as to why the schools aren't educating kids. That was the case with me, though I didn't leave after all.

This year was my third at the school, a hopeful year because a new principal had taken over. She was quite supportive of all my endeavors and gave me several positive evaluations. I was elated to finally get some positive feedback after years of having felt not good enough as a teacher.

In March, my principal sat me down to go over my formal evaluation, one that included many good remarks.

"Ms. Wind, what do you think in terms of next year?"

"Well, I'd love to be in the same grade again. It was challenging but I enjoyed it."

"You like middle school?" she asked.

"Yes, I do."

"Well, I'm not sure it's the best fit, after your last evaluation."

"But I did really well on that evaluation. I have a copy right here. This is the one you mean, right?"

My heart began to beat faster and faster.

"Yes, that's it. You did well in your instruction. You know the subject well. But I can't seem to figure out why we had so many problems in the middle school this year."

"Yes, there were a lot of problems. But the kids were adjusting to the new system, and all the classes had problems with it."

This was undeniably true. I wasn't simply trying to defend myself.

"That's true. It's just that . . . you know . . . you didn't really seem to have an effect on many of the kids. So many of the fights before and after school, the girls even getting into fights . . . I don't know what it is . . . what you didn't do to prevent those things."

"Mrs. Franklin, with all due respect, I don't think there was anything I could do. The kids come to school so angry, they have so many problems to work out . . . I can't possibly solve them all."

"But the fights, the arguing, it's all starting in your room. Ms. Wind, I'd love to move you down to a lower grade. I think you'd do well there. But I don't have a position open right now. I think there's just too much of a racial component at play once you get above fifth grade or so. The kids don't respond to you in the same way."

So there it was. The evaluation had been missing one category: race. And I had gotten a negative checkmark.

"I know you will be tenured next year, Ms. Wind. I could give you one more shot in middle school, but if it doesn't work out, then . . . then you'll be here on your terms."

That meant she didn't want to be stuck with a teacher with tenure, because she would then need a reason other than my skin color to fire me.

"I'm going to see what I can do. I'm not going to do anything without having many more conversations with you about it."

"I'd appreciate that, Mrs. Franklin," was all I could respond.

Two weeks later, on my way out the door, I was handed a letter stating that I would not be able to come back for the upcoming school year.

After three years at the school, that was that. It would have been easy to leave teaching at that point, to take a job in the business sector or in a nonprofit that supported education. But leaving my teaching career because of one unjust administrator would have been at odds with everything I've learned about life as an educator.

In four years, I've learned that teaching is about never giving up, no matter what anyone says, no matter how scared you are, no matter the risks. This year, I risked it all and some would say I lost.

I think of the fact that I showed up every day with a smile, with lessons that inspired and brought kids to the next level, with a can-do attitude when people tried to cut me down for who I am, and I think I succeeded.

I found another teaching job within the same system for the following year. I had to be honest and explain my situation with candor in order to make it happen, but that's exactly what I did. Real teachers never quit.

## 109.

Yesterday, the assistant principal strolled into my English class in his clean-cut suit and asked for my students' undivided attention. The girls in the room stared at him in a daze. My palms got sweaty. *This can't be good.* I gave him my fake, nervous smile. "I have some wonderful news." *Oh, thank God.* "You are the luckiest students at this school. Your teacher has been honored by the administration as this year's Teacher of the Year." The students all started clapping and cheering.

—*What? Me? Why would they pick me? I've only been here two years.* "She's a teacher who makes sure every student is successful.

No other teachers go above and beyond to the extent that your teacher does." In a short two years, I was able to gain the respect and admiration of the school's administration, but most of all, the time and effort I was putting into my students' success was not going unnoticed.

Looking back at yesterday's achievement, my family was enjoying a beautiful Saturday afternoon in my parents' backyard. Everyone was at the house, barbecuing and enjoying the beautiful spring weather. The kids were in the pool while the women and men were discussing politics and the economy. It was so nice to have everyone over, and to be congratulated as "Teacher of the Year" with every greeting.

The doorbell rang. "I'll get it," I said as I ran to the door, hoping it was my adorable two-year old cousin.

*Certified mail? What could this be?* I quickly signed for the letter and ripped open the envelope: "This notice of non-reelection is . . . We appreciate the services you have provided." I felt my face flush, tears gathered in my eyes, and I couldn't make out the rest of the letter. *Are you kidding me? How could they call me Teacher of the Year yesterday and slap me in the face today!*

Intellectually, I knew the letter was the result of a budget crisis. But emotionally, I was devastated.

Walking into the classroom on Monday morning is not going to be easy, but I need to remember that I went into this profession for the kids. If it doesn't work out at this school, I know I will be successful somewhere else. I cannot let this affect my teaching. I just wish I didn't have to deal with it. The political game just comes with the territory. I have to keep reminding myself, I'm here for the kids.

# REJUVENATION

Teachers live for the moment that their students "get it." When something clicks for a student and suddenly they want to talk to you and tell you exactly what they know, that's when the proverbial lightbulb turns on and all of the new information finally falls into place. These are the moments that reinvigorate your decision to become a teacher and make up for the times when a colleague belittles you in the dreaded teacher's lounge, or when you have to defer your student loans and eat cold pizza for breakfast.

These breakthrough moments don't come often, so I constantly looked for ways to make my students' education hands on and get them excited about the world around them. When Miep Gies arrived to speak with us, I saw the intensity written on their faces, the absolute respect for this one woman who made a difference by helping to hide Anne Frank in that attic. Every ounce of stress was well worth the effort when the Freedom Writers realized that learning did not just take place within the walls of a classroom. My students took this knowledge on our field trip to Washington, D.C. Standing on the steps of the Lincoln Memorial, there were no worksheets, quizzes, or tests needed. At that moment, I knew my students "got it"!

The great thing is that these moments generally fuel others, and before you know it, you have a classroom buzzing with energy. The stories in this section are about teachers who work tirelessly to engage their students and push them to have those "aha" moments. These teachers bring the world into their classroom by organizing field trips, inviting civil rights activists to talk with their students, and simply by giving their students a journal to find their voice. With a little energy, some sacrifice, and a lot of patience, these teachers are rewarded with the knowledge that they have passed the baton.

## 110

"Tell me they didn't make her cry," I begged the universe as I walked, bleary-eyed, across the parking lot, clutching my cup of coffee like a security blanket. I knew what I was in for. The students at my school can break even the most competent of substitutes. A friend once pointed out that leaving the school is three parts vacation and seven parts misery. I spend hours creating lesson plans the subs never bother to use, and then they leave me a list of handy teaching tips about how to run my classroom and fix my students.

As I wandered into the classroom, I was surprised yet happy to see it didn't look like a war zone. Shit. There it was on my desk: the note . . . and it was a long one. I had talked to my students about being polite, being good people, being leaders. Hell, I flat-out bribed them. They don't handle change well, and the subs pay the price.

I read the note, and it was appalling. The usual suspects: Jerome, Craig, Selena, and the list went on. I read all of the accounts of inexplicable rudeness and wondered, "Who are these kids?" Swearing, refusing to go to the office, creating aliases . . . The sub was meant to be there for two days but dropped the job after the first day. In my head, I was already composing the blasting my students would receive. Then I noticed another note below the first, probably from the second substitute. Super.

But the second note was not from the substitute but from the teacher of our special needs class. She wrote about how the boys in my class had invited Blake, one of her students, to play basketball with them. She said she had been impressed by their invitation, and then even more impressed because they really included Blake in the game, continuously passing him the ball and treating him like one of the guys.

I admit I was taken aback. My students take basketball seriously. There's an unwritten rule: If you can't play, you don't join the game.

When my class arrived looking rather sheepish, I asked them about the ball game the day before.

"It's great that you included Blake in your game," I told them.

"Oh my God, Miss! He was so bad—your grandma could kick his butt!"

"That kid couldn't dunk a cookie in a glass of milk!"

"Damn! He was so bad . . ."

I shot them a cautionary look, and they immediately backed off.

"Chill, Miss. It's just that we always saw the kid on the sidelines watching us and thought maybe we should let him play."

I repressed a smile and reiterated the fact that they had made Blake feel really good about himself. As I looked around the room, I could see smiles on the faces of some of my worst offenders. They knew they had done a good thing. The irritation I was feeling earlier dissipated, and I was simply filled with pride.

"Uh, Miss, did the sub leave a note?"

## 111.

"Who are you looking at?" Temika screamed as she launched herself out of her chair toward Maria. In an instant the volume in the class raised 50 decibels as twenty-five voices began to yell and cheer, and chairs scraped across the floor as students rushed toward the back corner of the room. It all happened so fast that I don't even remember crossing the classroom and pushing desks to the side to get to the girls. Fists were flying, curse words were being uttered, and Temika and Maria were completely oblivious to the sound of my voice trying to halt their efforts to pummel each other. I thought my heart would pound right out of my chest, and I tried desperately to grab onto their arms as they repeatedly struck out. With the help of other students, I managed to pull the girls apart. They were both disheveled, their hair falling down over their eyes, their fists clenched. We were all breathing hard as the realization of what had just happened began to sink in. The girls were escorted to the office, and the mood in the classroom became somber, because we all knew that the consequence would be another suspension. I was so frustrated that here was another disastrous day with Temika. She had instigated the fight, and on some level I felt that she had done so to spite me. The day before, I'd felt that we were coming to some sort of understanding, but if her behavior today was any indication, maybe I was simply kidding myself.

Temika was the student who challenged me the most. Her tiny frame was a facade for an explosive, sometimes violent personality. The "Who's Who" of the school had been placed into this class, and in September each student had walked into the classroom on the first day wearing his or her attitude like protective armor. Every one of them was prepared for another year of trips to the office and suspensions. Most of them had slowly started to come around—but not Temika. She was the only student who hadn't started to demonstrate any change. She resisted my every attempt to engage her. She was sullen and confrontational. She sucked her teeth in contempt when I tried to compliment her efforts or encourage her. She insulted the other students and refused to participate in any of the activities I assigned. Today was not the first day she had started fights with other girls in the class. The only time she seemed to follow direction was when I gave the students an opportunity to journal. However, she had never permitted me to read her journal, so I wasn't sure that she was actually writing. I always felt a sense of guilt at the immense feeling of relief I had when she walked out the door at the end of the day.

The day before, after the students left, I had sat down to read the journals, thrown haphazardly onto the shelf. The black-and-white covers were inscribed with graffiti. Despite the pseudonyms on the "name line," I could easily identify which journal was whose by the gang symbols and pictures on the covers. I was fully prepared to place Temika's journal aside (she had never tabbed any entries for me to read) when I noticed a lone Post-it Note marking an entry. With curiosity I flipped through her journal. I couldn't believe the amount of writing filling up the pages. I turned to the entry she had tabbed for me to read and began. I felt sick as I read Temika's journal entry. My eyes filled with tears, and I had to continually wipe them away so that I could finish reading. Her pain and frustration were clearly communicated in the words I read, and I felt that I was getting a sense of who she really was because, in finally allowing me to read her journal, she had reached out. None of her friends would know that she had let me in; her reputation was intact. But I had a better sense of who she was—and a connection had been made. I felt confident that by allowing me to read her journal, Temika was in essence telling me that she was ready to start to make a change. I expected that the following day would be different between us.

Despite the hope I had felt yesterday, today was just as hard as all the previous days. And now Temika was sitting in the office waiting to be "sentenced" by the principal. I would have to let the principal know what had taken place, and Temika would know that my account of what happened would seal her fate and result in another suspension. Yesterday I had gained perspective and a better sense of what Temika was dealing with, but she didn't seem to share my sense that we had crossed some sort of bridge. I realized that there would continue to be an ongoing battle between Temika and me. Despite that moment in which she reached out by letting me read her journal, she would continue to challenge and frustrate me. However, I was determined not to give up on her, because after reading her journal I knew that that was what she had come to expect from the people in her life.

## 112

I have heard that teachers make an average of ten thousand decisions a day. That afternoon, I decided I wasn't going to quit, I decided I was committed to my students, and I also decided I was going to get through to them today—damn it—if it took everything.

My students piled into the room. Chuckles and Ted were having a discussion about Tupac. Chuckles said, "Tupac got shot in a Cadillac." Ted said, "Tupac ain't even dead. They can't prove it." Chuckles said, "Tupac wants us all to think he's dead while he kicks it on the beach in Jamaica." *Elvis, watch out, Tupac has joined you in the halls of immortality.*

I teach at a psychiatric youth center. My students are all male. They live on site. They get therapy, food, medication, and education.

It was time to start class. "Be quiet, please, and sit down," I said.

"Tupac wouldn't put up with this place," Chuckles continued. "And by the way, white boy"—he was addressing me—"don't tell me what to do."

Chuckles looks uncannily like a sixteen-year-old Nelson Mandela. "I don't take orders," he said.

"Okay, Chuckles, would you please decide for yourself that you want to sit down? We need to start class."

Chuckles picked up a chair, said, "Fuck this class," and threw the chair across the room. It landed on a table in front of Max, who was reading. Max is a big guy who never smiles. He looked up at Chuckles, looked at the chair, then looked back down to his book. The other students in the classroom were equally unaffected.

Chuckles grabbed a table and lifted it. I ran up behind him and put him in a restraint. He couldn't move. He conceded and sat down.

I was off to a bad start. Not even five minutes into class and already one restraint. Something needed to happen. I had to reach them.

"All right, guys, line up in the hall. We're going back to your community room to have a group session."

The students stood and strutted toward the door, swearing, shoving chairs and tables out of the way. They lined up in the hall. Typically this group of kids has two large adult staff members to help out. That day, we were understaffed, and the only adult aide I had was a small Latina woman who typically works in the kitchen and was not trained to restrain large angry students. I realized the mistake I'd made, but it was too late.

I walked down the hallways. The angry posse followed. I opened one locked door after another with a magnetic key. I was rounding a corner when I heard a thud behind me. I turned to see a garbage can bouncing off the wall, its contents flying around the room. Max came around right behind it.

"Max," I said, "are you okay?"

"What're you fuckin' lookin' at, bitch?"

He punched me in the side of the head. I watched my glasses fly from my face and hit the ground.

He walked past and waited by the next locked door.

I picked up my glasses. They weren't damaged.

A woman staff member had witnessed the event. I asked her to call in a code yellow. A code yellow signifies that all available staff are needed to help with a situation.

I opened the door, and we entered the boys' living quarters. Max began raising hell on the furniture. I asked the other boys to sit down. Scott, an ally of mine in the group, approached me and said, "Don't get in his way. Nothing can stop him." I looked at Max. He was pulling a ten-foot bookcase, full of books, away from the wall. He tipped it over. The books scattered across the floor. "He'll kick your ass," Scott said. Max lifted his right foot up into the air and brought it down right along the spine of the fallen bookcase. It cracked down the center. "I'm serious, Max is crazy . . ."

I interrupted, "I get it. I'll take care of it."

Max walked near me. I took Scott's advice and jumped out of his way. The wall didn't. Max started punching holes in the wall. I turned to face the rest of my class. They were seated.

With one eye on Max, I began addressing the others: "I wanted us to come here so we can talk on your terms and come to an agreement." A couple of my students started chuckling.

Max had made his way to the water cooler. He grabbed the five-gallon water bottle and rested it on his shoulder. Water was spilling out of it. He approached me.

"Ya like ta talk, don't-cha?" he said.

"Uh?"

"Ya won't like talkin' when I pour water all over yo' face."

I thought about it. He was right; I wouldn't like talking if he was pouring water on my face. What happened next? I was laughing hysterically, and Max started laughing. We laughed hard and long together.

The tension dropped.

"Will you put down the water bottle?"

He did.

"You should sit down before the staff get here and try to re-strain you."

He sat down.

Just then the staff came running in for the rescue. They looked around the room. There were holes in the walls, books everywhere, furniture lying about the place, and a five-gallon wa-ter bottle on the ground in front of me, the teacher, laughing un-controllably. All of the kids were silent and behaving.

I had a lot of paperwork. When the residents hit staff or teachers, they get arrested and charged with assault. I didn't want Max to get arrested. He came to my class the next day.

"You know what happens to residents who hit staff?" I asked.

He looked at me and nodded.

"You're still here."

He looked at me for a moment, then said, "Thanks."

## 113.

Looking across the classroom, I saw that the pounding of my heart and the shaking of my hands were shared by one of my students. I continued to read her words: "Money is scarce. We don't exchange gifts at Christmas in my family unless it's something of my older siblings' that they no longer want." No other student in the room realized that it was a peer whose secrets and life were being displayed as I read the first diary entry. The night before, I had typed it up and six other entries, cut them apart, and taped them inside my copy of *The Freedom Writers Diary* in order to validate their writing among the toughest of crowds. I hoped that every student, outside of those whose entries I read aloud, would initially believe the writing was from the book.

It had taken some time for me to move past my own road blocks in teaching at the community court and probation schools. I thought, "I can't get students to write like that. My students would never share their personal stories on paper." Once I finally broke through these fears, my students delivered on paper in ways I could have never imagined. I was so amazed by my students' writing that I asked a handful of them if I could read their work anonymously in class.

After each of them agreed, I was uncertain how to present the writing. I wanted jaws to drop, doors to open, and students to believe in themselves. It was imperative that they walk away knowing that their writing was incredibly powerful and moving. As I sat at home planning for school, I decided to type up the entries. I carefully placed them on the page where I had left off in *The Freedom Writers Diary.* The butterflies in my stomach multiplied. The more I thought out my plan, the more nervous and excited I became.

As I entered the classroom the following day, I asked my street-savvy, ankle-monitored, and saggy-clothed crew to keep their copies of the book below their desks and to simply listen as I read. I instructed them to listen intensely and to connect with the words. My mouth was dry, and I could feel my heart move like a drum through my chest. What would happen? Would students blurt out that I was reading their entries? Would everyone know it was our class's entries and not the Freedom Writers'? Would someone make fun of an entry, causing me to destroy the trust I worked so hard to earn? Or would this be the springboard to writing I was so desperately looking for?

As I read the first entry, Samantha's words unfolded a life of being raised by a mentally ill parent in poverty. Her eyes were huge, and I imagine nerves were twisting her stomach just as they were in mine. Nevertheless, Samantha smiled and I knew she was okay with my deception.

"He's an addict, and that is all he thinks about, smoking meth and himself." I caught Pedro's eye, and he too sat up straight and had a focus I had never before witnessed.

I read four more entries, and one by one those students caught my eye and we shared a nervousness and excitement I still relish.

"My friend Rachel died, and I couldn't feel more loss if she were my mom or sibling."

"I hate having to share my life with probation."

"They swung a bat, hit my arm and then my face. I got home and waited to get even with them."

Twenty minutes after the journey began, I closed my copy of *The Freedom Writers Diary*. My hands were still shaking. One of my students asked, "Hey, were those all from here?" I told the students what I had done and said that they had just heard their entries, not the Freedom Writers'.

The students were shocked: "No way." "Really?" "Let me see your book." Two students actually stood up in class, walked over to me, and grabbed the book from my hands.

"Will you read something I wrote?" "Do we get to write again today?" "When will you do this again?" This moment changed my teaching. I opened a door I have refused to close. Over the past five years, journal writing has empowered my students, and they have shared the realities of their lives outside our classroom walls. What is now an anonymous exchange across cities and states has yielded an avenue for adolescents to safely vent, connect with others, and create a passion for putting words on paper.

### 114.

*Lord, grant me the serenity*
*to accept the things I cannot change;*
*courage to change the things I can;*
*and wisdom to know the difference.*

How many times had I returned to these words in my first few years of teaching? I'd always found them comforting, but they took on a whole new salience the day I stepped into the classroom. There is so much in teaching you cannot change despite your best intentions: the kid who sizes you up ("Who's this white guy? Does he think he's going to teach me? He looks like *he* should be in high school.") and shuts you out from day one; the lesson plan that you spend hours piecing together, that you're sure will be a hit—every conceivable learning style incorporated, a multimedia extravaganza—only to have your excitement pierced in the first five minutes of class by some knucklehead's dagger: "This sucks"; the student with so much potential—that you have *plans* for—there one day and gone the next, transferred to another school because of adolescent ennui and a spineless parent who "can't stand to see my kid unhappy"; and then this one . . .

"José, see me after class."

"Why?"

"Just do it."

It was José's sophomore year, and he was fading fast. Not that he had ever demonstrated much of an interest in school, but his attitude had recently reached an all-time low: head down constantly in class, little or no work turned in. I had always felt an affinity for José—our mutual love of baseball, our shared tendency toward perfectionism (when he applied himself)—and I hated to see his enrollment on the line. I confronted him.

"What's the deal?"

No response.

"The administration's not going to keep you here if you don't turn it around."

Eyes to the floor, mumbling: "So."

"I, for one, would hate to see you go. Where do you want to end up?"

"Don't know, don't care."

The conversation continued in this futile fashion until I ended it with some pathetic, exasperated plea that fell on deaf ears. José was in a place where he couldn't be reached. There are so many things you cannot change.

Or can you?

José hung on, barely, through the end of his sophomore and the beginning of his junior years. Midway through that junior year, he was slated to attend a week-long, intensive retreat with his classmates. A few days into the retreat and unbeknownst in advance to the students, they receive a bundle of letters from friends and family. These are letters of affirmation, wherein loved ones often end up expressing feelings that have long lain dormant. Arriving after several long days of intense introspection, the letters invariably spark a flood of emotion.

Although I knew the sentiments of one of their teachers

wouldn't come close to matching the emotional punch of letters from individuals more intimate to them, I decided—as was my tradition—to jot off a short, personalized note to each of the students. I even threw one in there for unreachable José.

Not surprisingly, José returned from the retreat to a mountain of overdue assignments.

"José," I said.

"What?"

"Stick around a second," I said, although I was already regretting my words because there couldn't be a worse time than the passing period to try to snag a struggling student. As I quickly scanned my grade book, barely finding time for eye contact, I said, "Hey, listen, I hope the retreat went well, but you've still got a ton of work to catch up on."

"Yeah, Mister."

"I mean, there's the book club assignment . . ."

"I know."

"Then you've got these movie-viewing notes I haven't seen yet . . ."

"I know."

"And the timeline activity . . ."

"Yep."

"Ya gonna get these taken care of?"

"Yeah, Mister." Then, just as the feverish pace of the passing period was about to sweep him out into the hallway and usher in the next batch of hyperactive hormones, I heard, "Hey, Mister."

(Distractedly) "Yeah."

"I'm just trying to do *this*." And there, tucked neatly inside the laminated cover of his U.S. history binder, was the following—words that I had included in my letters to all the students in the hopes that they might find in them some of the comforting value I did:

*Lord, grant me the serenity*
*to accept the things I cannot change;*

*courage to change the things I can;*
*and wisdom to know the difference.*

So much of teaching is a grind—an occupation in which, in the words of Woody Allen, "Eighty percent of success is showing up." Often you feel as if you're furiously spinning your wheels, trying to please the harshest critics but never really knowing to what effect. But once every so often, that furious pace slams to a halt, the barriers you've created to protect yourself are torn down, and you are confronted with the profound reality that lies at the heart of the teaching profession: the powerful prospect of meaningfully impacting young people's lives.

José and I exchanged a brief glance, but he didn't say anything further. He didn't need to. At that moment, we understood each other. It's as if we were both saying, "Thank you."

But just as quickly as things had slowed down, the pace picked right back up again. José gathered up his binder, strolled out into the hall, and flowed back into the rhythm of another school day.

## 115.

The wait was over.

I grinned and held up the manila envelope. Energy immediately began building in my students. Everyone crowded around me trying to get a peek at his or her letter first. I held up the first letter and said, "I have a letter for Miguel."

Miguel stood up. He wore sagging khakis, a long shirt, and spotless tennis shoes. In his right earlobe was an oversize earring. He swaggered to the front of the class. "Hey, that's my girl writing to me," he said. He took the letter from my hand and pressed it to his chest. Then he turned, looked at his classmates, and grinned. Friends teased him, and he told them they were just jealous. Smiling, he returned to his desk in an exaggerated stroll.

One by one, the letters went out and the class quieted. Those who didn't get a letter were crushed and looked at a neighbor's.

"Okay, class. We are going to group up in clusters of four students. I want you to pick the best letter from your group and put it on the bulletin board for Back to School Night. I want your parents to know about this project and how we are learning cultural tolerance through connecting to students who are different from you. Be prepared to defend your choice."

One by one, each student read his or her letter. Students laughed, asked questions, and listened. In the end, the students would score each letter and discuss which letter was best.

Words my students had never heard before appeared on our Word Board—hick, flannel, rural, mud womping. When it was time to write a reply, each student dug deep to write the best letter that he or she could possibly send. As time went on and letters were exchanged between my high school students in a southern California city and students living in rural West Virginia, "Sincerely yours," was replaced with "Love" or "Your friend."

One of the eleventh graders from West Virginia wrote about how she could no longer see her father. Her parents had divorced and both had remarried. New families were formed and she was now a stepsister. The girl's father didn't seem to have time for her anymore, and she felt like a guest in her own home. Her pen pal, who rarely wrote more than a few sentences, began writing with an intensity I had never seen in him before. He told his pen pal that he understood how she felt. He said he sometimes felt like a stranger in his own home.

He told his pen pal, a girl he had never seen, that his father died two years before. He understood how his new friend in West Virginia felt because he could never see his father again either. Now that his mother had remarried, there were times he felt unwanted and contemplated leaving. When he had told his mother how he felt, she reassured him, and the letter ended with a certain hope that all would be fine.

In another letter, a student from West Virginia wrote that he was gay and that his boyfriend had treated him badly. My ninth-grade girl began writing a loving letter back to her pen pal saying, "You are better than that. You should not let anybody make you feel badly about who you are." She shared a story about a friend of hers who regretted taking abuse from her boyfriend. She signed her letter "Love," and her name.

These pen pals, who came from such different cultures and homes, had discovered their common experiences and related to one another as humans without regard to appearance, dialect, or race. Something more powerful than a simple writing project was happening. Students were making friends, sharing feelings and stories of growth with students across the country.

Now, nearly a year later, students from both schools are planning to visit their pen pals. A second group of ninth graders are now writing to students in West Virginia, and some of last year's students continue writing even though they no longer have me as a teacher.

During Franklin High School's spring break in April, students from a rural West Virginia community are leaving their homes to visit our city in southern California, a place with nearly a half million people who speak more than twenty languages. While Mr. Wallace's students are here, they will attend classes at Roosevelt High School and experience what it is like to move around a campus that has forty-five hundred students. They will meet community volunteers who have come to the school to teach about the importance of cultural tolerance—Holocaust survivors, Killing Fields survivors, and a trauma surgeon from a local hospital who shares how he saved the life of a gang member only to watch him go back to the streets to shoot others. This city has seen too many young people die because of gang violence and poor choices. Those who can, teach tolerance.

The following week, a group of my students will journey to West Virginia to attend classes at Franklin High, see the rural countryside, build a campfire, share stories, and work on a farm for a day. I ask my students how they would feel hiking the Appalachian Trail if they were alone and lost. "Do they have bears?" one student asked. I nodded "yes." This student's troubled face said it all. Through their shared letters my students were ready for an adventure. They were prepared to take risks.

I ask if they think a student from Franklin High would be scared to be on the corner of 101st and Hawthorn at 11 at night. One of the boys shouts out, "Hell, yes! I'd be afraid, too." Laughter erupts.

Both groups of students will be leaving the security of their familiar surroundings, family, and friends in order to gain a new perspective about the people who make up this country. They are prepared to embark on a trail that will bring them to a new understanding because of the relationships they have developed through writing.

### 116.

Sweat dripped down my forehead as rivulets of paint ran down the wall. I wiped my brow with one hand, and with the other I used a roller to stop the paint from running. But there was nothing I could do about the midday Miami sun trying to fry my students, or about the two reporters asking intrusive questions about my students' home life, school experiences, and families.

The students were handling the press much better than I ever could, and they did not utter any complaints about the heat. Some, in fact, seemed quite at home in front of the camera. It never dawned on me that a small experiment in Brownsville, one of the poorest neighborhoods in Miami, could be this special.

Others had proposed murals at my school, but to no avail. I'm not sure what it was that changed my principal's mind this time. Perhaps it was the Freedom Writers brand, the equal rights theme, the money donated for materials—or maybe it was the breeze of the principal's upcoming retirement. Whatever it was, her decision afforded my students and me the opportunity to share a moment of giddiness the instant we rolled on the first layers of paint.

I have been painting murals for over a decade and wanted to share the experience with my students. The process first began more than three weeks earlier, when we sat down together to discuss the themes and images we would include in our mural. I gave one of the quickest Art 101 courses ever delivered to a group of high school students. I explained that art tends to have symbols that represent ideas, and we spoke about which images we felt would be the most important to portray.

After much discussion, we decided that the focal point of the mural would be a child leaning over a desk, writing in his journal. We agreed that to the child's right there would be an old Freedom Riders bus. Some students thought it was vital to have excerpts of a student's journal entry, so we decided to superimpose it over faint images on the piece. The elements took little time to think up, and, admittedly, they seem a bit obvious.

The component that the students tackled in the sweltering heat was the least conspicuous but one of the most important: the wide, open iron gates that would frame the mural. When I'd asked what the iron gates represented in their lives, my students had raised their hands eagerly. Some said the open gates represented freedom and a way out of prison through education. One student said that the open gates represented desegregation. As the discussion intensified, one shared with the group that she was living in a housing project where the gates were locked at the same time every night, so no one could get in or out. The enforced curfew was a severe security measure in this dangerous neighborhood. Education, she said, would be her key out of the projects.

Her words were like a splash of ice water in my face. Sometimes, I forget how far removed my students' lives are from anything I have experienced. Staying open to their stories has made me aware of many unpalatable truths. A large percentage of my students have parents in prison. Some of my students are abused; others are hungry.

I recently discovered that one of my students is homeless. He is usually positive and focused, and the only signs that anything was awry in his life were his consistent tardiness to school and his rare outbursts of anger. Discovering my student is homeless helped me realize that just when I think I have it all figured out, these young storytellers prove me wrong. They live in a world where "making something of yourself" is not a given, not entirely expected.

Today my students shrugged it all off enthusiastically. One girl's smile made it evident she was not thinking about her upcoming deployment in the U.S. Army. She left her worries in her journal. A boy next to her, the stocky football player in the group, accidentally stained a friend's shoe with paint. His friend said, "Nothing to worry about," cleaned it quickly, and carried on with his jokes. The hour was almost over. The time passed so fast that I could hardly believe it. We defied Miami's inferno and painted symbols of hope on one of the school's gray walls.

### 117.

I stepped away from my teaching career in 2004 to play music in Europe. Discussing the same sonnets, working within a set curriculum for the eleventh consecutive year, lacked the intrinsic appeal of life on the road, playing clubs in Amsterdam, Florence, Milan, and Paris. Did this choice signal my failure as a teacher? Being the son of a principal, I thought maybe it did. But I sought solace in the notion that I had at least become a halfway decent guitar player. After two years of stale beer, fast food, late nights, dirty clubs, doe-eyed girls, dial-tone promoters, grumpy soundmen, dead-end shows, dead-end conversations, dead-end dead ends, I was done. The dream was reduced to the chase, and I was out.

In my story, "out" meant back, back home. I was over thirty, unprepared to return to the classroom as I remembered it, and looking forward to starting a new "career." I bought a small building with the intention of opening a business—a music and sound studio. Located in Lawrenceville, a historic, working-class neighborhood in Pittsburgh, Blackberry Way Studio existed in a world removed from my life as a public school educator. To focus on making my new business a success, I closed the door on teaching—or so I thought.

As I discovered, building a business from nothing requires a lot of work. There were so many things happening at once, I did not spare a moment for nostalgia—no daydreams of desks and chalkboards, class bells, and recess for me. Besides, would you reminisce about times past, replay hard choices made, if you had just invested every material thing you owned into a new venture? Even the building, the physical structure, of Blackberry Way was of interest to me.

Fast-forward three years. I'm still making music and running a business, and I'm teaching. Who are my employees and what do I teach? Simply, I sign my own paycheck, and I aim to teach the skill that I hope to help all my students master: the ability to think critically. The primary difference between my past experience as a high school teacher and my present experience as a business owner is that man. I am now practicing in the present what I only preached in the past. I've descended from my ivory tower to mingle with the locals.

I never imagined my professional life would be as it is today. We work hard, often much longer hours than I ever did as a classroom teacher. We frequently take on less exciting corporate media projects, recording and engineering sound work by day. But at night, when all worldly responsibilities have been met, we come alive. Evening and early-morning hours are spent producing music—all kinds of music—because music is legitimate self-expression, regardless of genre.

I have learned much from my most recent students, now

more commonly referred to as "employees" or "clients." The curriculum has changed. No longer do my classes explore history's great works of literature. Now, critical thinking is encouraged through open discussions of several of life's major themes: Birth and death, building a life, are mandatory; love and hate are equally real but not equally powerful; humor can save; the practices of authentic self-expression and self-worth are directly correlated. Nowadays, I think of education from a different perspective. I think that my role as teacher and my role as student are not mutually exclusive but are unfolding simultaneously, which to me is the definition of a lifelong engagement in education. Of course, this is something my father taught me by example years ago; but for many students, including me, a lesson must be experienced before it is internalized.

At present, I smile every time I provide directions to Blackberry Studio. Indubitably, I left the traditional classroom in the past, and I replaced sonnets for sixteen bars on a "hot" verse. But I never stopped being a teacher because I learned that English poets and rappers are equally witty, deft with diction, and vulgar. And in the end, we all, even Shakespeare, have a little bit of "rock star" in us.

### 118.

A visible surge of excitement rippled through the impatient sixth graders when two school buses finally rumbled up the tree-lined drive. Young children from their sister school bounced out of the bus.

"I can't wait to see Abdi again," Jack said. He elbowed his friend Steve when the tiny kindergartener finally appeared at the bus door. "There he is. I knew he'd make it," Jack whispered.

Steve, busy looking for his own buddy, ignored the poke. Soon another little boy, in a red shirt and jeans, climbed out of the bus, and Steve's eyes lit up. Mohammed had come too. One hundred and five children, many of them refugees, bounced off the two buses and stared wide-eyed at the beautiful campus.

Abdi paused a moment on the bus step and scanned the group until he spotted Jack. A wide toothy grin spread across his face. He gave a shy quick wave then turned his attention to the teacher, who directed his classmates into the building.

Both schools had worked together all year, and this was a final celebration of the remarkable, though unlikely, partnership. The two schools involved couldn't be more different, one a tough inner-city elementary school, the other a prestigious private one. This year had proved that difference didn't matter.

Buddies quickly found one another and set off across the campus hand in hand. Jack and Abdi chose sidewalk art for their first activity and welcomed the warm sun and soft breeze. "What are you going to draw?" asked Jack. Without answering, Abdi grabbed a piece of blue chalk and knelt down on the cement walkway. A scrawling flower quickly took shape, and before Jack knew it, Abdi was standing back and admiring his handiwork. They soon headed for the next activity. No longer quiet or shy, Abdi skipped ahead, eager for what came next. Jack followed close behind. They called to Steve and Mohammed, who were waiting in line for the parachute game. The increasing comfort level of all the students was apparent. Everyone enjoyed lunch, complete with a visit from an ice cream truck, and a closing slide show featuring the visits the two schools had had throughout the year. Each young visitor was delighted with the small stuffed "study buddy" they all received as they climbed on their bus to go home.

It's hard to say what part of that day was the highlight. From beginning to end it was a success, even more than we had hoped. I watched teachers, parents, and students from very different teaching and learning backgrounds enjoy one another in the sincerest sort of way.

One could see that our sixth graders had truly found their voices and their passions through the year by searching, researching, and thinking about the difference one person can make in the world. I watched Abdi, Mohammed, Jack, and Steve wave as long as they could see each other. Jack commented as he watched his friends leave, "I think there must be two kinds of learning. There is learning the facts and there is learning from the facts. This year I have learned in both ways."

In the end this experience was about much more than games, ice cream, or stuffed animals. It was about students getting outside of themselves to learn of, and to become involved in, the plight of less fortunate individuals. It was about twelve-year-olds understanding that sometimes humanity exists under inhumane circumstances. They realized the untapped potential that is within those of different backgrounds and situations. They also came to believe that they personally could make a difference, even at age twelve. These goals had been both worthy and reachable. It had been a great year, and I hated to see it come to a close.

### 119.

I was uncertain what effect taking my students to Heifer Ranch would have. They were on their way to live one day in the life of a poor person in one of six poverty-stricken populations. Several of them had already experienced homelessness, and many more knew what being hungry felt like. As we rode from the city to the rebel-flag-draped porches of the countryside, I reminded myself of those who were already in the midst of these struggles. One of them, Zaphora, was a survivor of two suicide attempts and grew up as her father spent time in prison. She lived with her aunt but begged her mother to let her live with her. Her mother chose drugs and lacked the will to tell her daughter so. Once she said "yes" to Zaphora's begging and told her to go inside her aunt's house to pack her things. After doing so, Zaphora came out and found her mother gone. What did she have to learn about poverty or loss?

We arrived at a working farm where water buffalo cooled themselves in a small pond and a camel chomped on hay. After a brief tour, the group was split into six "villages"—Thailand, Zambia, Guatemala, Appalachia, urban slums, and refugees. Resources were unevenly distributed. Guatemala had water rights, Thais enjoyed a good quantity of rice, Zambia had carrots and potatoes, and Appalachians could barter with their wood. The refugees and the urban slum dwellers had only their labor. My anxiety over Zaphora deepened when she was randomly selected to join one-fifth of the world's population as someone who lived in what resembled chicken coops in the urban slum area.

Mirroring reality, in the Heifer Ranch simulation Zaphora and nine others were "pregnant." Their condition was indicated by a water balloon in an apron that they were to wear for the night. While other students flailed their arms and hammed for their friends when sent to the slums, Zaphora remained stoic, showing a smile without exaggeration. In class she listens without speaking but amazes us with her diary entries. She has everyone's respect because of her confidence and honesty. As the Thais hired the desperate poor to steal the Zambians' carrots and potatoes (the Zambians wouldn't trade, opting for self-sufficiency), Zaphora waited in the slums "for the sake of the child." The raid being successful, she got her milk and a small portion of half-cooked rice, potatoes, and carrots. As the sun set, her mood lightened even though she faced the prospect of sleeping on a dirt floor in a shanty with cardboard walls and no doors.

The night brought more arguing over resources. Because the Thais had taken advantage of others' desperation, especially the refugees', and used their own bargaining skills to commandeer everyone's resources, all of my students ate in the Thai village. Because Appalachia gave Thailand all of the wood for the huge cooking fire, the urban slum was dark and cold when Zaphora's group returned. At first, the sight of the four sheds that constituted the urban slums provoked astonishment—no running water, no lights, an outhouse roofed with strips of automobile tires.

As darkness fell, the sight of their shelters brought true horror. Being cold in the middle of the woods was not what their normal Friday nights looked like. The cheerleaders were wondering how the football team was doing, and others surely longed to be at the fair eating funnel cakes and flirting. Many out of the fifteen in Zaphora's group sought the comfort of Guatemala's concrete floor, walls, and closed doors and windows or Thailand's raised huts.

I waited to see what Zaphora's move was going to be. She looked at me and asked, "We can't change families?"

Taken by surprise, I could only offer, "People in these situations will take something better if they can get it. If they want to sleep on someone's floor rather than here, that's probably a fair picture of how it really works."

"They shouldn't be able to do that. And there should be a curfew," she said.

I agreed but stood by the Heifer Village's philosophy and rules for this real-world simulation. As long as there was a chaperone, everyone could pile up in one room if that's what they decided to do. Zaphora slept with a friend on the ground. As I drifted off to sleep in the shelter next to theirs, I heard chatter and giggling and rested easily.

This was the first glimpse I had gotten of her personality. She wrote honestly but was agonizingly quiet in class. Perhaps it was her dirty white uniform shirt or her aggression that lay just past the meek smile that kept her silent.

As the battery lantern dimmed, I saw her sense of belonging and justice meld. Despite her deep disappointments and pain, she held on to an idealistic view of community and responsibility. Zaphora was the only one of the ten "mothers" who gave birth and cared for her child. The families of the others didn't obtain milk, or the "mothers" burst their own or others' water balloons, thus failing to come to term. According to the village rules, if a group's mother lost her child, a twenty-minute period of silence should symbolize the tragedy. None of my students went so far.

At Heifer Ranch, Zaphora's real-life experiences of abandonment and powerlessness entered a larger context. As a teacher, I am often torn between wanting my students to delve into their pasts and identities and wanting them to protect their private lives. But if students do not know who they are and what shapes them, how can they decide to change anything? Zaphora showed me the value of such assignments. The lesson she learned goes far beyond the school's curriculum. As I saw her with her water balloon on the bus ride home, I thought, "What a good mother."

## 120.

The skinny, redheaded fourteen-year-old freshman was so shy that most of her classmates had never heard her talk and even fewer knew her name.

When she walked into my classroom on the first day of school, Tara slipped quietly into a desk, hoping that no one would notice her. But she stood out. Dressed in a perfect pressed skirt, she was the lone female in the class, and she was the only white student.

As I got to know Tara, I couldn't help but wonder how she felt, forced to take my public speaking course. Had it been her choice, she would have taken a class much more suited to her personality, like computer science. But the state of Texas requires high school students to take speech before they receive their diploma. So Tara and I were stuck together.

I looked into her panic-stricken eyes as I outlined the requirements of the course, which included making a number of speeches in front of the class, and I was transported back in time. Suddenly, I was in another class where I sat, much like Tara, skinny and shy. The class was sophomore English, and the teacher was telling us we would have to write poems and read them aloud to the class.

Our school is small, so I teach speech and drama and direct the school plays. In Texas, everything is a competition. From football to one-act plays, nothing is too big or small to escape the Texas tug-of-war.

This year, our competition play had a role for a twelve-year-old shy girl who comes to live with relatives. It was the perfect role for Tara. But first, I had to convince her to do it.

At the end of class the next day, I asked her to stay. Tara trembled and in her small, timid voice asked, "Did I do something wrong?"

"No," I assured her.

I stood in the doorway, waving kids good-bye. As the students left the classroom, Tara searched in vain for an escape.

When the last student filed out, I went to Tara and told her about the play and the character I wanted her to portray.

"I can't do that," Tara stammered.

"I won't take 'no' for an answer and will see you this afternoon at rehearsals."

Rehearsals began. No Tara. Disheartened, I started rehearsals without her.

A few minutes later, I looked up, and there sat Tara in the back row.

I motioned her to come onstage. Remembering that I would not take "no" for an answer, she made her way to the stage as if being led to her execution.

Tara gingerly took the script and read the lines of her character in a voice so low that I had to stand next to her to hear. She finished and hurried off the stage in tears, terrorized by the whole experience.

The next day, as rehearsal started, Tara walked in. My jaw dropped. She came up to the stage and in her timid voice said, "I want to be in the play."

Finally, after weeks and weeks of practice, it was time to perform the play. Our only hope was not to embarrass ourselves. We had no vision of advancing to the next level of competition. Our school had never advanced in the fifty years it had been entering this competition.

Tara and her fellow cast members gave the performance of a lifetime.

At the end of the day, we sat in the auditorium awaiting the results. Although we knew we had done well, our hopes were tempered.

The contest manager began to announce the two schools that would advance to the next level.

Tara suddenly yelled, "Mr. K, we're advancing!"

The surprises weren't quite finished.

The shy, skinny, redheaded fourteen-year-old who had been too scared to tell her teacher "no" won the award for Best Actress.

Next year, when it came time to begin rehearsals, Tara was the first student there. She participated every year until she graduated. Each time, she was named Best Actress.

The other day, Tara came to see me while she was home from college, where she is majoring in theater.

"Mr. K," she said, "I am going to be a drama teacher."

## 121.

"Oh no, please do not call on me," I thought. I hated reading aloud. "Is he going to call on me?" Everyone else in the class reads well, which only makes matters worse. "Why is he doing this to me?" It was my turn next. The girl who sat next to me read with fluidity. "I don't want to go," I thought. "Let me go to the restroom and just wait there until everything is done." I clutched my fists under my legs, held on to my chair for dear life, and awaited disaster.

A three-paragraph page in a book that should have taken one

minute took me five. "I want to leave," I thought. "Get me out of this classroom. I know the kids are holding in their laughs." I concluded that I was weird, strange, and different from everyone else and had a right to be quiet and reserved.

From when I was a little boy to adulthood, I suffered from stuttering. I avoided many "playing the dozens" or "cracking on others" environments that children love to get involved in because I did not want people to talk about something so sensitive to me. "Your mother was concerned that people were going to misunderstand you" was a comment I often heard from a dear friend of the family. "Boy, you sure need to learn how to talk," was a comment I often heard. I became so numb to the laughter and to being singled out as a "freak" by so many of my peers that I closed myself off from the world.

"My son stutters and has a hard time pronouncing his words. So can you work with him?" These were the words I heard when I met one of my students and his mother at the beginning of a school year. "The kids pick on him, and he clams up at times." I looked at the concerned mother with worry on her face—a mother who seemed to have had to fight her son's emotional battles and bandage his psychological wounds many times. She reminded me of my mom, who had equipped me by encouraging me, "Son, you are special and gifted in your own way. Don't let people tell you you are not."

I examined the young man from head to toe—a frail young man, no more than 90 pounds. His greenish hazel eyes spoke a message of desperation that I will always remember. He held his head down, and his weak, sweaty handshake reaffirmed for me that I had a purpose to fulfill in his life.

"Son, don't you ever let anyone tell you that you cannot speak." I remember pulling him to the side and saying, "You will one day be one of the greatest orators this world has seen." His glassy eyes became fixed on mine. He listened intently as I confronted him and charged him to work through his impediment. He listened and became.

He became confident, assured, and determined to speak so that others in the class would listen—and they did.

"Ooooh that boy is going somewhere" and "I want my daughter to be like him" were comments I heard after this young man presented a project. He spoke with great confidence, poise, and power. The applause he received from his classmates lit up his face. He appeared radiant, exuberant, and full of joy. It reminded me of the speech and poetry contests I'd won and the feelings I'd felt.

From being told that I speak with great articulation to being a sought-after speaker in my church and other arenas, I am grateful for my stutter. I have overcome much of the impediment by taking time when I speak and having confidence in myself. Many of my students never know that I battle such an impediment until I tell them. I have heard comments like "You speak so well," "You are so proper," and "You have a gift to speak so that others will listen to every word that comes from your mouth." But this would never have been the case without experiencing this impediment. Though it had the capability of impeding my success as a person and as an educator, it has proven to be the impetus to help me be the walking testimony to that hazel, green-eyed student who now has a sense of hope.

## 122.

"I'm sorry. Although I've passed, I feel I've let you down." In over sixteen years of teaching, I'd never had a student say anything like that.

It's about fifteen minutes before the end of the last class of the year for one of my eighth-grade Spanish classes, and as is my custom, I let my students know what their final grades will be on their report cards. Reina comes to my desk. I tell her that she has passed for the year, and I wish her the best for her high school career. After I finish giving the grade information to the rest of the class, Reina raises her hand and asks if she may speak with me. I call her to my desk and what she says surprises me.

Reina goes on to tell me that her mom is a single parent and that she has been raised primarily by her Italian grandmother. She tells me that she really never knew her father and that when she was finally able to contact him, he didn't want anything to do with her. She tells me that he is Hispanic and because of his indifference and neglect, she has held an inner grudge against anything related to the Spanish language and Hispanic culture. She goes on to say that her mom insisted that she take Spanish because of its value in today's society. I am taken aback by her story. I tell Reina that any father should be proud to have her as a daughter and that she has learned more Spanish this past year than she realizes. She gives me a hug and goes back to her seat.

Reina's story actually began in November of 2007. I was going to miss four days of classes with my students, and I advised them to treat the substitute teacher with the same respect that they give me. Naturally, in every class, the students wanted to know why I wouldn't be there. I let them know that I was going to Long Beach, California, to attend the Freedom Writers Institute. I asked if any of them had seen the movie *Freedom Writers*. In each of my classes, more than half of the students raised their hands. I then asked those who had seen the movie what they thought about it and what it meant to them. Reina told us that she owned the *Freedom Writers* DVD and had watched it numerous times. After class, I called Reina to my desk and asked why she had watched the movie so often. She told me that she loved the movie and that she identified herself with the character Eva (Maria in real life). She also told me that she was excited that I was going to the Institute.

Reina and I had many chats throughout the year. She was always excited to talk and read about anything related to the Freedom Writers. So when I told her that I was going back to California in April for another session, her eyes lit up. When I returned, I told Reina that I had met Maria. I told her how Maria was such a dynamic person and how she turned her life around to become the successful person that she is. I also told her that I brought her back a copy of *The Freedom Writers Diary* signed by Maria. Maria also graciously sent along a little inspirational note to Reina. I presented the book and note to Reina in her English class. She was so happy and proud, and the class gave her a healthy round of applause. I told Reina that as an English assignment, I thought it would be very appropriate for her to send Maria a thank-you letter and to let Maria know a little about herself.

In her letter, Reina told Maria, "I've changed a lot in the past year. I used to constantly be in trouble, getting into fights and thinking I was so cool. But I was only lying to myself. The life I was living was a living hell, and eventually I realized I deserved better." She went on to say, "I have so much I want to do in life. Travel the world. Write a book . . . I can't waste my days away by getting my face busted in and engaging in stupid arguments when I could be doing something to improve the world. Freedom Writers taught me a lot about myself and life in general."

I believe in the words of child advocate Father Chris Riley, who said, "If you save one child, you save the world." Reina just might be that one child. Certainly, any father would be proud of that.

### 123.

A little over a decade ago, I knew I had to make a change. I realized that my life of crime risked not only my life but also the lives of my two daughters. The restless nights, having to always look over my shoulder and watch my back, the houses, cars, and women my lifestyle afforded me weren't worth my daughters. I turned away from my "New Jack City" and became an educator.

I serve in a city that reminds me of my hometown, but now I am on the right side of the tracks.

When my students talk about not having a father in their lives, I step in and listen to them as the man that their lives are missing. "Damn, living without a father is hard," one of my students said one day. "I mean no one to talk to about males, or to give me advice." We have developed a bond. She's always honest with me; she always keeps it real. "Having all those kids, the baby mama drama and all that other crazy shit, I can see how he did illegal crime to get that money, even though I know in my heart that he could have done things legit. I know that there are dads out there that work two and three jobs to support their families. To be a black man, it's hard; and often you're not given many choices," she said. "But the bottom line is, what he did made me who I am today, and that is a student who is determined to be successful."

When a former student told me, "Mr. B, I have self-esteem issues. I don't live with my mom. I live with my aunt," I knew there was more beneath the surface, a pain that was scabbed over and festering. As I got to know her more, I learned she had been repeatedly molested by her stepfather. "It happened until I was about the age of fourteen or fifteen," she told me. "At the age of sixteen, I was finally woman enough to tell my mom. After she took me to the doctors, they couldn't tell if I had been raped. I lost her as a best friend."

In each of these stories I felt remorse and shame. Before turning my life around, I hustled illegally to put bread on the table to feed my daughters. I had sisters and aunts who were put on the streets and abandoned by my mother and grandmother just to please a man. I knew firsthand what my students struggled with. I told them both, "Use these personal tragedies as treasures to resurrect your life." When they asked me how I turned my life around, I told them I kept a journal, found hobbies, read self-help books, listened to CDs by some of the world's best motivational authors, prayed, and went to church.

And I told them to find a cause worth giving time to—a mentoring program like Big Brothers Big Sisters or other grassroots self-help initiatives that would empower them to heal through helping others heal. But first, I told them, healing begins with you. Self-affirmation is one of the biggest psychological and emotional boosters that the "greats" say they use. So I told them to talk to themselves daily, encourage themselves when they fall, and always, always get back up. I told them: "Think about all the positive things that you deserve, and those things will be drawn to your life."

In many of my workshops I tell the story of how, as a child, I wanted to be a policeman or a firefighter to help people. Since finding out what I love to do as an educator, I have expressed to my students that my career in teaching and counseling rewards me with success because it was what I was gifted in. Even as a student in college before the money came, I was always working or volunteering in some capacity as a student ambassador, mentor, counselor, or teacher. I want my exiting seniors to remember me saying, "You can only be what you were born and destined to be, so find your passion and live through your dreams. Live each of your days as if you have only one day to live."

## 124.

The smell of marijuana greets me at the door, followed closely by a disheveled woman. She asks what I want, and I tell her that I have come for the girls. She calls to them: "The lady is here." The girls dart to the door, excited and expectant, each asking what the plans are for the evening and what they will eat.

In this neighborhood grown men run around playing with toy guns only weeks after a neighborhood teen was shot to death on his front porch. In this neighborhood eight- and nine-year-old girls discuss rape in the way other girls might discuss the latest episode of *Hannah Montana*. I know of an alcoholic grandmother who has custody of her thirteen-year-old granddaughter. Here, drugs are rampant. The apartment complex grounds are littered with "Little Hugs" bottles and cigarette butts.

How does hope emerge from such a place? It comes with a field trip to a local college. It comes from meeting a woman who is vice-mayor. It comes from witnessing a performance of the Alvin Ailey Dance Company. It comes when the girls do community service, perform for elderly residents at a nursing home, or march proudly in a college homecoming parade.

I am often asked why I meet with the girls one day a week after working full-time with middle school students. I was a little girl once, I reply. There were women who gave my life meaning and who inspired me: my grandmother and mother, who believed in the power of books and reading though neither had a formal education; the teachers in my segregated public schools who valued me as a learner and believed, even in those tough times, that "education is the great equalizer"; the Sunday school teachers and ladies of the community who reinforced behaviors taught at home and at school.

The wonder that these girls express at things that I take for granted constantly amazes me. I am reminded of the Dr. Seuss book *Oh, the Places You'll Go!* and am convinced that these girls will go places that they never imagined for themselves. I am thrilled to encourage and inspire them to go to the "places they will go."

### 125.

The phone rang, and I instantly recognized the phone number of one of the high schools in my community.

"This is Mrs. Daley, Jamal's former special-ed teacher, and I want to make sure you know all about him."

Great, I thought.

Jamal had actually been doing well in the program, but any

additional insights into him would be helpful. His teacher went on.

"You know by now how difficult he is and what a failure he will be in your program. I know he won't last with you much longer either. But I need you to know that he is definitely not returning to my classroom."

My interactions with Jamal had been so radically different from those Mrs. Daley described that I didn't quite know what to say. But the call reinvigorated me to do all I could to figure out how Jamal could succeed.

A couple of years ago, juvenile justice asked me to start and run a program for suspended youth on probation. The minimal goal was to keep some of them off the streets for a few hours each day. The mission sounded simple enough, but the reality turned out to be complicated. All of the students were complex individuals dealing with multiple systems inadequately meeting their needs. It was time to try all the magic tricks I had up my sleeve and hope for miracles.

That's how I found myself driving a group of young men to Arkansas, hoping that the decrepit county van would actually make it there and back. Jamal had been ordered by the judge to attend the day program and had entered with little hope of succeeding.

We were going to Little Rock to visit Central High School, the site of the now famous integration of public schools. We would also be viewing the Emancipation Proclamation on display as part of the fiftieth anniversary of integration. In reality, the boys wanted to go because we were also camping out and fishing.

We toured the school, visited the museum, and fished. That evening around the campfire, Jamal was quieter than usual. He eventually spoke.

"We didn't catch any fish."

"Well, we'll try again tomorrow," I said. I was disappointed because I had been hoping for bigger responses to the history we had just witnessed.

"It's pretty cool, what those people did at the high school," Jamal went on. The moon was bright and illuminated his young and hardened face.

"Yes, it was," I replied.

Jamal attempted for the last time that evening to bait his hook and throw a line out into the river. As I stared at his silhouette against the sky, I found myself hoping he would not become one of the three thousand youth in our community this year to commit a crime and drop out of school.

We got home in one piece.

Once back, Jamal couldn't stop talking about the trip. Desegregation, slavery, camping, and fishing all blended together. He was beginning to trust adults again and perhaps even believe in learning in the most nontraditional way.

I dream of the day Jamal returns to a classroom like Mrs. Daley's as an example of perseverance and hope.

### 126.

Perhaps I'll never know how my assistant principal knew about my hopes and dreams for my students—that they may have the opportunity to expand their worldviews through life experiences of their very own. I was asked if I would be interested in researching a possible student trip to Washington, D.C. The thought of taking my students anywhere outside the city limits was pretty astonishing to me. I quickly got in touch with a travel agency that worked exclusively with school groups to plan what would possibly be the trip of a lifetime for many of my students. After I received all of the information, I quickly sprang into action. But I needed to be honest: A majority of my students came from households that simply didn't have the disposable income to plan family vacations, let alone a vacation for just one family member. So throughout the year my kids and I fund-raised as if there were no tomorrow, successfully raising enough money so that their parents would have to pay only $200 plus the cost of food and souvenirs.

The day after school let out in June, my assistant principal and I herded twelve of our kids into a stretch limousine to take us from our impoverished neighborhood to the airport across the city. After taking a red-eye flight direct from Las Vegas, we hit the ground running on our tour of historic Washington, D.C. Throughout our time in this city, we visited the Smithsonian museums, Arlington Cemetery, the Vietnam War Memorial, Mount Vernon, the Holocaust Memorial Museum, and the Lincoln Memorial. My kids were so excited. For most of them, it was their first time on a plane, their first time away from home, and even their first time on vacation.

After we had spent what felt like half the day in the Holocaust Museum, we took some time to reflect upon all that we had seen and felt while we were there. I was filled with pride because my kids were so well mannered and respectful the entire time we wandered through these powerful exhibits. After we were done and were able to collect our thoughts, one of my students, Marcus, who was of African descent, came up to me and said, "You know, Mister, I always thought it was only my people who suffered the most throughout history. I didn't realize that others had suffered as much. I can now see why we study history." When I asked him why, he simply said what I had been trying to get across to my students all year: "So we don't repeat the mistakes of others, and we learn to respect one another for our differences." Marcus's realization alone, I thought, made the entire trip and all of our hard work worthwhile for me.

But, as usual, my kids were about to impress me once again. The following day we went to visit the Lincoln Memorial. In their seventh- and eighth-grade social studies classes, my students had learned a lot about both Abraham Lincoln and Dr. Martin Luther King Jr. When we got to the steps of the Lincoln Memorial, I began to talk about the accomplishments of President Lincoln and how Dr. King gave his famous "I Have a Dream" speech on the steps of this memorial. When I was done, a group of my kids went charging up the many steps to get a picture of Lincoln's statue. As I turned around on the steps, I realized that not all of my students were bounding up the stairs ahead of me. As I looked for my stragglers, I noticed that a couple of my kids had stayed behind to slowly walk up with another student who was having some difficulty with the steep steps. I told them that we could walk around the corner to take the elevator, but they said, "No, Janet wants to walk up the stairs." I asked Janet if she was sure about it, and she replied, "Yes, sir, I want to climb the steps that Dr. King spoke on so that I could have equal rights, too." Janet had braces on her legs and also walked with two crutches. That hot June afternoon, Janet became my hero, much the same as Dr. King was hers.

With each trip that I have offered to my students, I have received from my students much more in return. As my students learn and explore their own humanity, I find my own life to be enriched beyond imagination. What have I learned? That's simple: There's no doubt that we face many challenges in life. However, it's not the challenges that matter. What matters most are the relationships we forge with one another and the experiences we share. We truly are companions on a journey. And my journey has led me to teaching second grade at an inner-city school in Las Vegas, Nevada.

### 127.

Manie was fifteen years old, tall and lanky with dark wavy hair and an olive complexion bespeaking his Middle Eastern roots. He was a talkative guy with a sense of humor that went above the heads of most of his peers, which was why he got along better

with adults than with people his own age. Diagnosed with a learning disability and partial hearing loss, he was held back a grade in his primary years, setting him apart from the others. But it was his right eye that attracted the most attention, because it was slightly smaller than the left and without sight. Often harassed by his classmates, Manie put up a good front. With adults, his tactic was a jovial veneer, but with his peers, he employed biting, sarcastic comments. Despite these challenges, he was an impressive artist and loved to draw. Wherever he went, he carried his sketchbook under his arm. Art was his escape. When I informed my eighth-grade students that I expected each of them to create an entry for the yearly Holocaust art and writing contest, Manie naturally made a drawing.

Students from all over the province submitted written or artistic pieces that reflected their interpretations of that year's theme. Four first-place winners would be chosen. All first-place prize winners were to be awarded a three-day, two-night, all-expenses-paid trip to Washington, D.C., to visit the United States Holocaust Memorial Museum.

Two months later, the local Holocaust Center contacted me and informed me that Manie had won first place. After the initial shock and disbelief wore off, Manie and I were filled with much joy and anticipation about the upcoming Washington trip. Initially, his parents refused to let him travel out of Canada; however, after persistent persuasion, he was permitted to go. I was given the privilege of going along as Manie's chaperone. The trip would be a defining moment in both our lives.

The highlight and focus of the trip was our visit to the Holocaust Memorial Museum, to which we devoted a full day. The towering, slate gray concrete construction gave little indication of what we might find inside. After passing through metal detectors, scanning devices, and tight security, we were ushered into a massive building of concrete, brick, and steel. We began on the fourth floor. We passed meters of glass cases that displayed

Hitler's scientific and mathematical "proof" that the Jews were inferior to other races.

We watched videos about the rise of anti-Semitism and how fear and ignorance of Judaism spread over the centuries. The information was vast; the photos were unsettling and upsetting. Not until we got to the third and second floors were we confronted directly with the horror, the terror, and the inexcusable. Manie and I separated from the rest of the group to truly absorb what we were seeing.

Here, all that we had read and studied, all that I had taught my students, was before us: the concentration camps, the barracks, the wooden bunk beds taken directly from Auschwitz, and the gas chambers. We passed corridors with photos, so many photos, of people now gone, murdered. Snapshots of smiling children riding tricycles, eating ice cream, holding well-loved dolls.

Manie did not speak the entire time; he stared for long periods or looked away, ashen and aghast. No room for words. Then we got to the boxcar, like the boxcars I had tried so hard to describe during our lessons. We had to pass through it. I hesitated, we hesitated. I stepped inside. It was empty, an empty boxcar, but it held great significance. It was empty, but we knew the truth; we knew what was in here once. Manie lingered for a long, long time, thinking, seemingly lost in thought.

Finally, he spoke, looking straight ahead to the far end of the boxcar's rough wall: "My family believes that what Hitler did was good. They told me that the Jews deserved it. They really didn't want me to come on this trip because they thought it was a waste of time. They were mad that I entered the contest in the first place. Then when I won, my family made fun of me and called me 'Jew lover.' "

He bent his head down, then slowly turned to look at me: "I used to think that way, too, because I didn't know any of this happened, but now I know that I will never, ever be like my par-

ents and I know they are wrong." Tears welled in his eyes, and he
exited the boxcar.

## 128.

Today marks the anniversary of the assassination of Dr. Martin
Luther King Jr. in Memphis, Tennessee. Last week during spring
break I was there at the Lorraine Motel where one dream ended
and another began. I jokingly called our trip a pilgrimage all
southerners must make, but it was not to the Lorraine Motel that
I referred. It was to Elvis's home, for Graceland, that southern
belle of the residence ball, is also in Memphis.

Although I did visit both places, the site of my epiphany surprised me. It wasn't in front of Elvis's grave where my past and
my present collided. Instead, it was at a balcony where a man
who filled people with hope and made a nation confront its guilt
breathed his last breath. It was there that I faced my own guilt
and realized that this truth belongs not to the adults in charge
but to everyone who waited in a white waiting room or drank
from a fountain marked for them—white or black. It belongs to
all who did not speak then and do not speak now.

I will be silent no longer.

Although the movement for equality started around the time
I was born in the 1950s, I remembered much of what I saw in
the National Civil Rights Museum exhibits at the Lorraine Motel
from my childhood in the Deep South. Waiting rooms at my doctor's office were labeled "White" and "Colored," and city water
fountains were labeled the same. Separation was not only established and accepted; it was institutionalized and taught.

I hate that these museum displays are still alive in so many
people's memories, but seeing it all made me understand
why there is still so much division, distrust, and even hatred.
Somehow it had never occurred to me that those wall signs and

water fountains would be kept and placed in a museum so that visitors could walk back through time and remember. Why would anyone want to remember? Didn't everyone just want to forget?

My journey through the museum took me past familiar signs and pictures and made me face parts of my history that I had never understood were mine. I remembered going home from school and telling my mother that the new "colored" girl and boy who were the first "token" black students to integrate my elementary school had arrived. The girl, Sherry, was seated in a desk next to me.

"Surely the teacher will move her around so that nobody has to sit next to her all year," my mother exclaimed in dismay over the news. I nodded in agreement, not because I believed it, but because it was what I was being taught by parents who had been taught by their parents before them. We have all since realized our errors in judgment.

"Can I touch your hair?" my friend Debbie asked Sherry one day in the restroom. I was shocked. Touch that black hair? Wouldn't it make her hands greasy or dirty?

Debbie did touch her hair, and she became Sherry's friend. I did not. Forty years later, I still regret that.

Pictures in the museum of innocent black children in starched dresses and braids made the memories flood back, and I was stunned by the depth of guilt I began to feel. I, who have spent a career treating students and colleagues without regard to race, was facing the fact that guilt was there nonetheless.

As my journey through the museum forced a journey through my past, I paused at the window looking out over the famous balcony of the Lorraine Motel where Martin Luther King Jr. was assassinated. I saw the spot on the concrete where his blood had spilled as the grainy black-and-white tape reel replayed in my mind of a proud man at the railing, smiling, waving, then falling, then shielded by his friends. I joined him on the balcony, assaulted with unexpected emotion.

Finished with the tour, I sat alone at a table in the snack shop, wrestling with the emotions that had thunderstruck me in a surprise attack. Using the only paper I had, the receipts from my museum admission and soft drink purchase, I worked through my emotions by writing, just as I had taught my students to do with journaling:

### THE PRICE I PAID

*For ten dollars I paid the price*
*of my forefathers' sins.*

*For two dollars more,*
*through rented headsets,*
*I bought a little more freedom from their sin,*
*my inherited guilt.*

*Panels of words and pictures*
*taught me why a dream was necessary*
*and how it became*
*deferred.*

*I listened to scratchy recordings*
*of voices now silent*
*as I moved through the short walk*
*telling of a long journey.*

*Discomforted,*
*dismayed,*
*disturbed,*
*I moved on.*

*And then I came face to face*
*with the balcony—*
*the spot on the concrete—*

*the very place of*
    *murder most foul.*

*I am sorry.*

*I am sorry*
    *for what people before me*
    *did under the banner of truth and justice.*

*I am sorry*
    *for my silence.*

*It will take more than $12*
    *for the wound to stop bleeding.*

*But I paid my price at the Lorraine Motel*
    *plus $2 more for audio.*

## 129.

Our guest speaker, a fiery old former SNCC (Student Nonviolent Coordinating Committee) member and friend of Stokely Carmichael, pulled out a noose.

"Just as you have given me the gift of hope, I have a present for you: a present that represents grit, perseverance, and courage. To me, that is who you are."

He continued: "The Ku Klux Klan sent this to me several years ago because they knew they would never catch me—that they could not use this as a weapon against me, because I was too strong-willed. I present this to you as a remembrance of your past and a reminder of your future: Stay strong and no one will keep you from your goals."

Tears welled in my eyes as I glanced at the twenty-five anxious faces staring curiously into Scotty B's face as he spoke.

I didn't see Kevin anymore, the crazy, outgoing, artistic, and socially intelligent sixth grader; or Lori, the girl who has caused more drama than any other girl; or Carla, my wildly excitable, overly loving sweetheart who had trouble finding her place in the world. This time I saw a group so closely woven together, so united, it was hard to tell where one ended and one began. Kevin was holding Carla's timid, slightly anxious hand. Lori's arm was around Reina, a girl who was her nemesis throughout the entire school year. And all of us were standing as a true family united by this common thread: We were the Class of 2014 on the trip of a lifetime through Birmingham, Selma, and Montgomery, and we had just been given a noose.

I turned to Scotty B. This short man, clad in overalls, chewing on a piece of his hip bone that he had hanging around his neck, had helped in our transformation from sixth graders focused on *High School Musical* into scholars focused on social injustice and the fight for human rights.

Knowing that it was odd for me to receive a noose, my students looked around with curiosity. An item that usually represents pure hate represented at that moment only perseverance, love, family, and our transformation. I heard whispers around the room, and finally someone spoke up: "Wow! How amazing. We have to hang that up in your classroom. This is all about us. We are persevering and will use our strong will so no noose will ever be used against us—of any kind." Leave it to Ann to perfectly synthesize our experience.

Four months earlier, this trip was a seed that wasn't ready to grow. No funding, not enough time to plan, and a thousand logistical reasons why it shouldn't happen. Yet through some miracle it became a reality. Relatives, friends, and New Orleans residents caught wind of our efforts and donated their money. Students wrote letters, planned out the journey, and studied the civil rights movement with a fervor often missing in the classroom, leading us up to that moment in June when we journeyed away from the comfort of our homes and embarked on an adventure not far in distance but millions of miles away from our comfort zone.

We lived together as a family for five days, met civil rights veterans, stood on the steps of the Sixth Street Baptist Church, and walked through Selma with a man who was in sixth grade at the time of the March. We were challenged to face our history head-on, to reflect on what those demonstrations, both nonviolent and violent, meant for our lives, and, most important, to connect the past to the present. While on a bus tour of Selma, we were unexpectedly shuttled off the bus. Suddenly, we were being screamed at: "Get over to the wall! Don't look up! Get your eyes down!" Unexpectedly, we were participating in a slavery reenactment. Soon, we were herded into a dark room. A few students were crying furiously next to me; others were desperately trying to catch my eyes. "Are we okay?" they silently asked. Tom, the baseball star, who usually had a tough-guy persona, grabbed my hand. "I don't think I can handle this alone," he whispered. Everyone was clinging to their team as we journeyed through the Middle Passage, an experience on the auction block, and an attempted escape from our plantation. Finally, we were brought into a well-lit room. Standing shoulder to shoulder as one united circle, we were led through a freedom song and brought back to our world. Soon Dehab was dancing, Shanae was singing, and Wade was smiling. Yet they had changed—we all had changed. Together, we had truly learned what the history books had told us.

We experienced our past over and over again that week. We felt for the marchers, cried for the four little girls in Birmingham, and felt proud when we learned of the children protesters. Every step of the trip led us to this moment, standing in a visitor center in Lowndes County, where decades earlier Scotty B had spent several months living in a tent, avoiding gunshots from passing cars, and fighting for human rights. Everything we experienced led to the moment when the Class of 2014 realized that together we could prevent a noose from being used against us. No one will take that moment away from us.

## 130

My nights are sleepless. During the day I cannot focus. At school I walk and smile. On the outside, things seem normal; inside, I am a ten-car pileup.

Today, teacher preference forms for next year were placed in our mailboxes. I have three days to consider which courses I would like to teach next year and submit the form. This one little form is the source of my emotional roller coaster. What appears to be a simple piece of paper—"List the courses and levels you would like to teach next year in the boxes provided below. Remember we cannot honor all requests, but we will try"—is, really, a constant thorn in my side. My department chair will ignore this form, just as he has ignored it the last three years. His mind is made up: I will teach African American history four times a day, and he will feed me a line of crap about how great I am. He patronizes me and feels his false flattery is convincing. He is cocky enough to think I once again will accept his decision and maintain the status quo.

One hundred twenty-five teachers teach at my school. Only sixteen of them are African American. The student population is over 40 percent African American, and most of these students are tracked into remedial classes. These students clearly understand that they are tolerated but not totally included in the academics at the school. I have held on to the African American history class because it provides a refuge for so many students. In the past I felt as though I had to keep the class because it is so important to so many students and parents. I do not want to turn my back on my students, yet I do not want to turn my back on myself and all that I can become.

I have prepared myself all year for the teacher preference form, and I am ready. I started the African American Achievers Club with two other teachers. The club focuses on culture and academic improvement. It provides a place for all students to gather and plan activities and field trips. I have created a place for my students, and I am relieved that they will not feel abandoned when I change my schedule. On the form, I list the courses I want to teach next year. I am so sure about it that I turn in the form the same day. I am done agonizing.

Two weeks later, I get the envelope with next year's schedule safely tucked inside. I walk through the office and watch my colleagues cheerfully open and share the contents with one another. I head out to my car, and I turn on the air conditioner and wait for the car to cool down before I open the envelope.

My cell phone rings. It is the African American literature teacher. "What did you get?" she asks.

"I haven't opened it yet; I'm waiting for my car to cool down."

"Well, I got four African American literature classes and one creative writing. Go ahead and open yours."

"Okay." I open it. I am not surprised. "Four African American history classes and one global studies. It looks like Soul Train once again," I said, referring to our joke about students moving from my room to hers all day long. "What are you going to do?"

"Nothing," she replies. "I am going out on maternity leave in October. I will decide my next move after the baby."

I decide to fight.

When I get home, I sit and put my thoughts together. I pray and ask God to remove all negative thoughts from my brain and to give me the solution.

The next morning I arrive at school wearing a black dress, and my hair pulled back neatly in a chignon and carrying my professional portfolio. I approach my principal and ask for a short conversation. When we go into her office, she comments on how nice I look. I thank her and place my portfolio on her desk and say, "I am here to interview for a job at this school."

She smiles. "You already work here."

"No, I work only with the African American students. I would like to work with all of the students. Each year I fill out the teacher preference form only to be given the African American history classes. Since our department chair changed three years ago, only the African American teachers have been given this class, and I feel that policy is racist."

"Don't you go there!" she says. "I never expected you to bring in race. I cannot believe this."

"Listen, you cannot tell me how to feel, and I feel that this schedule is racist, and I want a change."

After much debate, we both sat there, hurt but with a greater understanding of how we felt about racism in our school.

I am sure that if both of us weren't so tough, we would have cried and hugged afterward. Instead, we sat there wondering what was next. She agreed to look into the situation and get back to me.

Three days later, I received a schedule change. Next year I will teach three global studies classes and two African American history classes. I believe in my principal and in her ability to see what is hard to see. She actually listened.

### 131.

When people ask why I became a teacher, I blame my mom.

My first day of kindergarten I came to school not sure what to expect. The other kids in the class knew the songs the teacher led them into, but I sat with little understanding of what was being said. Later, during playtime, in my broken English I asked a girl if I could play with the blocks she had in front of her. Instead of inviting me to play, she called me a "dummy" and told me to go away. I knew she had called me something bad. I impulsively grabbed her ponytail and yanked so hard she fell to the ground screaming. Moments later, I was being whisked to the principal's office. I sat in front of him, not understanding a word he was saying. I said nothing. I stared at my red tennis shoes, hoping he would stop yelling soon. Our trailer was phone-less, so the principal walked me across the street to where we lived to talk to my parents.

He explained to my father what I had done and said I should not return to school because I might hurt someone. He also suggested I learn more English before returning to school the following year.

I stayed home, watching children enter the school and wondering if I would ever go back. I don't really remember wanting to go back to school. In the following weeks my parents somehow worked out a deal with the school: My mother would volunteer in my classroom every day to keep an eye on me and help the teacher. I wasn't thrilled. The stigma of being the wild Mexican kid who needed his mother to watch him in kindergarten lasted until I left the school in fifth grade.

At the time, my mother spoke very little English. Born and raised in a little farming village in Mexico, she had only completed the eighth grade. She had yearned to go to school but was not able to because money had been tight. This frustrated her for years and explained her determination to make sure her children were not denied the opportunity for an education. I know she felt uncomfortable and out of place a lot of the time during my kindergarten year, but there she was, every day.

The next year my mother secured a job at my school as a playground and classroom aide. School staff liked how she worked with the children despite her limited English. In the years that followed, she continued to learn more and more English and became interested in pursuing a higher education. Her work in public schools stimulated her interest in education as a career. She earned her GED in order to attend the local university. Starting with a few classes, she eventually enrolled in the bilingual/ESL teacher education program. I know she wanted to quit at times, but somehow she found the inner strength to stay focused on her goal of graduation.

She had to constantly remind herself that it would be a waste to quit with so much accomplished. She always reminded us that if she could make it through college with an eighth-grade education in another language, my sister and I had nothing to complain about when we moaned about school. All three of us had our struggles in school either academically or socially, sometimes both. Many times I didn't want to go to school because of the kids who rode by on the bus and yelled "spic" at me as I walked home. My mother assured me that I was there to get an education, and she urged me to forget what they all said. That was hard advice to swallow. I felt like fighting instead.

After earning a degree in education, my mother started teaching at the local university as an adjunct professor. Later that year, she was flown to Florida to receive the National Trio Achievers Award, given to first-generation college graduates who overcome extreme obstacles to earn college degrees. Determined to keep learning, my mother received a master's degree on Mother's Day in 1995. My sister and I received our baccalaureate degrees in bilingual/ESL education on the same day.

## 132.

*I can! I will! I must!* I wondered how I'd gotten this far in my life without really connecting. Somehow I was forty-six years old, neither a wife nor a mother. I was strong and independent, but my heart was wounded. Something was missing, and I had to keep searching to find it.

After college, I worked in restaurants and even owned a successful catering business. I enjoyed the work, but somewhere deep inside of me I heard a continual murmur: *What's the point? Why am I doing this?* I struggled with a sense of purpose despite support from my mom, brother, and friends. After my dad died, my anger and sadness seemed to distract me from feeling "normal." For a long time I believed that my life too would be cut short by a heart attack. It was this thought that anchored my actions yet eventually propelled me to change.

An acquaintance said to me, "You'd be a great teacher!" I'd never before thought of teaching as a career, and I wasn't sure I had the knowledge or experience. However, these words were the spark that ignited my journey into the world of education.

Some called my special education students "different." For years they had been laughed at and labeled in school. Little did these teenagers know, but I also felt different, labeled. As an adult, I was not invited to "couple" social functions, and I was often quiet while friends discussed their children and parental responsibilities.

I felt as though people wondered if there was something "wrong" with me because I had not participated in the traditional stages of a woman's life. Our classroom was full of "differences," which brought us close together, freed us all to be ourselves, and made everyone equal. Although I didn't wear the label "special," I realized that not judging one another united the students in my class in many ways. It was what made me feel accepted.

My kids, like a lot of other students, carry personal doubts and fears. I quickly learned that a few of them didn't believe in themselves or in their abilities to complete class work on any level, let alone class work similar to that of the "regular" education students. Even fewer thought they would ever graduate from high school.

Challenging fate with our class motto, "I can! I will! I must!" the class and I began a dedicated effort to increase self-confidence and academic abilities. I realized the motto wasn't just about them. When I began teaching, the sadness and meaninglessness I had experienced mirrored that of my students. But over time, it was replaced with joy as we motivated one another, laughed, and even danced in celebration.

It hasn't always been easy. There's been heartbreak and struggle within our class—teenage pregnancies, fights, jail time. My desire is to protect my students, knowing that they are fearful as they change from teens to adults, wondering what life will be like without the safety of school. As much as I am their cheerleader and supporter, I know that I will not always be there to keep them going forward.

All is balanced in my mind by the happiness of this group of students. I beam with parental pride when I think of their discussions of grade-point averages, the class clown who earned a place on the honor roll, and their willingness to read *Beowulf*. This is our senior year, and I feel that we are all graduating to new levels of pride and success.

I find it comforting that I am a teacher and a writer. I am following in the footsteps of my grandpa, who was a principal, and of my dad, who was a journalist. Even though they both left my life too soon, they inspire me daily in my classroom.

One student told me, "I didn't want to trust you, because I thought that you would leave me like all the rest." I can only hope that as my students move on, my words and actions will continue to motivate them to trust themselves. *They can! They will! They must!*

## 133.

Cute, bright, and admired, she could sing, dance, style hair, and design nails. She could be counted on to help check papers, run errands, and even lead a class discussion. But Kim barely made the honor roll and never had satisfactory citizenship. I was always on her about her school uniform, attitude, and academics. Many times I found her in the hallway because she had been put out of class. Other times, she was at my door, crying profusely. Calm and collected one minute, angry and distraught the next.

I was the teacher with whom she chose to confide. At first I thought, "Why me?" But as I got to know Kim, I realized she was another opportunity for me to make a difference. There were so many things that Kim had shared with me: She'd been told she was too light-skinned, too skinny, too ghetto, not smart enough. She was consistently tardy to school and full of excuses why her homework was not turned in.

When she told me, "Oh, my God, Ms. Z, I think he's going to kill my mother. I don't know what to do. I'm afraid," I knew we had gone beyond the standard teacher-student confidence.

"Kim, I'm going to have to report this because I'm a mandatory reporter. If a student ever tells me something that reveals they're in a dangerous situation, I'm obligated by the state to report it. So I'm sorry, but I have no other choice. Do you understand?"

"Yes, Ms. Z, I know," Kim said.

I thought, "Maybe that's why she told me." Then she left my room, and I knew her life was about to change. I just didn't know if the change would be for the better.

After Kim was removed from her home and taken to live with her aunt, she never stopped coming to see me. She began to call me "Momma Z." She told all her classmates and other teachers that she was my daughter. She yearned for discipline and structure, someone to tell her right from wrong yet still give her a hug at the end of the day. Day after day, week after week, she kept coming.

"Kim, I keep a journal to vent and get any feelings and frustrations out instead of being aggressive or hostile to anyone. Why don't you start one, too?" She did and it helped.

Throughout the year, Kim grew. She cared more about herself and made an effort to come to school every day on time. She did her work, and she participated more in class discussions. By spring, she'd even started a book club. She didn't run away, didn't get caught up with the wrong crowd, didn't let life beat her down.

I grew, too. I realized there is much more to teaching than is taught in college or expected by the public. It's the opportunities to make a difference—one Kim at a time—that give me purpose.

"Bye, Momma Z," Kim said, waving as she poked her head in my door for the last time as an eighth grader. I thought of Kim leaving and heading to high school in the fall. "I passed," she said. "I even passed my P.E. class that I skipped so much to come talk to you!"

"I'll miss you, Kim. Will you come back to visit me next year?"

"Momma Z, I'll never forget you."

And with that, she was gone.

## 134.

I thought I was a rock star! Every kid in the school knew my name and couldn't wait to be in my class. I had music blaring every morning to greet my students, and I led field trips to places no other teachers dared take their classes. I had received recognition from the administration and ridiculously generous gifts from parents each year. I was *the* big fish in this pond. So it was no big surprise that I was selected to join an exclusive group of teachers and fly to California as a "Freedom Writer Teacher" to be trained by some famous educator who'd had yet another "teacher triumphs against all odds" movie made about her.

During the weeks leading up to the seminar, I spent countless hours contemplating exactly which pearls of wisdom I was going to bestow upon Erin Gruwell and her colleagues. Was I going to share my infinite knowledge of student discipline and classroom management, or was I going to educate these English teachers on why mathematics was far more critical for the promotion of modern society? I was positive Erin was going to have the teachers sit in a circle and share their ideas and methodologies so we might all learn from one another, and I was bound and determined to share my wisdom with the group. But as is true so often in life, what we expect is not always what we get.

As I sat in the back of the van that retrieved the Freedom

Writer Teachers from the Los Angeles airport, I found myself in unfamiliar territory. The ten other teachers from all over the nation accompanying me were introducing themselves and sharing their stories of how they were selected for this training. As their stories unfolded, I began to feel my stomach sink. These teachers were truly incredible. The group included the Illinois State Teacher of the Year, a woman who worked in the prisons helping gangbangers find a way out, and a huge Saskatchewan gentleman who had developed an entire program to reach the at-risk children and help them find success.

All I could think was, "Holy crap! What the hell am I doing here?" My pearls of wisdom were quickly becoming a pile of turds. I, the "rock star" teacher who could stand in front of a classroom of teenagers or an auditorium filled with parents and command their attention, couldn't think of two words to put together that would sound halfway intelligent to this small group of teachers. As this horrible revelation washed over me, no one in the van seemed to notice I was trying to crawl under the seat. I was overcome with feelings of embarrassment and inadequacy. Then and there I made up my mind that I had been chosen for this training by mistake, that I had nothing valuable to share, and it would be best if I just kept my mouth shut and watched. This big fish got introduced to the real ocean.

While I sat in the back of this van heading to Freedom Writer hell, mulling over my paradise lost and planning my very own pity party, it hit me. There are students in my class who feel the very same way: inadequate and too embarrassed to raise their hands because they believe they have nothing important to share. Before the training had even begun, Erin had taught me the most important lesson. The smart kids, the jocks, the class clown, and even the troublemakers all had a voice in my class because it was easy to give them an audience. But what about the quiet kids, the average kids, the awkward kids, or the ones who want to crawl under their seats? Who was listening to them? It's easy to have a voice when you are a rock star. People want to hear you. It was then I truly realized that I was no rock star, I was a teacher. It was my job to give every kid in the class a voice. The names of those quiet students in my class who needed their voices to be heard ran through my head, and I remembered why I had become a teacher.

When the van pulled up to the Freedom Writers Foundation headquarters, an average unassuming woman was standing at the door, waiting for our arrival. As we got out of the van, Erin greeted each person with a heartfelt smile and hug. When that beautiful little woman wrapped her arms around me and said "Hello," she made me feel as if I was the only person in the room, I was welcome, and I belonged.

Isn't that the job of every teacher—to make every student feel welcome, to make every student feel she or he belongs, and to give every student a voice to be heard?

## 135.

Three finalists stood at the foot of the stairs to the stage in the Saroyan Theater. Standing next to two excellent teachers, I wondered how I could even compete with them. There was no doubt that one of them would be the next Teacher of the Year. Being the first teacher from juvenile hall to make it this far in the selection process, I saw no explanation other than God's providence moving me to be here.

As I stood there, my mind wandered back to what had brought me to that evening. My thoughts jumped back to the period before graduating from college. Because the Vietnam War was cutting men down like a threshing machine and my lottery number for the draft was 13, I joined the Army Reserve. After completing active duty and coming home, my goal was to get a teaching credential just to have one, because I didn't know what else to do. I had no plan to actually teach. The next year was filled with getting married, completing the requirements for a teaching credential, and finding a long-term substitute teaching job. Being inexperienced and having hardly any supervisors or other teachers who could have helped me through the tumultuous period all teachers go through, my frustration grew. Hearing me angrily crash through the door upon coming home, my wife would say, "You came through the door so hard, did you even turn the doorknob?" Because of my frustration, for the next thirty years I made choices that led me away from teaching school.

Passing the CBEST (California Basic Educational Skills Test) was a prerequisite to becoming a teacher. Not teaching and just on a whim, I took the test. Would passing this test be a benefit in the future? It took three attempts to pass the writing portion of the test. As it turned out, about fifteen years later I needed a job and I had a valid teaching credential. My wife said, "Why don't you teach?" Three months later I was teaching in juvenile hall.

I teach in a prison environment. My day is filled with one class of girls and two classes of boys in language arts and history. Students are marched from housing pods across a yard every morning into a school area of the facility. They are greeted warmly as they enter the classroom: High fives, handshakes, and fist bumps are exchanged along with "Good morning," "Cute hairdo," "What's up," "How are you today," "You look very pretty today," or some other form of encouragement. These comments get some very positive responses from each student filing in.

We are locked into a windowless classroom with only a radio and a probation officer. There is no view of the outside world, and razor wire is everywhere. The scene appears to be pretty scary, but in reality this is invigorating and exciting work. The classroom is covered with posters and students' work. The room is lively with music blaring. Calls come from next door—"Is there a party going on?" or "You are disturbing my class." Computers are going; assignments and quotations are written on the board;

videos are shown. One hears serious talk, banter, laughter, and crying and sees students having fun and working on assignments. I realize that this classroom is where I belong and teaching is my life.

Kids are here with drug problems, anger issues, mental illnesses, and learning problems that have led to various felonies. Some call or write after they get out. Some appear in the crime section of the newspaper. They will break your heart and at the same time fill you with a sense of joy, urgency, and purpose. One prays that these kids can find hope, purpose, and perseverance in their lives to conquer their problems.

I have always loved children. Becoming a teacher, I made connections with at-risk kids. Little things demonstrate this connection. Taking a student to lunch after his or her release; kids saying "thank you" at graduation ceremonies; phone calls to let their teacher know they are okay; their sincere appreciation when teachers feed the whole school hot dogs or pizza—these are a few events that mean so much to me. Also, a student writing about an experience in his or her life in an articulate and insightful way spurs me forward to help that student repeat this type of work. If you mix all of this with a group of teachers who enjoy helping kids, you have a recipe for love and hope.

I did not want to apply for the county Teacher of the Year award, although being the district Teacher of the Year made me eligible to apply. No one from juvenile hall had ever won that title. Reluctantly, I filled out the application at my boss's prodding. It was like writing a term paper about myself; I hated it. However, my selection as one of the three finalists gave our program great exposure at a time when a huge new juvenile facility was being planned and constructed.

Pausing in my reflections about the past, I heard my name being called as the 2005 Teacher of the Year. I am the first and only teacher chosen from the court schools. I am excited, humbled, and totally freaked out to be in front of all these people. The court schools will be recognized and honored through me. I am blessed to be working with at-risk kids. God has brought me home. On wobbly legs and with a mouth full of cotton, I ascend the stairs of the stage to accept my award.

# EMPOWERMENT

n the end, the sole purpose of teaching is to empower students to learn and excel on their own. On graduation day, we release our students into the world with the hope that they will continue to be lifelong learners, even after they receive their final grades and the last bell rings. If we are lucky enough to have had the chance to change a life, maybe one of our students will shake hands with us before leaving and say thank you.

I tried to empower my students with every lesson plan because I knew that eventually they would leave my classroom and need the tools I'd imparted to succeed. Helping my students understand the world outside their classroom was the most important lesson I could teach.

My proudest moments were seeing my students meet national leaders, civil rights activists, and individuals who make a difference every day. I saw my students transform into citizens who attended community meetings and thought critically about the rhetoric they heard and challenged ideas. In this way, the Freedom Writers have become activists in their own right. On rare occasions, these moments away from the chalkboards and desks were not just a part of my teaching experience, but also contributed to my life experience.

The stories in this section are the ones that I read when I need to be reminded that every teacher makes a difference. The students in these stories have endured the full gauntlet of classroom experiences. Some made a Toast for Change, some encouraged their families to change, and some were even able to break the cycle in their families and graduate from high school. These stories of empowerment are reminders that each student is worth every moment of anticipation, challenge, engagement, disillusionment, and rejuvenation.

## 136

"Why's this professor-guy making a big deal about *our* projects?" Luis asked again. He couldn't fully accept that a project he had completed in ninth grade might be valuable to a college educator. All of my students had been asked to research the heritage of their families. This had been one of the first projects Luis actually completed, and now he and three of his classmates were presenting their projects to a class of graduate students in the teacher credential program.

Dr. Andres, my friend and mentor, had invited us to his class, hoping that our presentations might help his graduate students see the benefits and ways of melding a multicultural curriculum with their standards-based lessons. As Dr. Andres's students meandered into class, Luis, Ethan, and Kate surveyed the adults to whom they would be speaking, and their eyes widened. Kate's hands began to shake the slightest bit. They looked like kettle corn jittering in the pan before it pops.

Dr. Andres began class by introducing each of us. Then I briefly explained the project and stepped aside to let the experts take over.

"My family came from Mexico," Luis began. "We left my grandmother and most of my family behind. I was so little that I thought we were going on a trip, like a vacation or something. My parents couldn't tell me we were moving to the United States because they were afraid I would say something when they checked us at the border."

Luis continued to describe the difficulties his family faced as illegal immigrants, and their struggle to become legal citizens. He talked about his family's dreams of life in the United States, and how they sharply contrasted with the reality they found. "America isn't what you expect," he said. "You think life will be easier. You'll have a better job and be sweeping the money in. But that's not how it is. You get here, and they sweep you."

"It was easier for my family once we were in the United States, because some of my family had already immigrated here before us," Ethan commented, following Luis's presentation. "Our struggle came in getting here."

Ethan's family lived in Palestine. He explained the politics and conflicts that forced his family to flee to Kuwait and then to the United States. "If we had stayed," he said, "my father would have been imprisoned or worse." He also spoke of the successful career his father had maintained in Palestine, and how difficult it had been for him to reestablish himself in the United States.

"My family also struggled to adjust to life here," Kate told Dr. Andres's class. Her family was originally from Russia and immigrated to the United States in 1889. "They lived in tenement housing when they first arrived. They endured prejudice from the natives who believed that the immigrants would 'outbreed, outnumber, and outvote' them." The historical setting of Kate's story was vastly different from Luis's and Ethan's stories, but her heritage further highlighted the obstacles and dreams common to immigration stories past and present.

"Thank you. Now if the four of you would please have a seat at the front of the room," Dr. Andres said, looking eagerly at each of us, "we would like to ask you a few questions."

We exchanged nervous glances and took our seats.

The class asked each of us a myriad of questions about teaching. I stumbled through my answers and was mesmerized by my students' articulate and even poetic answers to the very same questions. Although I had never discussed my teaching philosophies with them, all of their answers reflected everything I deeply believe about education. My face flushed every time Luis prefaced an answer by telling me, "Don't get all choked up, but . . ." He would then proceed to answer the question with such honesty that I would instantly tear up, and all three of my students would smile at my reaction.

"What do you think makes a good teacher?" one of the college students asked.

"I think you have to show your students that you love what you teach," Kate answered.

"And make it fun," Luis added.

"You have to show your students that you care about them. They have to know you care," Ethan concluded.

Finally, another college student asked our last question for the night: "What is each of your future goals?"

"I want be a teacher," Luis answered.

"An English teacher," Kate added.

"Actually, I want to be a history or poli-sci professor," Ethan said with a grin.

As I wiped even more tears from my eyes, I knew that I was fortunate. I had seen a glimpse of the future of education.

## 137.

Before his mother abandoned him, his parents had named him Charlie. His fellow students called him Loser, Freak, Idiot, Fool. He was still Charlie when his dad went away to prison for the first time. Then everything changed.

He needed to be accepted somewhere, anywhere. So he would do something foolish, anything ridiculous, to get anyone's attention. He attracted attention, and it didn't seem to matter to him if it was positive or negative.

That was the kid I met in September, still desperate for attention and seeming not to care what the consequences of his actions were. I couldn't blame him once I found out what he was facing outside of school. I went to speak to his teachers and his guidance counselor from the year before. Rolled eyes and deep sighs. They hadn't been able to figure him out or get him to manage himself in any way they found acceptable.

Suspensions piled up for the asinine things he did in the hallways and on the streets to impress his friends, enemies, anyone. At meetings with his grandmother, Charlie would be terribly irritated and insolent to her. I couldn't figure out how on earth he could behave this way to the last relative he had who would or could take care of him and give him shelter. Behind my back, I didn't know what he was doing in class. To my face, he was fairly reasonable, if not exactly engaged. In his self-imposed isolation in the back corner of the classroom, abuse piled on him. How was I ever going to help Charlie begin to turn his life in the right direction?

If ever a class needed the writing program I had tailored for them, this was it. They were a serious mess. I had to do something. The class and I were desperate to build a cohesive and caring community.

Students began writing about their lives and standing up to read their intimate stories with their classmates. I was pretty shocked that this class was able to write and read such profound material after all the bickering and lack of academic engagement I had seen for the past four months.

Students who had said little to nothing up to this point suddenly found their voices and were writing lovingly crafted essays.

I watched Charlie closely.

His eyes locked on each reader, but he said nothing. He was silent. Ordinarily, he would have been the first student with an outrageously insulting remark about the writer. He took note of the attention his classmates, especially his usual target, Sahara, were getting from each other.

His first two pieces were weak and generally unfinished, but then something beautiful happened. Charlie realized he had something to say and had a unique way of saying it. He watched as I gave out bound journals to students who had written powerfully for their initial pieces. He wanted one. He set out to craft a rich explanation of the things he fears on Earth. He wrote of fearing he would never be good enough to have his mother back in his life, of his father never getting himself together enough to stay out of the prison system, and of doing something so bad some day that his grandmother would put him out on the street.

His classmates, who usually scorned his every word, sat silent as he read. His former tormentors stared in amazement that he was willing to be nakedly honest about such painful issues. When he finished reading, he looked up from his paper, his vulnerable, hopeful eyes brimming with tears. They overflowed when he heard the clapping and shrieks of amazement. I can't forget the look on his face as tears trickled down his cheeks and across his giant smile. "Oh, Charlie," were the only words that registered, and then Sahara stood to hug him. What was going on? They regularly said the most outrageously insulting things to each other, but this day they shared a hug and much more. She wanted to comfort him and was dealing with some of the same fears. This was the first chance Charlie took to try to get acceptance for something positive and worthwhile. No longer will he be Loser, Freak, Idiot, or Fool. Finally, for him, there was something, and he wasn't going to let it go for anything.

### 138.

Dirty Kleenex, cough drop wrappers, and stacks of journals litter my desk. Hoping the heavy clouds will produce a snow day tomorrow, I open Leslie's journal, anticipating commentary on whether the girls' basketball team will make it to the state championship. Instead, I read:

> *I found myself watching Sarah in basketball practice tonight. I had an excuse in case anyone called me on it—that I was admiring the consistency of her three-point shot. The truth is, I was admiring the way she looked when she made those three-pointers. No one in this town gets me. Sometimes I want to run down the halls screaming, "Don't you get it? I'm gay."*

My stomach knots up. I teach in a small town in the middle of the Bible Belt. Everyone here is Christian, Republican, and straight—or at least pretends to be. No openly gay people live here, just a few "roommates" and prayer team leaders in denial. Instead of a support group for kids with sexual issues, we offer morning Bible study.

In search of caffeine, I wander past the counselor's office, where conservative talk radio is blaring into the teachers' lounge. I check the folder where students can submit work for the school's literary journal. As usual, it feels thin (our school is really too small for this project, but I keep trying). I find one lone piece of paper—a poem by Leslie, beginning with the line "You think you know but you don't." Staring down at the neatly printed words, I overhear the principal and math teacher discuss the upcoming Valentine's Day dance.

"Amber wants to bring her friend Emily to the dance, but I told her we're not getting that sort of thing started." My principal taps her acrylic nails on the counter.

The math teacher nods and asks what she should bring to the church potluck dinner on Sunday. What would their reaction be if I published Leslie's poem, which ends with the line "I'm gay, and I always have been. That's who I really am"?

After school, I grab Leslie out of the hallway, knowing I have to keep this short so she can get to practice on time.

"Have you told your parents yet?"

"Are you kidding? They'll totally freak. My dad thinks gay people are all perverts. And I'm not sure my mom knows what it means."

"So how do you think they'll feel when they find out from a literary journal that their daughter is gay?"

Leslie studies the carpet. I get her to promise she'll talk to her parents before we publish the poem.

A couple of weeks later, Leslie shares another journal entry:

*I told my parents. It wasn't as bad as I thought, but they're worried about how people will treat me. They think I'll lose my babysitting jobs. My dad says I'll never get any scholarships,*

*and my mom thinks coach will find a way to bench me. What
if they're right? What if my friends think I'm a freak? What
if I get kicked out of youth group?*

Leslie pops her head into my room after school that day,
and says, "I think I want to publish my poem anonymously.
That way I won't have to deal with all the stupid people in this
town."

*Oh, honey,* I want to say, *publish the poem anonymously and
you'll have the entire school playing "Who's the fag?"* Instead, I say,
"Leslie, this is a small town. Not that many kids write poetry.
They'll know that it's you."

"I can change enough details so they can't tell it's me. Besides, my Facebook page still says I'm straight. No one will know.
And it's pretty vague. They might think it's James," she grins,
mentioning another student who sports facial piercings and a
Mohawk.

"I'm confused. If you're not ready to come out, maybe we
shouldn't publish a poem that makes it pretty clear that you're
gay. Are you sure you're ready for this?"

"Oh, no. I want to publish the poem." Leslie glances at the
clock, grabs her duffel bag, and sprints down the hall to practice.

I sit down at my desk, buried under a new pile of journals to
be read. Are Leslie and I ready to confront sexual politics in small-
town America? Plucking a journal from the top of the stack, I
glance out the window at the snow clouds and wonder what
awaits me next.

### 139.

"It doesn't matter what I do. This is my third year in the eighth
grade. I know I'm not gonna pass." It seemed that Ramiro had finally succumbed to what all of his former eighth-grade teachers
said about him behind closed doors: "Isn't he a member of that

gang?" "I heard he became violent with many of his former teachers." "It's not like it matters—he's never going to make it."

Despite everyone's denial of any possibility that Ramiro would ever be successful, Ramiro proved to be quite capable.

"So what is the moral, or theme, of *Born Worker*?"

The murmuring of the class was suddenly interrupted by Ramiro's boisterous, "Hey, Miss! Ain't it that just because certain people have certain expectations don't mean you gotta be that way your whole life?"

"Good, Ramiro, what expectations did Jose overcome?"

"You know, everyone thought that all he was ever good for was working, but he was really smart and even helped that one dude."

As Standardized Testing Week approached—and with it, the tests that would determine if Ramiro would remain in eighth grade for yet another year—I began to see a sharp decline not only in his confidence but also in his behavior.

"Man! Get the hell outta my face or else!"

I rushed into the hall to discover two teachers pinning Ramiro against the wall and shouting at him to "Shut up" and "Calm down." I could tell that Ramiro was past the point of being able to calm down—he was trapped and looking for any escape, ready to muscle his way out of his captors' reach if need be. As an administrator escorted Ramiro to the office, Ramiro glared threateningly back at the two teachers, the tattoo on the back of his neck heaving with fury.

The next day I approached him and asked, "Ramiro, what's going on with you? What's with the attitude lately?"

"Man, you know it don't matter what I do. Everyone knows I'm gonna fail."

"Why would you say that? I happen to know you are passing every one of your core classes."

He simply shrugged his shoulders and refused to talk, or to listen, any further.

Despite his claims of "knowing" he would not pass, I saw

Ramiro exert more effort and concentration than any other student during the week of testing. He struggled through every passage, every question, and was the last to complete the test.

When scores arrived, I was anxious to verify what I knew had to be true: Ramiro had passed his tests and would be moving on to high school the following year. But I was wrong.

"Ramiro, you will be given the opportunity to retake the tests. I know you tried really hard, but sometimes . . ." I began.

Ramiro locked eyes with me and very matter-of-factly said, "I told you so."

I saw his defenses reemerge, and I was afraid I had lost him.

For the next four weeks, he was assigned to my "remedial" class for students who had not passed. He attended each class, but I could never tell whether he was actually understanding or retaining anything. Only days before retesting, I stood with Ramiro in the hallway. His frame wilted against the wall, he refused to look me in the eye. Then he said, "Why should I care? Why should I try? It never makes a difference."

I lowered myself to eye level with him, forcing him to see the truth in my eyes: "Ramiro," I said, "you are amazing. You make a difference. You have made a difference in my life, and I will never give up on you."

Once again test day came. As Ramiro came into class that morning, his eyes were troubled. Slumping, he stared somberly at the test booklet and ran his fingers through his hair. I walked by and very gently squeezed his shoulder and then gave him a reassuring smile. He sat up a little straighter, opened the book, and began.

Two weeks later, the results were in. I was giddy awaiting his arrival in class. As I reported that he had passed all four core exams, I also handed him a brand-new Freedom Writers journal. On the first page I had written a note about how proud I was and I'd decorated it with every positive phrase I could think of to describe him: "Inspirational, dedicated, genuine, tough, determined, brave . . ."

"That's all you, Ramiro. I knew you had it in you. You did this."

Finally recovering from his initial shock, Ramiro looked at his journal, looked back at me, and simply said, "Thank you."

## 140.

With two weeks left in my first year of working with at-risk students, George was assigned to me. The administrator described how George would be a "perfect fit" for my classroom. His behavior included taking off from school, being verbally abusive to staff, being verbally and physically abusive to fellow students, and having no desire to succeed at school. Add in criminal behavior, combined with drug and alcohol abuse, and I was left wondering how I could have any success changing the behavior of my "perfect fit" in only two weeks.

Unfortunately, George stabbed someone the summer before school started, and was being held until the judge decided if he should be released. I didn't know it at first, but George's mistake would end up being an opportunity for positive change. Working with his parole officer, I got him released, but he always had to be accompanied by his parents or by me. He wasn't even permitted to walk by himself the half block from his home to the school for his required daily attendance.

"New George" didn't hug me, begin a campaign to have me selected Teacher of the Year, or make a public announcement describing his dedication to academic achievement. In my second year of working with him, however, he did begin to have some academic success. We still had to have regular meetings with his parole officer, but a glimmer of hope seeped from within George.

It came time for Christmas holidays, and George had won a Student of the Month award. Sadly, after Christmas, "Old George" returned. The reason why became clear to me when I leafed through his journal. A road map of emotions, written in various colors, showed his greatest roadblock: worry. He knew that he had hit the big time at fourteen years of age because he now faced two counts of aggravated assault with a weapon. His trial date was coming up, and he masked his worry in poor attendance and behavior. We had to talk.

My promise to be in court with him encouraged him to talk—a promise he trusted because we had been there before. I explained that I would describe the good and the bad of the past five months but I said there was much more good than bad. I shared that I didn't want to tell the judge that "Old George" was back.

"Improved George" returned, and I went to court with him. The prosecutor's case was solid, and George's witnesses were weak and lacked credibility. Sadly but predictably, George was found guilty. Now his worry also shared a darkening room with anger and sadness.

At sentencing, his parole officer and I spoke of the successes George had had. Our reports encouraged the judge to give George a four-month conditional sentence. That meant no jail time, but George had to remain in school, abide by curfew, and stay out of trouble.

George went out to celebrate that weekend and promptly broke curfew. He was arrested and was once again in jail, where he was scared of being sent away because he had messed up. When I saw him, I asked if there was anything I could do for him. "Actually, there is," he replied. "I was hoping that you could get me my copy of *The Freedom Writers Diary*. And could I also have some chapter books?"

Eight months ago, George would have growled at the suggestion of reading. Now he wanted books and not comics or magazines with lots of pictures. I rushed out to get them. I was so proud. "Wow," I thought, "he wants to read." Unfortunately, his desire to read didn't change his mistakes. The judge ordered him into custody until three days before the end of the school year.

While in custody, George called me a few times. He explained what it was like "inside," he spoke of family stresses, and he asked about the class.

With about three weeks remaining in the school year, I got a surprise phone call from George. Expecting the worst, I answered the phone. My worry was unwarranted. In fact, it may have been one of the most exhilarating and rewarding phone calls of my teaching career. George had broken into the office in the correctional center to phone me. He wanted a favor. His parole officer told him he wouldn't have to go to school for those final three school days. But George wanted to come back and was asking to return to my class.

The class was already overfilled with students. "What will I do with a student who is there for the final three days of the school year?" I asked myself. My brain said "no," but my heart overruled and shouted "Yes!" I encouraged George to come back to my class at the end of his sentence.

I marveled at how far we had come together—George wanted to be in school. What a heart-pounding way to end my second year of working with at-risk youth.

### 141.

At the hospital's reception desk, I demanded to see my brother. As I argued with the receptionist, a police officer came over and interrogated me about my brother's case. According to the officer, my brother was shot during the course of a robbery. Stunned, I realized the time had come for the preacher's son to rely on his inner faith. Two weeks later, when I encountered Justin, my brother was in my heart.

Justin was a hard-nosed type who liked attention. Every day he walked into class with his "Justinian" swagger. I knew he was very intelligent, even though he tried to hide it behind the company he kept. A star footballer who was always dressed to impress off the field, Justin was quite a ladies' man. He was clearly a star—in his own mind and everyone else's. So I wondered how I would be able to reach him. But it was Justin who would show me the door to his heart.

One day, he stopped me after class. "Mr. $H_2O$, may I have a word with you?" Justin asked.

"Sure, what's up?"

I had noticed that he was reserved during class. Usually, he was lively and cracking jokes.

"I got a story to tell you that I've been hush on," Justin said.

Justin told me that he missed his twin brother, with whom he had been very close. Justin and his two brothers grew up in a dysfunctional home. After their parents separated and gang violence had claimed the lives of his two brothers, Justin was sent to live in various group homes. He told me how he struggled every day to stay clear of the law—which was tough because every day he was faced with fights or another friend under arrest. He encountered so much trouble with the courts that after his last hearing, he was offered the opportunity to enter a second-chance program that would help him start fresh. I had signed on to the program to serve as a mentor.

When someone says I am crazy to choose to work with at-risk students, I tell them that I recognized the need to be an agent of change in my students' lives—to serve where I am most needed. As I listened to Justin, I could feel the pain he had endured. Justin had to become a man at an age at which most kids begin learning how to ride a bike. Justin's beloved twin brother was found beaten and floating in a pond outside the city limits, and it made me think of my brother, still lying in the hospital.

"I left the game to save my life in order to be something," Justin said. The brothers had dreamed of going to college and eventually being drafted to play in the NFL. Justin vowed to continue this dream while keeping his brother's spirit with him and his memory alive. But when Justin visited his brother's grave, he found that his family had not placed a grave marker to identify his brother's burial site.

"My only reason for working is to be in a position to buy a grave marker to place on my brother's grave," he said. After a pause, Justin finally said, "Thanks for listening to me, Mr. H$_2$0."

I was the ear that Justin needed to hear and really listen to him. Since that day, I have come across several students who have similar stories of struggle. I strive, every day, to provide them with a source of hope and to help them find ways of redirecting their lives to reach their full potential.

Today, Justin is working toward his dream of graduating from high school. My brother and Justin showed me how to value life. And now my brother and I have committed to meeting underneath the "Friday-night lights" to help support Justin. With each touchdown or big play that Justin makes, we are there to cheer him on. We have made Justin our honorary brother.

## 142.

When people have goals in life, they have something to live for; they have hope. Learning work ethics during soccer practice helped my soccer team to develop work ethics in the classroom. Not too long ago, my senior class made me a special guest at their senior prom. My date and I arrived late. The students were already eating when we arrived. When they saw me, they immediately stood up and chanted: "Salazar, Salazar, Salazar, Salazar!" Their love and their affection sent me running to the restroom. I had to wipe my tears away. They know I'm a Marine, a tough man who never gives up, never quits, and never cries.

I know that every day I have the power to change their lives, so I focus on motivating them, guiding them toward their goals. And when it comes to dreams and goals there are no boundaries. In December 2002, an opportunity presented itself. While I was an adjunct professor at Miami-Dade Community College, I was invited to participate in a conference for the World Peace Federation in Washington, D.C. During this conference, I had the great opportunity to meet wonderful people and community leaders from all over the world. They informed us that during the summer of 2003 they were going to have the first Inter-Religious Sports Peace Festival in South Korea.

The festival was for young athletes between ages sixteen and twenty-three (Youth Olympics). The American Federation was looking for young people who were highly talented athletes to represent the United States in several sports. After the conference, I met a woman in charge and assured her that I had the best team in the country. Several months later she called and requested more information about my young soccer team, asking for pictures and evidence of our talent. It was unbelievable! We were chosen to represent the United States at the Inter-Religious Sports Peace Festival in South Korea. But unfortunate events happened. Two of my players told me that they were undocumented and therefore unable to travel out of the United States. I felt powerless. They had worked so hard but would not be able to play. We did not have money for uniforms, so we borrowed uniforms from another team, packed our bags, and headed to Seoul, South Korea.

The South Koreans treated us with love. We met other soccer players and athletes from many other countries. A couple days later, the moment of truth arrived—the moment we were waiting for: We had to play our first game. While watching the first game between two other countries, we saw our opponents, the soccer team of Thailand, on the other side of the benches.

The Thai team had twenty-two players, probably three or four coaches, and very nice uniforms, and was very well organized. I noticed my players spending a lot of time watching the Thais and talking about them. I did not say anything. Moments later, when we went to our lockers to change right before the game, a couple of my players started complaining out loud.

"Look at us!" exclaimed one. "We don't even have good uniforms, we are only eleven players, we don't have any substitutes, and we are going to make fools of ourselves!"

"Coach, it's your fault we are not prepared to compete at this level," said another. "We are not good enough to play against well-organized and rich teams from other countries. In Miami we are good because we only play among ourselves."

I reminded them: "If I remember correctly, a few weeks ago when we were in Miami, all of you were very excited to come to South Korea. You were willing to do anything to be here. You considered yourselves the best soccer players in the whole world. You considered me the best coach in the world. Now that we have made it to the other side of the world, are you too afraid to play?

"All you have to give is all you have. I am sure if you give me your best on the field it will be more than enough. Just remember: You will always miss one hundred percent of the shots you don't take. Go out there and take a lot of shots. If the eleven of you give your very best and we still lose the game, then you can blame it on me, and you will have the right to call me the worst coach in the world."

We defeated Thailand 6–1. The next game we defeated Indonesia 4–0. The following game we beat Japan 3–0. We made it to the semifinals and beat Nepal 6–0. Before we knew it, we were going to play the final game against South Korea just before the closing ceremony.

After seeing us play day in and day out, the U.S. Federation was so impressed that for the final game they bought us new jerseys. I knew that because of the humidity and summer heat of South Korea, some of my players were suffering from athlete's foot. Each of them had only two pairs of black socks for practice and play every day. So to reward their outstanding effort, I took a taxi from the Olympic Village to the city and bought them new soccer socks for the final game.

The night before the final, we met in my room, as we usually did before a game. I surprised them with the new jerseys and new socks. Once again I said how far we had come and how proud I was of them.

"Tomorrow," I told them, "we are playing the game of our lives. All I want you to do is to give it your best. Tomorrow all you need to give me is all you have. Let's go—let's get the gold!"

I would love to report that we won the gold, but I would be lying. We lost 2–1 in the final. The South Korean team was very professional, well trained, and well organized, and in better shape and much faster than my eleven warriors. But my eleven students went from being students playing for fun to feeling like professionals playing at the World Cup. We did win the silver medal and a golden opportunity because we all became better students, better people, and better friends.

My eleven warriors did continue playing soccer with me in Miami. We still see each other when they visit me at my school or come to play soccer at the park. Very often I hear "Salazar, Salazar!" and "You are the best!" I just smile with lots of love and tell them: "Yes, I know, I know, I am the best! I am the best— thanks to all of you!"

### 143.

"Coach, how have you been doing—great like always? Has everyone told you I'm in the training school? I'm sorry I let everyone down by selling drugs. Could you please help me get out of here? My court date is August 24, 9 a.m., fifth floor. Please be there to help me. I'm sorry for letting you down. I'm begging you to try and get me out."

Jared was one month shy of his seventeenth birthday when he wrote this letter to me from the Rhode Island Juvenile Corrections Center. I had been Jared's and his twin brother's basketball coach for seven years. Jared was a national-caliber point guard who led his AAU team to four national tournaments and two state championships.

When I showed up for the hearing to testify on his behalf, Jared sat in court, scared and in tears, broken down by his first taste of what was in store for him over the next few years. He was living an all-too-common story: a dad in jail and a mom who was young enough to be his sister. A young black man with a chip on his shoulder chasing hoop dreams while growing up in a home that changed addresses every few months when the rent money ran out, where Dunkin' Donuts napkins are used for toilet paper and bedroom sets are purchased from the Salvation Army. Living in a home where you fight for every meal and where you use all your resources just to make it to the next day.

Jared was a difficult player to coach. One day he could lead his team to championships, and the next day he would refuse to practice. At one tournament in New Jersey, a parent became so frustrated with Jared for leaving the court during a game to sit in the stands that she removed Jared's belongings from her car and told him to find another way back to Rhode Island.

Yet Jared was a good kid who volunteered his time to help raise funds for the local Boys and Girls Club, and he was always welcome and trusted in my home, as he is today. He continues his friendship with my son, his former teammate, who has since graduated from college and now works in New York City. He still generously shares gifts with us at Christmas just as he did as a teenager.

I stayed involved in Jared's life after he walked out of the corrections center. And Jared, whose inner resources and determination are remarkable, has become a contributing citizen in his community, making a life for himself. But if you ask me if he reached his full potential, the honest answer would be "no." The truth is that even if Jared had stuck with basketball and gotten a college scholarship he would not have had some of the basic intellectual and life skills needed to make it through a four-year college curriculum.

A few months after Jared graduated from high school, I set up a meeting for him with the admissions director at the local junior college. I was shocked to hear that Jared was not prepared to begin taking college-level courses without remedial help. Jared still has not earned a college credit—never mind a college degree.

Jared's letter should have marked a new beginning and should have been the platform for a new education program for him. Instead, the state solution: "training school." What exactly are we training Jared for? Shouldn't we aim higher than just "productive citizen"? Why not aim to develop kids who want to succeed, who want to help, who want to fulfill a dream?

Eight years after receiving Jared's letter in my mailbox, I revisited the corrections center with him, not as his coach but as his mayor. During my visit, I listened to Jared speak with the teens who were now reliving his journey. As we stood in the room where Jared had penned his letter to me, Jared spoke to me of his hope of still attending college and shared his feelings of shame that he did not have a job. He expressed his concern for those who sat in front of him, fully understanding that they too will find it difficult to get an education and be gainfully employed.

I am enormously proud of Jared and believe he has great things ahead of him. But he is also a testament to the fierce urgency of this moment. When I look at the Jareds in the community I represent, I think, "If we don't invest in them right now, if mayors don't take the lead and get it right on education, how will they ever invest in us?"

## 144.

Upon our arrival at Philadelphia's City Hall, the mayor's scheduling secretary greeted us. She looked pleasantly surprised to see that we had brought a bag of supplies for our ten-minute photo session. I explained what I intended to do, and she responded, "The mayor is a very busy man. I hope he'll have time for what you have in mind." I knew she understood when she moved us from the mayor's reception room straight to his board room.

Moments later, Mayor Nutter's press coordinator entered the room with two local television station cameramen. "Are these the members of the mayor's new cabinet?" the cameraman playfully asked.

The night before, I had called and e-mailed every newspaper, television station, and radio station in Philadelphia, insisting our visit with the mayor was a must-see event: "We aren't here to just take a picture to hang on our refrigerator. We want our voices to be heard—our concerns, frustrations, hopes, and dreams for our city."

One reporter was curious about the twelve champagne glasses and sparkling cider I began to pour. "Oh, that's one of our traditions," I said. "We're here to have a toast for new beginnings with our new mayor."

"We can't vote yet," said Aaron, "but our voices will be heard today."

Minutes later, Mayor Michael Nutter walked into his cabinet room for the most important meeting on his agenda that day. My students sprang to their feet and applauded their city's new face of hope. He walked around the room and shook hands with every one of us. He then looked at me, a little confused as his eyes moved over the bubbling sparkling cider that sat in champagne glasses on his important decision-making table.

"Perhaps you want to speak of our agenda today?" he asked.

"We come today to toast with you," I explained.

Ronaee loudly interrupted, "To toast for change."

"As long as these news stations report that there is sparkling cider in these glasses, I would like you all to begin," the mayor responded with a smile.

Aaron, one of my "rough and tumble" students, insisted on speaking first: "In a place nicknamed the City of Brotherly Love, why is Philadelphia's homicide rate more than twice the national rate? I toast that all guns come off our streets, and we create a safe city to live in. I toast for change."

As Aaron finished, his eyes locked with the mayor's. It was

obvious a connection was forged between them. Aaron knew he had been heard, and the pain of violence in his life was validated by our city's top official.

Michael, a soft-spoken student, went next: "In the place where our Founding Fathers declared independence and insisted that 'all men are created equal,' that we hold 'certain unalienable rights, that among these are life, liberty, and the pursuit of happiness,' I toast that we can prevent hate crimes from occurring in our schools and communities by accepting all people for who they are. I toast for change."

My eyes began to water at Michael's words, for his courage to speak, for the pain in his body that drove him to speak about hate crimes, but, most important, for the space and place in which he was able to speak his dream today.

The mayor handed me a tissue. He whispered, "This is unique."

Karen quietly began to speak next: "I toast . . ." The reporter moved the microphone closer to her. She paused and looked at me, and I gave her an encouraging wink. She started again, speaking more loudly as her voice shook: "I toast that all people, currently employed or not, have health benefits to ensure adequate medical care. I toast for change."

I watched as the magic I had imagined in my office over the last few months unfolded. Here, ten middle school students, their teacher, and the mayor of the sixth largest city in our country came together to hear about a vision of change—a vision created not by businessmen and politicians but by a new kind of mayoral cabinet. The mayor focused as each remaining student spoke. He responded thoughtfully to each.

My students' toasts concluded with Monica's: "I toast that all children can learn in a safe environment—in their schools, on their streets, and in their homes. That they work to create everlasting change from the bottom up to ensure a promising future. I toast for change."

And with that, we all raised our glasses in the air. Mayor Nutter turned to my students and me, and together we spoke our words of hope for the future of ourselves and our city. Ten middle school students, their teacher, and the man who vowed to try to make it happen pledged: "I toast for change."

## 145.

Jacob is doing his Grim Reaper impersonation again. He pulls the black hood of his DC sweatshirt low over his eyes and slumps forward onto the desk with his chin placed in the crook of his arm. Earlier in the school year I made him sit up and straighten his back against the chair, but this morning the bags under his eyes weigh heavy on us both.

"Jacob, is everything all right?" I whisper as he raises his head slightly.

"Yeah."

He buries his eyes once again before I can continue.

"Jacob," I say, settling into the seat beside him. "Is there something you want to talk about?"

A half-muffled "no" escapes through the side of his hood as his head remains pushed against his arm, like a baby finding comfort in the womb. Then we're both silent.

It's the second-to-last day of school, and Jacob and I are still not seeing eye to eye. Silence is what we have shared best the entire year. Tomorrow the front doors will swing open and then close. The last student will leave on the final day of school, and the building will exhale, emptying its lungs for the summer. Jacob will walk away from our classroom, and I will be left to wonder if I have helped him. My challenge now is to say good-bye with the right words.

*This year's end will be different.* For two weeks I've woken each morning chasing that thought. I'm always on the verge of believing it too, if not for the vision of Jacob shaking his head and turning his back to me. I am suddenly the proverbial man walking the beach trying to throw all the stranded starfish back into the ocean. I need to give my students something that will not break, wither, fade, or vanish. A gift they will perhaps carry with them for years to come. A gift that will outlast the brick and cement walls that surround us, and that will be stronger than both. A gift that can undo silence.

So I give them some yarn: fifty-one pieces, give or take a few. One long piece of yarn tied around fifty shorter pieces, creating a necklace. It is something that the Freedom Writers call a "warm fuzzy." Everyone is given the warm fuzzy and then each person removes a piece of yarn from his or her own necklace, and ties it to the other person's necklace. Each time a piece of yarn is exchanged, a compliment is given and gratitude is created.

On the final day of school, eighty-seven students and six teachers proudly place a warm fuzzy around their necks. I hold my breath and shake the blood back into my hands. The students move around the room hesitantly at first. Then smiles erupt, and the room fills with energy like a soldout crowd before a Led Zeppelin concert.

We spread out in a living lava lamp of giggles, hugs, and thank-yous. Shuffling, sidestepping, tripping over chairs, I try to listen to different students giving more than taking while letting their words navigate their emotions. Their words are simple, but all are sincere.

Jacob moves slowly toward me in the closing moments of the activity. He is tall for his age, but his shoulders droop and he keeps his head down as if he is ducking under a low doorway.

"Thanks, for being a good teacher," he says while tying his green yarn to my own yarn necklace.

I wait until he looks up; his eyes are the same color as my father's.

"Jacob, I'm hard on you because I care about you. You're a good kid."

"Really?" His eyes are direct now, searching me for doubt, searching me for hesitation, searching for what so many have given him.

I place my hands gently on both his shoulders, and his posture straightens.

"Really, Jacob."

He strides away after a piece of my necklace is tied to his own. A slight smile pushes itself into a grin on his face. I step back and swallow hard. The world slows for just a moment, and I know someday, even as other memories have left me, I will think back to this.

The unique last day is soon over. A quick hug at the door or a casual high five and they turn the corner at the end of the hall and are gone. The buses roll away, while students wave frantically from half-open windows and shout emphatic words. Waves pull gently at the barren sand as starfish come to rest in the depths of the ocean. Then, silence.

## 146.

"Then I'll just drop out."

The words spilled from the sixteen-year-old boy's mouth as if they had been rehearsed. But this was not your typical dropout, and he had never uttered those words before.

Mike was a bright kid who had transformed over the course of a year from a perpetually tardy slacker to a kid with potential. A kid with brains, with a future. It was like he woke up one day and realized that his education might actually be worth taking seriously.

Now he was going to drop out.

His decision came after he failed his portfolio presentation. At our school, all sophomores are required to give a presentation at the end of the year proving that they are ready to be upperclassmen. If they don't pass their presentations, they don't pass for the year.

Mike failed his because he was missing one piece of his portfolio: the creative expression of learning. He simply left it out. The good news was that students at our school are given multiple opportunities to present if they don't pass the first time. The bad news was that Mike decided that this whole school thing was a load of crap, that he had better things to do, and that he was going to drop out.

"Mike, *don't* drop out," his friends begged.

"Mike, if you drop out, you're not welcome in our home," his parents warned.

"Mike, you can do it over," his teachers insisted.

But Mike had made up his mind. He was out.

At this point, another student, Jason, entered my classroom with an announcement: "Sorry to interrupt, but the principal asked that the entire sophomore class go outside to the front steps."

Whether the principal actually ordered this, or simply okayed this, or had no idea this was going on, I still don't know. But suddenly ninety-eight sophomores and six teachers were standing on the front steps trying to convince Mike to please just walk in the door.

For forty-five minutes, the entire sophomore class and their teachers stood outside and begged. Pleaded. Cajoled. Beseeched. Implored. Cried. Sounds unbelievable? It was.

"Mike, listen to me," started Carolina, a student who had struggled in my class at many points during the year but had made an academic turnaround recently. "Whatever you need to do, we'll help you. What do you need to pass? We'll go in school and do it right now. I'll help you!" Here was a girl who fought every assignment I had ever given her, but now, when her classmate needed her most, the truth came out: She believed in herself, in the school, and in Mike.

"Mike," spoke up Rodney, "I am eighteen years old, and I haven't given up. I'm only in tenth grade. When I came to America, they said that they couldn't accept my transcript, and that I had to start high school all over. If I can do this, you can, too."

Rodney had emigrated from Jamaica. When I met him as a freshman, I was shocked at how little English he knew and could write. I never knew how old he was, his story, or his level of determination before that moment.

The kids spoke one by one and shared their stories with Mike and offered all their help. As I looked at the community before me, I saw one hundred students who had all crossed the line together—written and read memoirs of their pasts together, role-played, debated, participated in Freedom Writers activities, and cried together. I knew that if these kids hadn't been pushed out of their comfort zones or shared their deepest secrets Freedom Writer–style, they wouldn't be out here. Though everyone else seemed to be crying, I was overtaken by the huge success this calamity had exposed.

Nonetheless, Mike remained obstinate.

Finally, the teachers took over and coaxed the kids back into the building. "Mike has to make his own decisions, and you need to get back to class," they said. The students couldn't believe we were giving up so easily, but we all knew that Mike would be back tomorrow.

But he wasn't. Not tomorrow, nor the next day, nor the next. Soon, kids stopped talking about him, and teachers thought about erasing his name from their grade books. Our school began to feel like a typical urban school, where dropping out was accepted as the norm.

As the school year wound down, teachers scrambled to grade all the papers that had been sitting on their desks for the last hectic month, and I was no exception. I had found and graded Mike's final paper. It felt wrong not to.

I decided to hand back papers and have the students reflect on their work as a way to close the year. As my students entered my classroom, they had big smiles on their faces, and I didn't know why. Then I saw Mike walk in the door and sit in his usual seat.

"Good work," I said, beaming, and I handed him his paper. I was even more proud of him when he passed his portfolio and moved on to eleventh grade. Now, if you ask him, "Remember that day you dropped out?" he smiles as if it never happened.

## 147.

My left knee twitches nervously as the butterflies flutter in my stomach. From the graduation stage, my eyes scan confidently over the audience packed into the community center for the big event. Babies cry. Toddlers teeter from relative to relative packed in the long, narrow aisles of chairs laid out like a gauntlet, daring anyone to stumble down to find an empty seat. There is no standing room to be found. Parents, cousins, uncles, friends, and grandparents overflow out the door and into the lobby, where they can only listen to the festivities. "I hope the fire marshal doesn't pay us a visit today," I think to myself.

I turn my gaze toward my students, looking proud in their silver and maroon caps and gowns. Some shift nervously in their seats, awaiting the big moment when it will seem as though the whole world will focus only on them and their accomplishments. I have known some of these students since their eighth-grade year, when I practically dared our feeder junior high schools to assemble their most at-risk eighth graders in one room—alone. I believed these students could swim through their sea of dysfunction to a high school diploma—with the right escort. An equally idealistic colleague and I both believed we could keep this group of students together for four years. We would go to our feeder junior highs and recruit the most at-risk students just as honors programs recruited their target audiences.

Scanning the auditorium, I lock eyes with Pablo. He doesn't

know it, but I can't look at him without thinking of Frankie. Two boys. Same neighborhood. Same gang. Same class. Same story—two different endings.

Near the end of his freshman year, Pablo cut his regular English class to attend mine. Technically, I should have sent him to the office or back to his official class. Besides, what teacher really wants a five-foot-ten, 200-pound, hairnet-wearing, up-and-coming gang member in his classroom if he doesn't have to be there? You could have fit a small arsenal of weapons into Pablo's baggy jeans. But he was always respectful. He followed along as we read *The Freedom Writers Diary,* shook my hand before leaving when the bell rang, and even contributed to our class discussions from time to time. One day, he stayed after the bell and asked if he could be in my class next year. I smiled proudly as I met his firm handshake. "I don't know why you weren't in my class in the first place, Pablo," I told him.

Over the next couple of weeks before school let out for the summer, Pablo and I had several conversations about his gang: what it meant to him; the significance of the ink on his chest, biceps, and hands; and the numbers and slogans he flaunted on his CD player and binder. Sometimes he'd stay after class at the end of the day to talk at my desk. Sometimes I'd write him a note—often with a pointed question about his gang-oriented lifestyle. I tried not to preach at him, but I also wanted him to know that I cared enough to ask honest questions and expect intelligent answers in response. Although he turned in class assignments only intermittently, Pablo *always* wrote me back.

Frankie had been in my class from day one. Small in stature, large in reputation, Frankie didn't want to be in my class, or in any other class. Frankie was obviously "down," but he never wore clothes, colors, symbols, or any markings that would identify him with his gang. He didn't have to. His last name—Mendoza—said it all; it was practically synonymous with the gang.

In class, Frankie talked out of turn, gave flippant answers, flirted shamelessly with girls (boyfriend or not), and generally claimed to "run thangs" in my class. His most impressive score would have been on a drug test. Frankie often had the look of someone who had just smoked half of Colombia—before 10 a.m. Not surprisingly, he loathed any activity requiring thoughtful reflection or introspection, especially my "open letters" to the class. Open letters were a method I used to share my perceptions about class progress and to get students to write about their personal lives. Frankie never stayed after class to talk and rolled his eyes when I passed out my open letters. Frankie made it clear to me that the topic of gangs was off the table: "You just don't get it, man, and I ain't writin' about it." Frankie never wrote me back.

Sophomore and junior years went much the same way. But then Frankie was arrested for a gang-related murder. At sixteen, he was tried as an adult, convicted, and sentenced to eighty-five-years-to-life. Two months later, Pablo transferred to our continuation high school to make up the credits he missed.

I crossed paths with Pablo again at the beginning of his senior year. He looked fit and trim and showed no obvious signs of gang affiliation. He greeted me with the same confident, reserved smile, firm handshake, and direct eye contact that he had given me that first day three years earlier. Yet something had changed in him. He began distinguishing himself as a leader on campus. I observed that he clearly was on good terms with his homies but he never really kicked it with them, choosing instead to hang out with his girlfriend or work in a teacher's classroom on a leadership project. Other high schools had one or two students present their updates to the school board, but Pablo made sure our school had no fewer than eight students on hand—wearing matching school T-shirts. He addressed the board confidently and articulately, with unmistakable ownership of his school and its activities. On campus, we checked in with each other all the time, as a general would with his best captain. I counted on him to help shape my school's culture the way older gang members once relied on him to shape the minds of younger wannabes in the neighborhood. Choosing never to ask Pablo what happened, what made him choose to slowly drift away from his gang, I was left to wonder.

Until the day before graduation when he came into my office to receive a special award I had made for him: a specially embroidered graduation stole. His eyes widened in surprise as he held it up. We chatted casually for a minute before he got up to go back to class. As he walked out of my office, he stopped and turned around toward me. He looked at me and said, "I don't even want to *think* about where I would be right now if I hadn't met you."

I blink quickly, awaking from my daydream. The crowd is boisterous. It's diploma time. As Pablo locks eyes with me, the confident, reserved smile breaks into a toothy grin as he makes his way toward the stage to receive his diploma. Our hands clasp one last time as teacher and student as a most improbable graduate crosses the stage to camera flashes and joyful cheers.

When I get home that evening, I find a letter waiting for me on the counter: "State Prison . . . Cellblock C-5 [stamped in red ink] . . . inmate number 26784 . . . Frankie Mendoza." Curiously, I open the letter and read the first lines: "You were right about everything you said, everything you warned me about . . . I know you're busy but I would be very grateful if you would write to me. I don't really have anyone but my parents now . . ." It had taken him four years and a murder trial, but Frankie had finally written me back.

## 148.

"It's my mom," Liza breathed deeply. "She was picked up again for prostitution last night, back on the crack. My grandmother borrowed two hundred dollars to bail her out." She was desperately trying to sound matter-of-fact, and even my crappy cell service couldn't hide the anger, sorrow, and hopelessness in her voice.

She was a beautiful, brilliant, sarcastic, volatile, violent, and vulnerable sixteen-year-old. Big-boned and striking, dressed in black with chains and studs, and sporting a pierced tongue, she walked into my class ten minutes late, cocky, mouthy, and ominous. She wordlessly fired a pass onto my desk with black painted nails. Her hair ranged from ebony to fiery red. Her deep green, catlike eyes were outlined in thick kohl, and three black teardrops were drawn under one eye. Her narrowed eyes flashed, confronting me, and one corner of her mouth curled hatefully.

"Are you Liza?" I asked.

"It's right there on the pass."

She was irate at the world, and everyone else would be miserable too. She was constantly absent or getting thrown out of her classes. Liza's anger management counseling twice a week was failing. It simply supplied material for her cynical outbursts. For months I struggled to gain her attention in class. A very talented writer, she loved journaling. She wrote that writing helped her relieve the stress and anger that were eating her alive. I also read that Liza and her siblings had been taken away because of their mom's addictions. She had beaten Liza repeatedly with various objects, including an ashtray and a frying pan.

Her journals brought back memories I had buried long ago. My dad was an Old World Sicilian with two clearly defined categories for women: Madonna and whore. I was neither, but rather was the daughter of a man who saw me as the embodiment of all he worshipped and despised in women. I wanted to be loved. Ranting for him was a high art. "If it weren't for Eve, we'd all be running naked through the Garden of Eden without a worry in the world" would inevitably lead to "No daughter of mine is going to disgrace me." One night, a flat tire on the highway caused me to miss an 11 p.m. curfew. It didn't matter that I was eighteen. I had no time to get my explanation out before his "golden gloves uppercut" slammed into my head. When I came home from the hospital with a concussion, he screamed, "See what you made me do!" My little brother got the worst of it. In ninth grade Dad beat him in front of our entire high school. It happened in the parking lot. His hockey coach and friends saw it all. Then Dad pulled him into the car and started driving away. He finished it off Tony Soprano–style. "Daddy Dearest" pushed him out of the car while driving away. The entire school was shocked, and my brother was never the same emotionally.

Maybe that's why one of Liza's journals hit me so hard. Before Liza's younger brother and sister were taken away, Liza had been diverting her mother's attention away from them. She had been taking all the beatings to protect them. I admired her courage. She had incredible "balls," and I admire that in a woman.

Like so many of my students, Liza had so much drama to deal with in her life that very little excited her in the classroom, until I assigned a documentary film project. After studying the media, I asked the students, in groups of four, to produce a film of their own. It could be as simple as a PowerPoint presentation. Liza worked alone and told the story of her mom's graduation from rehab. She edited it, adding graphics and music. Her classmates and my department chair were mesmerized by it and moved to tears.

Liza had used the film as an intensive therapy session. During filming, her mom took ownership of what she had done, told Liza how much she loved her, and asked for forgiveness. Liza forgave her wholeheartedly. Her mom had enrolled at the local community college to start a degree in sociology. Most important, Liza's relationship with her mom blossomed. For the first time her mom felt understood. The audience became part of a very profound journey. Everyone in class responded intensely to the film and to Liza. She became a kind of celebrity. Classmates were saying she should go into television. She became very serious about her future and going to college. She went from being short on credits for graduation to being on track to graduate with her class the next year.

I spent lots of extra time with Liza after her mom relapsed, trying to convince her that her mom's problems were not her fault. I knew Liza was feeling better when she asked, "Hey, should I work on a sequel to my mom's documentary?" Her indomitable spirit made me smile.

A gravelly voice interrupted my thoughts: "Here goes our girl!" Liza's mom hugged me for a long time. Her face was gaunt and pale, but her deep green eyes shone with tears. We cheered as Liza's name was announced. She crossed the stage and looked joyously at us, squealing and waving her diploma triumphantly. On that morning in June, there were no black tears drawn under Liza's sparkling green eyes.

## 149.

Yesterday morning I went to the bus stop to bring DeJuan into school to finish his assignments before graduation last night. His body odor was so bad that I could hardly stand to be near him, and it was clear that he was high. DeJuan is living from place to place because he actually has no home. His parents kicked him out and want nothing to do with him.

"DeJuan, please. Please walk back to school with me and finish your work. You have so little to do, and this is going to make such a great difference in your life."

I kept my cool but I wanted to scream at him. I was so angry.

"What happened to you? I was so worried about you. I thought we had a great relationship, and I haven't even heard from you in two weeks. You're letting yourself and me down. What were you thinking? I have one word for you, 'Graduation,' and you are going to graduate."

Here I was "hand-holding" again and with a guy who was so

high I wasn't sure he could accomplish what he needed to do. He gave me no answers; he just walked quietly back to school with me. I made him drink some coffee and eat a snack so he could wake up a little before we went to work.

There was very little left for him to complete before receiving his final credit, but he had to be forced to do it. He knew he had to complete the assignments because we don't just give away diplomas. He completed his assignments, proving how smart he really is. I high-fived him as we walked his last credit to the registrar. He did it.

Is that why he showed up at the bus stop? Did he know that someone would report seeing him and that he would be "brought in"? I had not been able to locate him for days. Anyway, he finished his work. Would he come to the ceremony?

Fast-forward. The tassels were moved, the hats were thrown high, "Pomp and Circumstance" began to play, and fifty-eight graduates (including DeJuan) marched proudly out of the ballroom. He really graduated. The ceremony symbolically ended one phase of the seniors' lives. Now they would move on without me.

As I searched the faces in the audience, I realized that no one was there for DeJuan, no cheering section to see his triumphant walk, no support group to greet him after the ceremony. Didn't his family know he was graduating? This was a big deal—he was the first in his family to graduate. Didn't anyone care?

If only I didn't have doubts. Did I help or just enable DeJuan? He had been in an alternative school setting for so long. I'd pulled him along, cried with him when his life was slammed by senseless and endless violence, stepped into the middle of his arguments and fights, and rejoiced with him over personal and educational victories.

The principal said the graduates were "conquerors," and the guest speaker told them to proudly play the "hand they were dealt" without giving up or giving in to peer pressure. Would they do it? Would they conquer all the barriers of injustice, poverty, broken families, drugs, alcohol, violence, and all the other difficulties that would continue to bombard them?

While I was teaching DeJuan and the whole time I was at graduation I kept thinking, "Have I really done these students any favors? Have I made them codependent on me, or have I prepared them to face the future with assurance?" My mind wouldn't stop rerunning this endless quandary.

I thought about the four students who were caught in a drive-by shooting a couple of months ago. Would they make it?

Two of them were able to come back to school and complete assignments before graduation even though they are missing parts of vital organs and have multiple gunshot wounds. Jermaine wheeled across the stage to receive his diploma. He may be in a wheelchair the rest of his life. Marcus hopped across the stage on crutches. The other two students said they would try to complete school assignments this summer, but will they?

I wanted to go with, and protect, each graduate. I wanted to help them through college or other training and then watch them become productive members of society. *Stop. Enough. I have done my best. I will let go of them. They will succeed and conquer. Why? Because I showed them I care, because they are educated, and because they have already achieved greatness. Each one is bright, creative, and energetic—especially DeJuan. I know my students are equipped; they will choose the best future for themselves and their communities.*

I'm not just placating myself. I believe this. I'm a teacher.

## 150.

I open the heavy metal door and walk into an empty room. There are round, oak tables, each surrounded by complementary black chairs. Cherry-stained bookshelves are shoved against the walls. The remaining wall space is covered—posters with happy messages of encouragement are now year-end wallpaper. At the front of the room are a white board and a smart board. All of this, yet the room is still empty.

We held our second graduation yesterday. These two days are the hardest days of the year. From the first day of the school year, when my students were still afraid, not knowing what to expect or when to expect it, to the last day with its uncontainable excitement because they are heading home, all the memories we created together stay with me. My once-wingless angels are leaving to strengthen their wings and soar.

My head still aches from the tears I cried yesterday. My kids cried with me. Then we said "See ya," because "good-bye" is never allowed. We aren't going to be separated forever, only for a few months. Now is the time to put to use all they have learned. They have to fly on their own. We never say "good-bye," because I will be that arm that shows up whenever they need me.

So today, I am in an empty room. No more laughter, no more dancing, and no more hugs. But before my class experienced joy, we first had to make sense of the past. My students arrived already labeled. They believed the shorthand that others used to describe them. When I told them that they would get a clean slate just by walking into my room, they didn't believe me, even though I could see that they wanted to believe. By the time they left, though, they had found their value and their worth. They left with goals, bigger dreams, and purpose. For the first time in their lives they are prepared for their purpose, ready for life's successes.

Milestones are made every day in this room. When one of my kids looks at me and says, "I really am smart," when one of my students finally gets it, it makes my day, my month, my class. I tell my kids, "Just because you have made bad choices, doesn't mean you are a bad person." I tell them that over and over, until finally it sinks in and I can see that they believe it—in their posture and, most important, in their eyes.

Now that they are gone and beginning a new life, I am left,

trying to move on. I have posters to trace, supplies to buy, and a room to fill. My room may be empty today, but soon another group of winged-angels-in-waiting will appear. When that happens, we will fill this room again. We will fill it with love, laughter, music, and, most of all, success.

# FREEDOM WRITER TEACHERS

**ALABAMA**
Jenni Currie
Jesse Schmitt

**ALASKA**
Jason Marvel
Jennifer Angaiak

**ARIZONA**
Chris Tafoya
Mike Sissel

**ARKANSAS**
Karon Parrish

**CALIFORNIA**
Bill Feaver
Brent Marlowe
Brian Hagman
Cameron Lymon
Dave McKay
Debbie Sidler
Devon Day
Erin McPeek
Gail Anderson
Giovanni Torres
Jenn Laskin
Ken Williams
Eduardo Ochoa
Lisa Kopp
Michelle Halimi
Nicole Hsu
Robert Rojas
Scott Bailey

Torhon Barnes
Veleda
  Tiyaamornwong

**COLORADO**
Dan Schaller

**CONNECTICUT**
Leslie Dalenta
Lynn Frazier

**DELAWARE**
Ken Fugowski

**FLORIDA**
Carlos Ardaya
Claudio Picasso
Katie Williams

**GEORGIA**
Charles Allen
Forrest Walker
Henry Wright
Robert Waller

**HAWAII**
Crisoforo Angel Perez
Monalisa Siofele

**IDAHO**
Emiliano Beagarie

**ILLINOIS**
Juanita Douglas-
  Thurman

Kristin Wynkoop
Kyle Miller

**INDIANA**
Alanna Oatts
Connie Heermann
Kate Hogg

**IOWA**
Cody Cochran

**KANSAS**
Karen Burrows

**KENTUCKY**
Quincy Murdock

**LOUISIANA**
Bridget Mann
Christine Neuner

**MAINE**
Kevin Coombs

**MARYLAND**
Nomsa Geleta

**MASSACHUSETTS**
Eileen Pereira
Elizabeth Dunn
Megan McDonough
Peter Panchy
Sarah Akhtar

**MICHIGAN**
Aqua-Raven Davis
Cathy Capy Cantu
Melissa Jennings

**MINNESOTA**
Katie Gagstetter
Marcia Nelson

**MISSISSIPPI**
Suzanna Maddox

**MISSOURI**
Jan Werner
Judy Kendall
Laura Vilines

**MONTANA**
Joe Anderson

**NEBRASKA**
Corey Degner
Natalie Russell
Paul Smith

**NEVADA**
Bradley Shaffer-Ortiz

**NEW HAMPSHIRE**
CarolAnn Edscorn

**NEW JERSEY**
Didi Schiele
Jennifer Clyde-Lewis
Renee Cleaves

**NEW MEXICO**
Toni Purrachio

**NEW YORK**
Joaquin Noguera
Jon Paul Pedergnana
Susan O'Rourke

**NORTH CAROLINA**
Corey Waters
Sophia Jackson

**NORTH DAKOTA**
Mary Jean Dehne

**OHIO**
Aalaa Eldeib
Crystal Russell
Lori Pyles
Steven Ward
Sumaya Brown

**OKLAHOMA**
Heather Meldrum
Mary Kevin
  McNamara

**OREGON**
Debbie Baker
Joseph Thornton
Karen Sojourner

**PENNSYLVANIA**
Anne Schober
Charlotte Fong
Eric Graf
Jason Fritz
Marlon Barbour
Michael Farrell
Michael Galbraith
Zac Chase

**PUERTO RICO**
Abigail Medina-
  Betancourt

**RHODE ISLAND**
Daniel McKee
Tom Scully

**SOUTH CAROLINA**
Carol Jackson
Mahwish McIntosh
Robin Gary

**SOUTH DAKOTA**
Sherie Bauer

**TENNESSEE**
Hardy Thames
Noelle Taylor

**TEXAS**
Diana Stock
Fermin Muñoz
Fernando Alejandro
John McGee
Kerrie Bourland
Lori Low
Marco Franco
Richard Kotrla
Sefakor Amaa

**U.S. VIRGIN ISLANDS**
Susan Diverio

**UTAH**
Jennifer Clyde
Jeremy Asay
Ryan Anderson

**VERMONT**
Megan Dorsey

**VIRGINIA**
Doug Ball
John Tupponce
Nick Lincoln
Norma Trotman
Perez Gatling

**WASHINGTON**
Darence Shine
Janette Levandusky
Kirsten Jensen
Matt Yarkosky

**WASHINGTON, D.C.**
Kelli Taylor
Patrick McNabb
Tara Libert

**WEST VIRGINIA**
Chad Spencer

**WISCONSIN**
Carol Shaw
Lisa Sanford

**WYOMING**
Angie Schultz

**ONTARIO, CANADA**
Darwin Chan
Erin Dietrich
Jamie Coburn
Kelly Dhatt
Mike Ross
Robin Meehan
Xochitl Lugo

**SASKATCHEWAN, CANADA**
Marc Cheriyan

# ACKNOWLEDGMENTS

n the spirit of Margaret Mead, who urges us to "Never doubt that a small group of thoughtful, committed citizens can change the world. Indeed, it is the only thing that ever has," we would like to personally thank the "committed citizens" who have helped us change the world by changing education!

In bringing *Teaching Hope* to fruition, we have been blessed to have so many corporations and philanthropic leaders help the Freedom Writer Teachers. We would like to personally thank Microsoft (with a special thanks to Karla Tharin Hakansson and Mike Tholfsen) and Hewlett-Packard (with a special thanks to Liz Crawford), for providing mini-HP laptops loaded with Microsoft software for each of our 150 teachers to create this unique book! We'd like to thank: Southwest Airlines, for flying the teachers to our Institute in Long Beach; Paramount Studios; Washington Mutual; Merrill Lynch; COSTCO; CSULB; Facing History and Ourselves; the Museum of Tolerance (with a special thanks to Avra Shapiro, Renee Firestone, Matthew Boger, Tim Zaal, Eddie Ilam, and Gloria Ungar), for providing the venue to teach tolerance; the Ayres Hotels and the Newport Beach Marriott (with a special thanks to Roger Conner), for providing hotels for our teachers; the Kayne Foundation (special thanks to Ric Kayne), for providing the funding for scholarships and our educational evaluation; Stars and Stripes (with a special thanks to Dick Gebhard); Fight Night (with a special thanks to Bo Marconi); Kingston Technology (with a special thanks to John Tu for his unwavering support); the Sherwood Foundation (with a special thanks to Susie Buffett, for being such an advocate of public education); and Wahoos (with a special thanks to Wing Lam for always believing in our cause!).

We'd also like to thank the individuals and dedicated educators who have helped train, touch, and inspire the Freedom

Writer Teachers: the Freedom Writers Foundation (with a special thanks to Sonia Pineda, Robyn Marotta, Maria Reyes, Sue Ellen Alpizer, Tony Becerra, Steven Barnes, Lisa Smith, Paige Ratleff, David Jones, Fathia Macauley, Susan Olmstead, and Larry Hochendoner); Urban School Imaginers (with a special thanks to Dr. Carl Cohn, Dr. Karin Polachek, Dr. Lynn Winters, Dr. Kristen Powers, and Monica Cordova); the Freedom Writers Educational Advisory Board (with special thanks to Dr. Dan O'Connor, Horace Hall, Dave Beard and Marcia Nye); and the Freedom Writers Foundation's Board: Dave and Ellen Dukehart, Peter Long, Karen Clark, Karyn Furstman, Greg Mech, and Josh Richman. And our loyal supporters Carol and Marvin Levy, Peter Thum, Michael Rogers, Sonny Savoie, Dr. Otto Graf, Joe Werlich, Doug Mancino, Jorge Arcinega, Han Jason Yu, Noah McMahon, Rich Archibald, and Congressman Patrick Kennedy.

We would also love to thank our incredible team at Random House for allowing us to write what needs to be written, with a special thanks to Janet Hill, Christian Nwachukwu, Rebecca Cole, Christine Pride, Annie Chagnot, and Michael Palgon. We thank you for allowing us to tell what needs to be told!

Erin Gruwell, center, with the Freedom Writer Teachers, April 2008

# FREEDOM WRITERS FOUNDATION

Erin Gruwell founded the Freedom Writers Foundation with the vision of changing the educational system one classroom at a time. With the help of the Freedom Writers, the Foundation trains teachers in the Freedom Writers Method and advocates for improved educational policies and support. The Foundation fundamentally believes that by engaging, enlightening, and empowering young people, teachers can help their students reach their full academic potential.

To support the work of the Freedom Writers Foundation, please send your contribution to:

Freedom Writers Foundation
P.O. Box 41505
Long Beach, CA 90853

The Freedom Writers Foundation is a 501(c)(3) tax-deductible nonprofit charity. Tax ID number 04-3678807

www.freedomwritersfoundation.org

## ABOUT THE AUTHOR

Erin Gruwell is the founder of the Freedom Writers Foundation, a nonprofit 501(c)(3) organization that funds scholarships and promotes innovative teaching by training teachers at the Freedom Writers Institute. She lives in Long Beach, California.